D0947097

The Amish *and the* Media

Young Center Books in Anabaptist & Pietist Studies

Donald B. Kraybill, *Series Editor*

The Amish *and* *the* Media

Edited by

Diane Zimmerman Umble
and David L. Weaver-Zercher

The Johns Hopkins University Press
Baltimore

Printed in the United States of America on acid-free paper
2 4 6 8 9 7 5 3 1

The Johns Hopkins University Press
2715 North Charles Street
Baltimore, Maryland 21218-4363
www.press.jhu.edu

Library of Congress Cataloging-in-Publication Data

The Amish and the media / edited by Diane Zimmerman Umble and
David L. Weaver-Zercher.
p. cm. — (Young center books in Anabaptist and Pietist studies)
Includes bibliographical references and index.
ISBN-13: 978-0-8018-8789-5 (hardcover : alk. paper)
ISBN-10: 0-8018-8789-5 (hardcover : alk. paper)
1. Mass media and the Amish. 2. Mass media—United States.
I. Umble, Diane Zimmerman, 1952– II. Weaver-Zercher, David, 1960–
P94.5.A46A47 2008
070.4′492897—dc22 2007033669

A catalog record for this book is available from the British Library.

Special discounts are available for bulk purchases of this book. For more information, please contact Special Sales at 410-516-6936 or specialsales@press.jhu.edu.

The Johns Hopkins University Press uses environmentally friendly book materials, including recycled text paper that is composed of at least 30 percent post-consumer waste, whenever possible. All of our book papers are acid-free, and our jackets and covers are printed on paper with recycled content.

To

Ron, Kate, and Eric

Valerie, Samuel, Isaiah, and Henry

Contents

The Amish *and the* Media

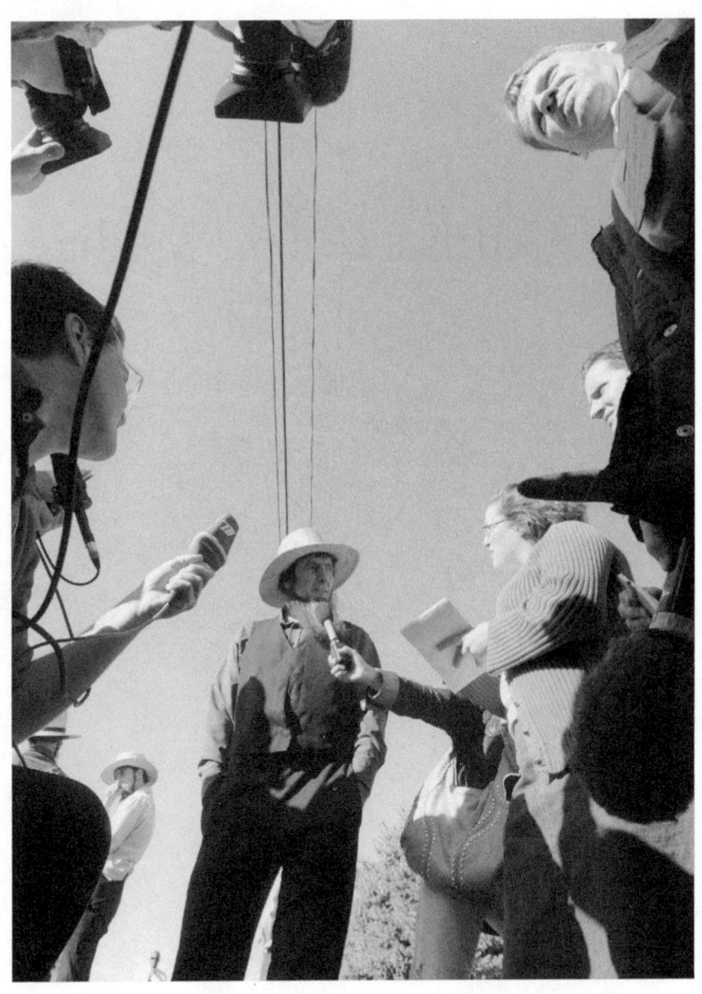

A man is interviewed by reporters near the scene of the West Nickel Mines School shooting.
Used by permission of the *Lancaster New Era*.

Introduction

The Amish and the Culture of Mediation

Diane Zimmerman Umble and David L. Weaver-Zercher

The world is desperate for something to satisfy its hunger. . . .
While they focus on our beards and buggies and bonnets,
they miss entirely what our faith is all about.
—Amish editor Joseph Stoll, writing in *Family Life*

Forgiveness. On Sunday, October 1, 2006, no one would have predicted that by week's end a word mostly reserved for sermons and country music would be a prime topic of discussion across the United States. But the events of Monday, October 2, changed all that. On that day, at around ten o'clock, truck driver Charles Carl Roberts IV barricaded himself in a one-room Amish school in Nickel Mines, Pennsylvania, armed with a semi-automatic pistol, a shotgun, a rifle, and six hundred rounds of ammunition. An hour later ten Amish schoolgirls had been shot, five of them fatally. As the police stormed the building, Roberts fired a final shot, ending the blood-bath by taking his own life.

For a day and a half, the media focused their attention on Roberts's heinous acts, asking questions about the killer's motives and pondering the long-term effects the shooting would have on the Amish way of life. Then, as if someone flipped a switch, the story line changed. Although questions about the future persisted, the accent now fell on what the Amish had already done: they forgave. Although the details were not always clear—who extended forgiveness? to whom? what exactly did they say or do?—print and broadcast media alike found themselves telling a story dramatically different from the one they had set out to tell when they first converged on Nickel Mines.

As scholars of Amish life, we hadn't anticipated that story line shift either. Had you asked us on the day of the shooting, Will the Amish forgive the killer? both of us would have answered, Certainly. But that's a different question from, Will the morning news shows later this week devote significant airtime to the topic of forgiveness? Even though we like to think of ourselves as media savvy, we were as surprised as anyone that Amish forgiveness became the top story in the days following the shooting. Even the Amish were taken aback by their newfound celebrity. While a few outside observers wondered if this forgiveness granting was calculated to win public relations points, the Nickel Mines Amish merely did what Amish people have done many times before in similarly painful circumstances. Thus, they too were surprised that, in the days following the shooting, many commentators branded them the world's most gracious people.

This leads us to an important question: when it comes to producing media portrayals of the Amish (or any religious group, for that matter), who is running the show? Is it the media, with all their resources for discovering, shaping, and communicating information? Is it the religious community, which actually lives, breathes, and acts in ways that capture others' attention? Or is it the media-consuming public, with its insatiable curiosity, its leisure-time preferences, and its disposable income? The answer, of course, is complicated, for there is agency everywhere in this equation. Everyone has power, and everyone has choices—but everyone's power and choices are constrained by the social systems in which they participate.

This volume explores that complicated mix of agency and power, using the intersection of "the Amish" and "the media" as its focal point. We realize that this coupling may seem peculiar, for of all the religious groups in contemporary America, few demonstrate as much suspicion toward the mainstream media as the Old Order Amish. In most Amish communities, church regulations proscribe television watching, Internet surfing, and movie going. Listening to the radio is a little more common, especially among Amish youth, but even that is considered taboo by the Amish leaders who enforce the rules. Print media sources likewise meet a wary eye. Although most Amish communities do not forbid reading matter like *Time*, *Newsweek*, and *USA Today*, Amish subscribers would hardly keep the presses running overtime. The Old Order Amish may not observe a "media fast," as one commentator recently wrote, but they do adhere to a very strict diet.[1]

The irony in this, of course, is that even before the Nickel Mines school shooting, the media-wary Amish were a media-friendly phenomenon, making regular appearances in feature films, romance novels, newspaper stories, magazine features—and yes, "reality television." Take a minute to Google the Amish, and they are everywhere. The reason for their ubiquity is hardly a secret. The Amish are fascinating, at least to those of us who operate from different assumptions about dress, travel, education, technology, and success—or, to put it more sociologically, different assumptions about individuation, specialization, and differentiation.[2] Religiously informed decisions that the Amish have made over the past 150 years have produced not only a visibly distinct culture but also a viscerally fascinating one. To be sure, the Amish did not pursue their particular path of piety in order to capture their neighbors' fancy, let alone to become the media's darlings. Indeed, most Amish people would be glad if their public renown would wither away, taking with it the tourists who sprout like beans in the summer sun. Regardless of their wishes, however, these publicly reticent sectarians will likely remain among America's most recognizable and renowned religionists for decades to come.

The media have played, and will continue to play, an important role in this celebrity. It is one thing to say that the Amish are "viscerally fascinating" due to their cultural eccentricities. It is another thing to consider how Americans *think about* cultural differences, or even how they *become aware* of those differences that capture their attention. In that sense, it is crucial to recognize that we inhabit a world in which people and institutions are invested, both literally and figuratively, in mediating information to other people. For these mediators—in other words, "the media"—there is money to be made and there are careers to be advanced in the mediation of the Amish. We do not say this to be critical of those who do this sort of thing, most of whom have more than their own interests in view. At the same time, we must recognize that widespread public interest in the Amish is not an inevitable, let alone accidental, result of differences between the Amish and the English.[3] Rather, this fascination has been created and sustained to a large degree by the media.

We begin, then, by exploring ways in which the Old Order Amish have been represented by a variety of mainstream media, starting with Hollywood films and concluding with reality television. The second half of this volume moves beyond a consideration of the Amish *as mediated images* to consider the Amish *as actors*—that is, as agents who produce and consume their own media and, in various ways, interact with and respond to mainstream media endeavors. Our goal in all this is an optimistic one: we believe that this rather focused subject provides a window for exploring larger issues about religion and the media in contemporary American life. Furthermore, we believe that a comparative approach—setting essays that consider mainstream mediations of the Amish beside essays that consider Amish interactions with and uses of the media—will enable us to shed additional light on the relationship of religion and the media. We will revisit our volume's objectives near the end of this introduction. First, however, we turn to brief considerations of some crucial terms: *the Amish* and *the media.*

The Amish

The Amish are theological heirs of a nearly five-hundred-year-old Christian tradition known as Anabaptism. This tradition first emerged in Zurich, Switzerland, around 1525, when a band of young radicals broke ranks with Ulrich Zwingli's Protestant reform program, which they deemed too timid. In particular, these radicals found Zwingli's continued embrace of infant baptism theologically unsound. Believing that the New Testament demanded the baptism of adult believers, the radicals took it upon themselves to baptize one another, an act that earned them the derisive label

"Anabaptists," meaning "re-baptizers."[4] For the next two hundred years, those who joined the Anabaptist movement would be considered theologically and politically suspect by other European Christians. Harried, imprisoned, and sometimes put to death by Catholic and Protestant authorities alike, Anabaptist martyrs eventually numbered in the thousands.

Despite persistent efforts to stamp it out, the nascent Anabaptist movement survived—and divided. One place where Anabaptists found sanctuary from persecution was the Alsace region of present-day France. Migrating there from Switzerland in the mid- and late seventeenth century, these Swiss-Alsatian Anabaptists nevertheless maintained fellowship with other Swiss Anabaptist churches, at least for a time. Under the leadership of Jacob Amman, however, some chose to break from the more established Swiss Anabaptist churches in 1693, citing Swiss church leaders' lack of faithfulness to the original Anabaptist vision. In particular, Amman and his faction complained that Swiss Anabaptists had become lax on a variety of lifestyle and ecclesiastical issues, most significantly their commitment to church discipline. Invoking earlier Anabaptist precedents for shunning wayward church members, the Ammanists demanded a reinvigoration of this potent form of spiritual rebuke.[5] When Swiss Anabaptist leaders rejected the Ammanists' demand, the Amish church was born.[6] Three centuries later, it still survives.

The term *Amish,* then, is best understood as a particular brand of Christianity and, more specifically, as a particular manifestation of Anabaptist Christianity. As Trinitarian *Christians,* the Amish affirm the existence of one triune God: Father, Son, and Holy Spirit; moreover, they affirm the salvific life, death, and resurrection of Jesus Christ, worship him as Savior and Lord, and endeavor to live faithfully until his return. As *Anabaptist* Christians, the Amish espouse a particular set of ideas that distinguish Anabaptist churches—Mennonites, the Amish, and some Brethren groups—from other Christian traditions. For instance, like other Anabaptist groups, the Amish reject the notion of infant baptism in favor of baptizing only adults. Indeed, in the Anabaptist tradition, thinking of oneself as a Christian only makes sense in connection to a commitment to follow Jesus' teaching and example, and only adults are equipped to make that sort of life-altering commitment. For Anabaptists, that decision is indeed life-altering, for it entails, among other things, the rejection of violence. Perhaps more than anything, this particular commitment distinguishes Anabaptist churches from other expressions of Christianity: the belief that following Jesus entails an intractable commitment to nonviolence, even in the face of persecution.

In these and other ways, the Amish are clearly Anabaptist Christians. They are not, however, *merely* Anabaptist Christians. Rather, they comprise a *subset* of Anabaptist Christianity, exhibiting a mélange of differences that distinguish them from other Anabaptist peoples and groups. Given the variety that exists today even among persons who consider themselves Amish, making generalizations about "the Amish" vis-à-vis other Anabaptist groups is a perilous endeavor. One relatively safe generalization, however, pertains to church discipline, an element of church life in which contemporary Amish churches continue to manifest the three-hundred-year-old concerns of Jacob Amman. Although details may vary among Amish communities, Amish churches nonetheless demonstrate a strong and abiding commitment to church discipline, a commitment that is more thoroughgoing than in most Mennonite and Brethren churches. Moreover, Amish communities have tended to produce longer, more determinate lists of lifestyle expectations than have their Mennonite and Brethren counterparts.[7] These expectations, when combined with an ardent commitment to church discipline, have given rise to religious communities that manifest a degree of uniformity in both belief and practice that is much higher than most other Christian communities, including most other Anabaptist ones.

It is one thing for a community's membership to possess a high degree of uniformity. It is another thing to incarnate that uniformity in strikingly visible ways. One reason the Amish are so renowned in contemporary North America is that certain shared features of their community life (e.g., traveling in horse-drawn buggies) are both culturally unusual and visibly distinct. This was not always the case, of course. As late as 1875, a full 140 years after Amish immigrants first settled in eastern Pennsylvania, the Amish community's use of horse-drawn vehicles, its nonuse of electric technology, and its reliance on the Pennsylvania German language (also called "Pennsylvania Dutch") would not have distinguished the Amish from many of their non-Amish neighbors.[8] Correspondingly, most outsiders who took an interest in the Amish in the late nineteenth and early twentieth centuries did so in the context of a wider interest in the Pennsylvania German culture, which included Lutherans, Moravians, and the German Reformed in addition to the various Anabaptist groups already mentioned.[9] Over the years, however, and especially after the twentieth century's turn, the Amish became distinguishable from their rural neighbors in ever more visible ways, a visibility that set the stage for the renown they experience today.

Historians trace the roots of this distinctiveness to two contrasting but interrelated developments, one progressive and the other unprogressive. From the 1870s on, ever larger segments of American society partook of the fruits of progress, consuming both the technological and cultural blandishments of an industrialized, market-driven mass culture.[10] In response to this development, though also in connection with debates about revivalism, dress codes, and church disciplinary practices, some Anabaptist communities (including *some* Amish groups, *some* Mennonite groups, and *some* Brethren groups) chose the path of resistance. In other words, they deemed the fruits of progress—cultural, religious, and technological—forbidden. Over time, these contrasting responses produced a significant lifestyle chasm between what became known as "Old Order" Anabaptist groups and the more progressive Anabaptist communities.[11] Moreover, it transformed the Old Orders into a particularly recognizable segment of the larger Pennsylvania Dutch subculture. For even as other Pennsylvania German farmers, including many Mennonites, embraced motorized cars and tractors, the Old Orders continued to drive horse-drawn buggies and plows. Similarly, even as most rural Americans hooked happily into the electric power grid and public telephone service, the Old Orders opted for less technologically sophisticated ways of life.

Some onlookers interpreted this cultural resistance, which was further accentuated by unconventional dress and a tenacious retention of the Pennsylvania Dutch dialect, as the last gasp of a dying religious culture and forecast a quick acquiescence to mainstream practices. The Old Orders not only proved these prognosticators wrong, but they obliterated their predictions with a degree of numerical growth that, a full century later, shows no signs of abating. Indeed, the Old Order Amish now number around

225,000 children and adults scattered across 372 settlements in at least 27 states and the province of Ontario.[12]

Still, as impressive as Old Order numerical growth has been, it pales in comparison to the growth of their renown, a celebrity that is typically—and rather simplistically—awarded to "the Amish." This two-word term, while linguistically convenient (we, the editors of this volume, often use it ourselves), is fraught with problems, for it frequently obscures as much as it illumines. In the first place, the term "the Amish" too often obscures the existence of other Old Order Anabaptist groups (e.g., Old Order Mennonite groups) that, like many Amish communities, manifest a marked degree of resistance to modern technology, contemporary dress styles, and other mainstream cultural habits. Second, popular invocations of "the Amish" often conceal the existence of self-identified Amish churches that have not, in fact, rejected standard North American technologies—for instance, the Beachy Amish, who farm with tractors, drive late-model automobiles, and use various electronic devices in their homes and businesses. More generally, the term masks the variety that exists among churches, communities, and people that think of themselves as Amish, a variety that ranges from the world-resisting Swartzentruber Amish to the technologically assimilated, evangelically oriented Beachy Amish on the world-embracing end of the scale.[13] In most cases, the distinctions between these various Amish incarnations are clear and significant to persons who think of themselves as Amish. To outsiders, however, the differences are often indistinguishable or at least baffling. To these observers, some of whom mediate information about Amish life to enthusiastic consumers, it is often easier to forgo the subtle distinctions and simply talk about "the Amish."

This brings us full circle to the topic at hand: the Amish and the media. The aforementioned variety of Amish and Old Order cultures, which is manifest in a wide array of Amish, Mennonite, and Brethren communities, has profound implications for the mediation of the Amish. Perhaps most significantly, this variety can be quite confusing to the uninitiated, a confusion that almost certainly catalyzes consumer desires for additional information. For their part, English mediators—writers, filmmakers, tour guides, and others—are happy to produce and deliver this information, sometimes for the mere satisfaction of setting the record straight, but more often for a mix of pedagogical, ideological, and pecuniary reasons. In some cases, these English mediators are very careful to delineate the cultural and religious distinctions outlined above, taking pains to note the variety of Amish life. In other cases, mediators demonstrate little or no obligation to outline these distinctions. For them, dealing with the complexity of Amish life and culture may be inconvenient, perhaps even impossible (e.g., in the case of a short newspaper article), though it may also be that an undifferentiated invocation of "the Amish" serves a mediator's purposes in ways that a more exacting representational approach would not.

Of course, Amish church members are likewise mediators of the Amish. In other words, it is not simply outsiders who use the term "the Amish" as they talk about Amish life and culture; Amish people do as well. Moreover, some Amish people have embraced rather sophisticated means to communicate their views of Amish life to large numbers of people. These Amish-initiated media endeavors, most of which are modest by mainstream standards, almost always assume other Amish people as their primary audience. Only occasionally do Amish persons produce media representations of Amish life expressly for English audiences (e.g., letters to editors of mainstream newspapers). Still, in an exploration of the Amish and the media, it is important to remember that the Amish are not just virtual images created and circulated by English mediators. They are also actors who create their own images of Amish life and, in various ways, respond to the images they encounter.

The Media

The term "the media" refers to various public, popular forms of communication that are part of the contemporary cultural landscape. For many observers this two-word phrase conjures thoughts of the mainstream *news media*—that is, it refers to print, radio, television, and Internet journalists who, at the behest of their editors and publishers, report current events to a news-hungry public. For the purposes of this volume, "the media" is that—and much more. In addition to exploring the news coverage of an incident in which two young men from Amish families were arrested for selling cocaine, this volume considers media representations of the Amish that have very little to do with "the news," including feature and documentary films, poetry, nonfiction travel narratives, and reality television. We also consider tourism as a medium of representation, recognizing, of course, that Amish-theme tourism is really a system of messages presented by a variety of media situated in a particular geographical region. Finally, in this volume's second half, we look at media endeavors in which Amish persons generate public forms of communication, most of which provide observations about the nature of Amish life for an Amish readership.

In all these instances, three distinct elements can be identified: (1) mediators of information; (2) the medium by which the mediators transmit their information; and (3) consumers of the mediated information. The first two elements taken together comprise "the media," and the work they accomplish in concert with their consumers is "mediation." In other words, *mediation is the process of creating and recreating meaning to be shared.* The media provide the raw materials—images, stories, and explanations—that media consumers use to make sense of the world in which they live and, in many cases, to make sense of their own lives. Of course, because mediation is a cultural practice that is socially situated in particular places and times, the transmitted images, stories, and explanations reflect a "point of view." Although mediators hold the potential to communicate the world's buzzing, blooming reality in countless ways, every media endeavor offers a *particular* way of making sense of the world, in contrast to some other way of telling the story. The process of mediation thus produces a vocabulary for creating and recreating shared meaning about "the way things are."

Because the media are plural and, from an operational standpoint, independent from one another, the meanings that circulate about a given subject are rarely monolithic. At the same time, certain meanings do tend to predominate in particular times and places. This has certainly been true of the Amish, whose meaning in the mainstream media has taken various forms and various turns over the course of the twentieth century. At the beginning of the century, for instance, the Amish "meant" next to nothing, for their presence in the mainstream media was practically nonexistent. As the twentieth century unfolded, however, the Amish came to mean a great deal to the media and their consumers, not because they altered their way of living, but because the world around them changed. From 1910 to 1930, for instance, the primary significance of the Amish was their stubborn resistance to progress, which struck most cultural observers as a dim-witted and shortsighted response to technological advances. Stories accenting the "dumb Dutch" were common, and commentators frequently speculated about how long it would be until the Amish came to their senses and forswore their foolish ways.[14]

By no means did this viewpoint disappear in the 1930s, but the Depression did compel some observers to reassess their views, particularly as they witnessed the Amish ability to weather the nation's most brutal economic crisis. Indeed, one Depression-era commentator determined that the chief significance of the Amish lay in their communal self-sufficiency that, in his view, rendered New Deal policies unnecessary.[15] Not everyone agreed with this politically motivated interpretation of Amish life, though other commentators concurred that the Amish community's resistance to a homogenizing mass culture was worthy of respect, if not emulation. Contributing to this reassessment of Amish life was the late-1930s attempt by some Lancaster County Amish families to preserve rural community-based education, an endeavor that enabled the media to connect the Amish to a picturesque national icon: the one-room schoolhouse. With the help of the national news media, including the *New York Times,* the Amish quickly became repositories of America's treasured (if somewhat imaginary) past, a status they continue to hold today.[16]

Still other meanings of Amish life came to the fore in the latter half of the twentieth century. With the decline of the family farm and the advance of urban sprawl, the Amish assumed the mantle of America's premier and archetypical agrarians.[17] The media helped to advance this view, which was abetted by striking visuals of Amish farmland—this despite the fact that in many Amish settlements fewer and fewer Amish families were actually farming. But even as "family, faith, and farming" became the triumvirate that drew increasing numbers of tourists to Amish settlements in the 1960s, '70s, and '80s, it also laid the foundation for news stories about the Amish that, had the actors been Baptists or Presbyterians, would not have been considered "news." How else can one explain the intense media attention devoted to the June 1998 arrest of two Amish-born men for selling cocaine to other Amish youth? Given the incongruity between "Amishness" and cocaine dealing, this otherwise ordinary event was deemed newsworthy by media outlets, many of whom quickly broadened their lens to consider the Amish rite of passage known as *Rumspringa* ("running around").[18] Only with the horrific Nickel Mines shooting in 2006 did the media's predominant image of the Amish shift once again, this time toward the notion of forgiveness and extraordinary grace in the midst of tragedy.

From this cursory historical overview of the Amish in the media, it should be clear that creating shared meanings about "the way things are" with respect to Amish life is neither simple nor uncontested. Part of this complexity stems from Amish reality itself, which is neither monolithic nor unchanging. But even when mediators draw from the same well of information, the mediation of the Amish reveals struggles over the interpretation of experiences and events, struggles that reflect competing values—those of the consumers as well as of the producers. The mediation process is further complicated by practices of commodification; that is, media images frequently take the form of economic commodities bought and sold on the open market. That being the case, most mediators must be attentive to what their intended public is willing to pay to receive mediated information. At the end of the day, even Amish persons involved in mediating information must pay attention to the balance sheet, despite the fact that Amish media endeavors are typically less profit-oriented than those of English media.

In sum, mediation is a holistic, dialectical process that includes not only those who produce public accounts of Amish life, but also those who consume these accounts. As participants in the mediation process, consumers recreate these accounts from the perspective of their personal and cultural identities and their own quests to make meaning. Indeed, one of the key questions raised by the following essays asks just what identities are being created and sustained in the mediation process. Are those who critique Amish religious practice as oppressive seeking to promote their own enlightened perspectives in the process? Are those who celebrate the simplicity of Amish pastoral life yearning for a solution to their own sense of fragmentation? What is accomplished by documenting the coming-of-age struggles of Amish youth? Is it merely voyeuristic pleasure, or is there some larger lesson to be learned? And what should we make of tourists who visit Amish Country? In what ways do their consumptive practices reflect their hopes and fears at the dawn of the twenty-first century?

The foregoing questions pertain almost wholly to the English and what they have to gain through producing and consuming representations of the Amish. In addition to probing English identities, we are also interested in the role of the Amish community in the mediation process. Although the Amish have assumed a unique role in the mainstream American imagination, they are nonetheless members of living communities that thrive in the present. They too participate in mediation. They speak, write, publish, and read. Although they do not make movies or engage public relations firms to communicate their messages, they participate in mediation processes on their own terms, for their own purposes, using their own means. The second part of this volume thus shifts the focus from English mediations of the Amish to the Amish as mediators in their own fashion. At one level, the Amish would say that their community life is their message, representing who they are and "speaking for itself." Nevertheless, the Amish do communicate more formally among themselves and with outsiders. Through their own reading, writing, speaking, and publishing, they tell their stories and engage in meaning-making processes for the purpose of creating and sustaining identity. To what degree is their engagement in the mediation process the same or different from the rest of us? How does what they do engage us?

We offer these inquiries as a window on wider cultural conversations about the nature of religion in North American culture. A leading scholar in the study of media and religion has written that, for most twenty-first-century Americans, a strict distinction between religion and the media is no longer realistic or relevant. Instead, he argues, "it is most helpful to think of religious practice inhabiting an emerging 'religious-symbolic marketplace' constructed at the confluence of religion and the media."[19] That is, the media provide both a context for and a repertoire of practices and symbols for use in finding religious meaning and creating religious identity. Recent sociological studies of American religion, which almost universally attest to an increased orientation toward the self in American religious life, likewise document the tendency to shape religious identities with reference to symbolic resources offered via the media.[20] What, then, does the fascination with community-based Amish religious practice offer to the autonomous, postmodern seeker? What might the construction of Amish religious practice as Other say about the values we espouse for religious identity? What can we learn about our treatment of religious minorities from this study of the mediation of the Old Order Amish? And what might the Old Order Amish teach us about the creation of religious identity on the basis of their own mediation practices?

Although this volume may raise more questions than it will answer, its conclusion—which uses the media coverage of the Nickel Mines shooting as something of a lens—endeavors to highlight themes that hold particular relevance for the study of religion and the media. The conclusion also affords us, the editors, the opportunity to focus our analytical lenses, however briefly, on people like us, that is, on scholars who are themselves mediators of Amish life. Suffice it to say here that we do not perceive ourselves as rising above the fray of complicated questions about the mediation of Amish life. Nor do we think our inclusion of Amish voices as epigraphs to each essay remedies the problems inherent in the English mediation of Amish life. To be sure, our intent in including these epigraphs is to give real-life Amish persons some voice in a volume conceived and written by non-Amish persons. At the same time, the fact that *we* selected, excerpted, and placed these writings indicates that these Amish voices are far from unmediated. We too are complicit in this process of mediating the Amish. We do not apologize for pursuing what we believe to be a worthy project, but we do admit that our mediating work is not above analysis or reproach. In that sense, we can only hope that our efforts will invite further conversation on this important topic of mediating religion in twenty-first-century America.

Notes

Epigraph: This July 1989 entry from Stoll's "Views and Values" column is reprinted in *The Amish: In Their Own Words*, comp. Brad Igou (Scottdale, PA: Herald Press, 1999), 271–72.

1. Thomas W. Cooper, "Of Scripts and Scriptures: Why Plain People Perpetuate a Media Fast," *Journal of American Culture* 29 (2006): 139–53.

2. For a sociological analysis of Old Order Amish life, see Donald B. Kraybill and Marc A. Olshan, eds., *The Amish Struggle with Modernity* (Hanover, NH: University

Press of New England, 1994), especially Kraybill's chapter, "The Amish Encounter with Modernity," 21–33.

3. Amish persons often refer to their non-Amish neighbors as "the English," a designation based on their neighbors' use of the English language and nonuse of Pennsylvania German.

4. Since the first Anabaptist Christians had been baptized as infants in the Roman Catholic Church, their baptism as adults actually constituted rebaptism. For an account of early Anabaptism, see J. Denny Weaver, *Becoming Anabaptist: The Origin and Significance of Sixteenth-Century Anabaptism,* 2nd ed. (Scottdale, PA: Herald Press, 2005).

5. One obvious precedent was the 1632 Dordrecht Confession, written and adopted by Dutch Mennonites. The confession's seventeenth article, "Of the Shunning of Those Who Are Expelled," outlines both the objectives of and parameters for shunning excommunicated members. See "The Dordrecht Confession," in John H. Leith, ed., *Creeds of the Churches,* 3rd ed. (Atlanta: John Knox Press, 1982), 292–308.

6. See Steven M. Nolt, *A History of the Amish,* rev. ed. (Intercourse, PA: Good Books, 2003), and John D. Roth, ed., *Letters of the Amish Division: A Sourcebook* (Goshen, IN: Mennonite Historical Society, 1993).

7. These lifestyle expectations, called "the *Ordnung,*" are typically unwritten, though nonetheless well understood.

8. Even at this time, the Amish exhibited some distinguishing factors that occasioned comments from observers, for example, their use of hooks and eyes to fasten clothing instead of buttons. Still, these distinguishing marks were far less conspicuous than certain ones they exhibit today.

9. A perusal of this early ethnographic literature reveals a great deal of confusion with respect to the terms "Amish," "Mennonite," and "Pennsylvania Dutch." Some writers used the term "Mennonites" when they were really talking about the Amish. Even more writers invoked the broader term "Pennsylvania Dutch" in reference to the Amish, a conflation of terms that perturbed many non-Amish members of the Pennsylvania German ethnic family. Although this frustration was justified, it is nonetheless important to recognize that, on the late-nineteenth- and early-twentieth-century Pennsylvania landscape, the Amish were not as distinct from their rural Pennsylvania German neighbors as they would soon become. In this regard, see Steven M. Nolt, "Finding a Context for Mennonite History: Pennsylvania German Ethnicity and the (Old) Mennonite Experience," *Pennsylvania Mennonite Heritage* 21, no. 4 (1998): 2–14.

10. For reactions to the advocates of progress, see T. J. Jackson Lears, *No Place of Grace: Antimodernism and the Transformation of American Culture, 1880–1920* (New York: Pantheon Books, 1981), and especially Christopher Lasch, *The True and Only Heaven: Progress and Its Critics* (New York: W. W. Norton, 1991).

11. Each Anabaptist family we have identified—Amish, Brethren, and Mennonite—spawned both Old Order and progressive factions during the last half of the

nineteenth century. In each case, the progressives and the traditionalists parted ways in answer to this question: How open should godly people be to the practices of the surrounding culture? For the Amish divide, which produced the Old Order Amish and progressive "Amish Mennonites," see Paton Yoder, *Tradition and Transition: Amish Mennonites and Old Order Amish, 1800–1900* (Scottdale, PA: Herald Press, 1991), 115–71. For consideration of the other Old Order groups, see Donald B. Kraybill and Carl Desportes Bowman, *On the Backroad to Heaven: Old Order Hutterites, Mennonites, Amish, and Brethren* (Baltimore: Johns Hopkins University Press, 2001).

12. These numbers represent the findings of a survey conducted in September 2006 by the Young Center for Anabaptist and Pietist Studies at Elizabethtown College in Elizabethtown, Pennsylvania.

13. For the variety that exists in Ohio's Holmes/Wayne/Tuscarawas County settlement, see Donald B. Kraybill, "Plotting Social Change across Four Affiliations," in *Amish Struggle with Modernity,* 53–74. In Amish life, a "settlement" is a geographical region that contains at least one church "district," a local church that meets regularly in members' homes for worship. Districts, which typically entail twenty to thirty families, are "affiliated" or "in fellowship" with other likeminded districts, some of which may be geographically proximate, though not necessarily so.

14. For instance, Katherine Haviland Taylor, "Pennsylvania Dutch," *Travel,* June 1921, 10–11, 42.

15. Albert Jay Nock, "Utopia in Pennsylvania: The Amish," *Atlantic Monthly,* April 1941, 478–84.

16. See David Weaver-Zercher, *The Amish in the American Imagination* (Baltimore: Johns Hopkins University Press, 2001), 63–78.

17. See David Walbert, *Garden Spot: Lancaster County, the Old Order Amish, and the Selling of Rural America* (New York: Oxford University Press, 2002), 101–15.

18. For instance, David Remnick, "Bad Seeds," *New Yorker,* 20 July 1998, 28–33. For a nuanced look at this rite of passage, which varies dramatically from settlement to settlement, see Richard A. Stevick, *Growing Up Amish: The Teenage Years* (Baltimore: Johns Hopkins University Press, 2007).

19. Stewart Hoover, "Religion, Media and Identity: Theory and Method in Audience Research on Religion and Media," in *Mediating Religion: Conversations in Media, Religion and Culture,* ed. Jolyon Mitchell and Sophia Marriage (New York: T & T Clark, 2003), 11.

20. Wade Clark Roof, *Spiritual Marketplace: Baby Boomers and the Remaking of American Religion* (Princeton: Princeton University Press, 1999).

Part I

The Old Order Amish as Media Images

Mainstream media presentations of the Old Order Amish track a long history. As early as 1869, when Phebe Earle Gibbons published her travelogue, "Pennsylvania Dutch," in the *Atlantic Monthly,* non-Amish media consumers have been treated to portrayals of the Amish by the English media. Gibbons's journalistic piece prefigured other textual representations of the Old Order Amish that appeared in the late nineteenth and early twentieth centuries, portrayals that were accompanied sometimes by photographs but more often by hand-drawn sketches. These primitive visuals anticipated a teeming market in Amish-theme postcards, which originated in Lancaster County during the twentieth century's opening decade and continues today in many other places where the Amish can be found. Other sorts of visual representations would follow: slide shows, documentary films, feature films, television shows, and, most recently, Internet Web sites. In the meantime, Amish-theme tourist attractions fashioned additional representations of the Old Order Amish. These tourist sites, like other media outlets, found consumers willing to pay a few dollars to learn something about the Amish. Of course, knowledge of Amish life was not the only thing these consumers were seeking, for most of them possessed desires that, like the lives they were living, were multifaceted, complicated, and sometimes even contradictory. For them, learning about Amish life was often coupled with other goods, like consuming their favorite ice cream or, in the case of the Hollywood blockbuster *Witness*, viewing attractive movie stars.

Part I of this volume analyzes a variety of mainstream media representations of the Old Order Amish. That being the case, non-Amish people who produce and consume representations of Amish life constitute the primary actors in the chapters of part I. Conversely, the Amish who appear in these chapters do so primarily as media productions—images—of Amish life. Most of the media fare considered here appeared relatively recently, though a few of the following chapters reach back twenty years or so to explore particularly influential offerings. Given the variety of media that exist in contemporary America, it is simply impossible to consider every media genre with respect to its treatment of the Amish. The media that are considered, however, offer instructive case studies both for exploring the ways in which the Amish have been portrayed by English mediators and for discerning what English consumers hope to receive in their consumption of the Amish.

Part I begins with Crystal Downing's exploration of two Amish-theme feature films, *Witness* (1985) and *For Richer or Poorer* (1997). Twenty years after its initial release, *Witness* continues to be the most influential media representation of the Amish ever produced. More people have learned about the Amish from *Witness* than from any other media portrayal of Amish life—though, as Downing shows, instructing viewers about the intricacies of Amish life was not the primary intent of those who made *Witness*, let alone those who followed it up with the more farcical (but no less mythical) *For Richer or Poorer*. Rather, these filmmakers sought to tell entertaining stories that highlighted the virtues of pastoral life, virtues they presented in contrast to the decadence of urban living.

Documentary filmmakers are far more inclined to instruct viewers about cultural intricacies—and are much more devoted to ethnographic accuracy—than are Hollywood directors. Still, as Dirk Eitzen observes in chapter 2, documentary filmmakers have a similar need to produce consumer-friendly cinematic products, which, in the case of documentaries, means telling a compelling story that holds the audience's attention. Eitzen explores this tension by way of four documentary treatments of Amish life, beginning with the sympathetic, myth-enhancing *A People of Preservation* and concluding with the myth-busting (and, for reasons that Eitzen explains, far more entertaining) *Devil's Playground.*

In chapter 3, Julia Spicher Kasdorf considers a less market-driven media genre but one that is similarly beholden to traditional forms and practices: poetry. If the Amish-theme films considered in chapters 1 and 2 participate in long-standing cultural myths about pastoral life, the poems in chapter 3 reveal how particular persons appropriate and respond to the Amish in the present. As Kasdorf notes, the dominant mode of poetry in twentieth-century America took "objects in the world as catalysts for self-discovery," a practice that "parallels the social construction of mainstream identity." Not coincidentally, the poems that Kasdorf considers employ the Amish to imagine a sort of collective mainstream identity that stands apart from the "whiter-than-white" identity the Amish represent.

David L. Weaver-Zercher continues this exploration of personal identity in chapter 4, in which he examines two nonfiction narratives about encounters with Amish people. These narratives, Sue Bender's *Plain and Simple* (1989) and Randy-Michael Testa's *After the Fire* (1992), recount their respective authors' emerging fascination with the Amish that, in both cases, led them to live with Amish families for significant periods. Drawing on the work of Victor and Edith Turner, Weaver-Zercher casts the authors' journeys to the Amish as religious pilgrimages in which "previous orderings of thought and behavior are subject to revision and criticism." Still, as Weaver-Zercher notes, Bender and Testa undertake their journeys with different sorts of existential angst, which contribute to radically different portrayals of their touristic experiences and their Amish hosts.

Chapter 5 moves beyond the experience of a few isolated seekers to explore the production of Amish-theme tourism for the masses. In it, Susan Biesecker notes the importance of authenticity in the enterprise of cultural tourism, a significance that she illustrates with respect to Amish Country tourism in Ohio's Holmes and Wayne counties. These tourists, like the filmmakers in chapters 1 and 2, find themselves participating in the myth of the pastoral. At the same time, they are negotiating identities that have largely been shaped by a capitalist, consumer culture that has little resonance with the pastoral. For Biesecker, this dissonance helps to explain the relative popularity of tourist destinations in Ohio's Amish Country, where the more authentic sites tend to attract fewer tourists.

In the final chapter in part I, Dirk Eitzen examines a relatively recent Amish-theme media creation, the reality television series *Amish in the City*. The series, which premiered in July 2004, featured five young people from Amish families who, according to the show's producers, were wrestling through the decision of joining (or not joining) the Amish church. Placed in a trendy house in southern California with six other young adults, the Amish youth served as experimental subjects in Hollywood's latest laboratory, an experiment that garnered millions of viewers every week. Eitzen notes that, even though *Amish in the City* was relatively tame compared to most reality series, it nonetheless garnered a great deal of criticism. How should we think about the ethics of this media endeavor? From an ethical standpoint, did it make any difference that these young people were Amish and not, say, Episcopalians?

This last chapter in part I serves to remind us that the Amish are not just media subjects or media creations but actual people who, for the most part, seek to live their lives out of the public spotlight. Of course, the Amish-raised participants in *Amish in the City* complicate that claim. Not only did they willingly place their religious quests before the camera (for a reported $20,000 each), but they also blurred the line between "media creation" and "real life." Of course, the line between what is created by the media and what constitutes real life has always been rather fuzzy, a fuzziness that is not restricted to the productions of the mainstream media. We will revisit that blurry line in part II of this book, when the Amish become the primary actors in the production and consumption of the media.

Harrison Ford in the 1985 movie Witness,
filmed in Lancaster County, Pennsylvania.
Photo by Dan Marschka; used by permission of the *Lancaster Intelligencer Journal.*

Chapter One

Witnessing the Amish

Plain People on Fancy Film

Crystal Downing

Jesus commanded us to come out from the world, and be separated, and touch not the unclean things. . . . We shall not be conformed to this world, but be transformed.
—a Lancaster County Amish man

The first time I witnessed "the Amish" I cried. Admittedly, a good part of the tears expressed the relief of escape. Having recently moved to central Pennsylvania from a lifetime in California, I drove for an hour in search of the Amish, only to find myself mired in the stop-and-go traffic of Lancaster County's Route 30, a billboard-infested highway pockmarked by tawdry enterprises with names like "Ye Olde Amish Inn" and "Amish Play World." Reminded of the first time I cruised along a derelict Hollywood Boulevard hoping to witness a movie star, I had begun to think that "the Amish" were just a public relations ploy of the Pennsylvania Tourism Board. Finally, in frustration, I turned off Lancaster's camino real of commodified kitsch. Suddenly, it seemed almost miraculously, I was surrounded by soothingly green farmland. And in another heartbeat I drove by two women in plain dress, hoeing a garden in bare feet. I stopped the car at the side of the road, sobs blinding my sight.

The Amish industry must be fueled with responses like mine: reverent amazement for a people who have resisted the conveniences and luxuries of mass culture in order to live in harmony with nature, caressing life-giving dirt beneath their feet. This, at least, is what "the Amish" have come to symbolize for "the English"—those outsiders who use technology to depict the famed repudiators of modern technology. Some depictions are written at word processors; others are photographed for picture books; and some, perhaps the most controversial, have been placed in motion pictures. Hollywood Boulevard and Route 30 have crossed in more than my own imagination.

Controversy about the most famous crossing, *Witness,* has already been well documented.[1] As a film critic and cultural theorist, I plan to discuss, in contrast, what Amish depictions on film tell us about English culture. Focusing on two commercially successful examples—*For Richer or Poorer* (1997) and *Witness* (1985)—I will argue that actors portraying the Amish do not represent the "real" Amish so much as perpetuate an American dream: that the idyllic agrarian harmony and simple rural peace idealized by the likes of Wordsworth and Thoreau still actually exist in North America. Films about the Amish, I suggest, present an age-old fiction known as "the pastoral."[2]

The Pastoral

Among literary scholars, the word *pastoral* refers to mystified depictions of rural life, the genre dating back to the Greek poet Theocritus in the third century BCE. The Latin poet Virgil adapted Theocritus's Idylls in his *Bucolics* (43–37 BCE), identifying the ideal realm with "Arcadia," a rural part of Greece. Art historian Erwin Panofsky describes Virgil's Arcadia with words that anticipate the Amish fiction: "The Arcadians were renowned for their rustic virtue, their hospitality, and primordial simplicity, as well as for their complete ignorance of what was happening in the outer world."[3] This ignorance leads some—Juvenal in the early part of the second century and

Helen Reimensnyder Martin in the early part of the twentieth century—to disdain the Arcadian/Amish ideal, emphasizing in their writings "negative aspects of primordial simplicity."[4] However, contempt for the pastoral ideal merely proves its power, a power abetted by tensions between rural and urban economies that are as relevant today as they were in Virgilian Rome.[5] Throughout the pastoral tradition, authors who celebrate bucolic purity write from the city, weary of the impersonal nature of urban constructions, both architectural and social.

In *Garden Spot: Lancaster County, the Old Order Amish, and the Selling of Rural America,* David Walbert cites the pastoral genre to discuss conflicting attitudes toward agricultural America still manifest in the twenty-first century: the push toward "progress" versus the pull for "preservation." He repeatedly quotes idealizations of rural America reminiscent of pastoral conventions. *New York Times* architectural critic Herbert Muschamp, for example, effused in 1998, "You can't drive more than a mile through Lancaster County's rolling farmland without thinking you've already entered one of the world's great sacred spaces, a landscape consecrated over the centuries to a peaceful way of life."[6] The alignment of Lancaster farmland with consecrated peace implicitly invokes the Amish pacifists who sanctify the land by farming it.

For urbanites like Muschamp, the agrarian Amish are the preservers of an idealized rural America. It therefore makes sense that, when they appear on film, the Amish represent the mystified realm of Arcadia in contradistinction to the contaminated city. Hollywood films about the Amish, then, are not really about the Amish; they are about the urban longing for consecrated rural peace. Such films, in other words, are pastorals. Thus, they should not be watched with expectations for documentary accuracy and sociological realism. In fact, as Dirk Eitzen demonstrates later in this book, even documentaries about the Amish have a vexed relationship with "accuracy" and "realism." This provides all the more reason that we view feature films about the Amish with an openness to "pastoral's moral capacity for addressing the social and political problems" of the technologically advanced society that makes them.[7] As William Rose Benét notes, a "major function of pastoral has been the implicit or explicit criticism of the corruption, sterility, and falseness of life in city or court."[8]

For Richer or Poorer

No film better illustrates the pastoral's explicit criticism of corruption, sterility, and falseness in the city than *For Richer or Poorer,* a lightweight movie directed by Bryan Spicer. The 1997 film opens with a montage of consumerist activity set in a glamorous New York City backdrop. Close-ups on champagne bottles, jewels, jets, flight itineraries, and receipts for expensive purchases are intercut with images of Manhattan buildings frequented by the rich and famous. While capturing a luxuriously extravagant lifestyle, the montage shows only parts of the human body—hands presenting credit cards, a neck wearing an emerald and diamond necklace—as though to communicate the dehumanization of greed. Bodies become defined by the commodities they purchase.

The first entire body we see in the film is that of a corrupt accountant sitting behind a conference table, framed by Manhattan architecture through the window behind his back. As he is grilled by a collection of IRS suits, we realize that people—his clients—have spent money they do not have. Next we meet the spenders—at an upscale party to celebrate their tenth wedding anniversary. Brad and Caroline (Tim Allen and Kirstie Alley) seem perfectly happy—at least until they leave the party. At that point, acerbic arguments begin, ending only when they retreat into separate bedrooms in a pricey Park Avenue apartment.

True to pastoral tradition, the film repeatedly signals that city life is complicit with the couple's unhappiness. In Brad's real estate development office, where he learns of his financial problems, even the chair backs are in the shape of famous New York City skyscrapers. Significantly, for his next project he plans to create a theme park called "Holy Land," erecting constructions alluding to biblical themes: The Water into Winery; Torah, Torah, Torah, the Waterslide "for his Jewish guests"; and Tora! Tora! Tora! the Waterslide "for Japanese guests." Brad's Holy Land, as we see from the model he displays, is all architecture, no land. So when Brad describes it as "a theme park inspired by God himself," we are being prepared for a different holy land that will lead to his redemption: the Arcadian land of the Amish, the authenticity of which is inversely proportional to the theme park developments along Route 30 in Lancaster County.

In the remainder of the film we witness how the consecrated land of the Amish subverts Brad and Caroline's dependence on urban consumerism. Their change in sensibilities is signaled by contrasting bovine figures. In Manhattan, as Brad runs from a gun-toting IRS agent, we see over his shoulder a huge bronze statue of a horned Wall Street bull. As he hides under the bull's tail, Brad mutters, "This is bullshit." Though played for slapstick laughs (like much in the film), this image prepares us for the next scene when Brad and Caroline escape to Pennsylvania in a stolen cab, veering off the road to avoid hitting a horned cow. Having to sleep under a tree, Caroline discovers that she has literally encountered bull shit—slept on it, in fact. She has been initiated into the pastureland of the pastoral.

As part of the pastoral tradition, city dwellers who enter Arcadia are at first repulsed by the earthiness of rural people. However, they soon become attracted by the natural beauty of an environment that seems to inculcate simple, unsullied expressions of love among the rustics who dwell there. In Shakespeare's most famous pastoral romances, *As You Like It* and *The Winter's Tale,* wealthy members of the court experience an idyllic pastoral community only because they have disguised themselves as simple rural folk. True to this form, Brad and Caroline steal some Amish clothing and pretend to be relatives of Sam and Lavinia Yoder, visiting to help with the farm: a pristine flower-trimmed clapboard house and tidy barn, both brightly white, nestled in the gorgeous green of a Pennsylvania valley.

We see the disguised city dwellers settle in the first night, she in a bed and he in a chair, only to have an aged Amish man, wielding an axe, interrupt their attempt to sleep. It soon becomes clear, however, that his thump at the door is actually the wake-up call at 4:45 the next morning. His sudden appearance in the film, without any conventional signal of a time lapse, communicates how suddenly morning comes to these city folk. Their bodies are not yet attuned to the natural cycle of the sun.

And what the couple wakes to are down-to-earth chores—literally, in the case of Brad, who is thrown to the ground several times as he attempts to tame a horse. Caroline complains about her share in all the "paring, pickling, and plucking," saying "prison couldn't be worse than this." But slowly both become transformed, starting to love not only the land but also each other, fulfilling another pastoral convention.

As Panofsky notes, Virgil often revels "in the contrast between the Utopian beauty of Arcadia and the sadness of unreciprocated love."[9] In *For Richer or Poorer,* it is quite clear that Brad wants to make the marriage work but Caroline does not reciprocate his feelings, banishing him from their bed in the Yoder house. Through the wall, however, they regularly hear the bed rocking from the Yoders' lovemaking, the fertility of which is manifest in multiple Yoder children. At one point, the Yoders discuss the lack of love they see in their visitors' marriage, Lavinia telling her husband, "God has sent them to us. I don't know how we can help them. But we must try." However, all they have to do is be themselves, living the pastoral ideal. Significantly, when Brad and Caroline first disguise themselves, they take off their wedding rings—Caroline's studded with multiple diamonds—since the Amish do not wear rings. The film employs this accurate reflection of Amish practice to symbolize the consumerism of city life—expensive rings signifying marriage—in contrast to a culture that needs no commodified constructions to achieve contented love.

Fulfilling both Hollywood and pastoral convention, Brad and Caroline fall in love again, consummating their renewed vows in the bed from which Brad had initially been banned. To symbolize the pastoral nature of their love, the axe-wielding Amish grandpa allows the couple to sleep in the morning after their sexual reunion. The film then cuts to a low-angle shot of five-inch corn stalks growing from the fertile earth, the shot of rich dirt and intensely green shoots filling the entire screen. Brad comments on the tender growth to his Amish host, "It's so honest; you plant it and it grows." His comment prepares us for what Caroline later tells him: that he has planted a growing seed in her womb. True to pastoral tradition, authentic love is tied to agrarian fertility. The film ends with the endorsement of Arcadian hope as Caroline and Brad, expecting a baby, decide to buy land adjacent to their Amish hosts.

Significantly, the weakest moments of *For Richer or Poorer* occur when the screenplay detours from pastoral convention. Degrading both the film and the Amish, several scenes show how Brad and Caroline's city-sense helps their rustic hosts. The agonizingly worst scene occurs when Caroline arranges a fashion show, complete with Amish runway models, in an attempt to change the community's *Ordnung* proscribing colorful clothing.

Even though the Yoders explain that they belong to an unusually "conservative" Amish order, the community swiftly abandons its *Ordnung* once Caroline teaches them the value of color. What makes this incident so distasteful is its inconsistency with the film's thematic structure. Implying that Caroline is transformed because the Amish are completely Other to her lived experience, the film undermines that which mediates her healing: Amish purity from outside influences. After all, any pastoral community that quickly adopts the ideas of city dwellers will not remain Other for long. Thus, the film unwittingly deconstructs its own pastoral premises.

The would-be constructor of Holy Land is a deconstructor as well. When Brad discovers that a young Amish man is in love with the Yoders' daughter, he advises him to follow his heart rather than the *Ordnung* requiring a two-year courtship. In other words, Brad advises the young man to do what he himself did: propose impetuously (and we know how that marriage turned out!). Nevertheless, when the young man follows Brad's advice, boldly asking for the daughter's hand in marriage, the *Ordnung* is dismissed, Samuel Yoder endorsing the engagement immediately. Hence, the Hollywood creed reigns supreme: erotic love trumps submission to community values.

Both Brad and Caroline thus release a bomb in their pastoral Gilead, but of course the fluffy feel-good film does not want us to think about that. In fact, to offset implications that it took savvy city folk to loosen up the naive Amish bumpkins who were too dumb to recognize an urban couple in disguise, we are offered a palliative at the end of the film: Samuel Yoder tells Brad that he knew the whole time that his visitors were fakes. This, then, gives substance to something Samuel told Brad in the fertile cornfield: "The English view us as hiding from reality. But this [gesturing toward the cornfield] is reality. It is not we who are hiding." The pastoral escape, Samuel implies, is not escapist; farming cultivates not only corn, but psychological health as well.

The pastoral, then, is more than an arbitrary literary genre that idealizes rural environments; it reflects human psychology. David Halperin explains: "Critics are justifiably unsure whether to locate the identity of pastoral in certain enduring literary norms and conventions, or in a specific (if perennial) subject, or in some continuity of feeling, attitude, 'philosophical conception,' or mode of consciousness which informs the literary imagination but originates outside it."[10] The "mode of consciousness" is about human wholeness and its dependence on rural fertility, generating a "feeling" that a humble tiller of soil is more fully human than a city dweller. Perhaps this "attitude" is subconsciously tied to the etymology of the word *human;* like *humble,* human comes from *humus,* the Latin word for ground, or soil. Desires for the pastoral arise, then, when rural land—the soil—seems compromised by the depredations of urban life. In contemporary America, as Glen A. Love noted several years before the release of *For Richer or Poorer,* the genre developed by Theocritus and Virgil takes on "heretofore unprecedented significance" as the "green world of pastoral is beset by profound threats of pollution, despoliation, and diminishment."[11]

It is no coincidence that the protagonist in *For Richer or Poorer* is a real estate developer who, after his sojourn in Amish Arcadia, finally realizes that "Holy Land is the worst idea I ever had." Ironically, not long after the release of *For Richer or Poorer,* something called "The Holy Land Experience" was constructed in Orlando, Florida: a theme park offering attractions not that much different from those in Brad's bad idea.

Witness

When Brad suggests putting on an Amish disguise in *For Richer or Poorer,* Caroline asks him how he knows what to do. "I saw *Witness,*" he blithely responds. One wonders if the screenwriters of *For Richer or Poorer* were influenced by rumors that Kelly McGillis, researching her role for *Witness,* disguised herself as a seeker in order to live for several weeks with the Amish.[12] Of course, *Witness* itself focuses on disguise: a detective, John Book (Harrison Ford), dresses in Amish clothes, collaborating with his hosts in order to protect himself and a young Amish boy, both of whom have witnessed police corruption in Philadelphia.

For Richer or Poorer alludes to the earlier film in other ways as well. The axe-wielding grandpa who awakens Brad and Caroline explicitly echoes a scene in *Witness* when a similar-looking grandfather awakens the detective at daybreak. And the "bullshit" joke is anticipated in *Witness* when a corrupt narcotics officer (Danny Glover), having traced Book to the Amish farm, utters a similar expletive after stepping in cow dung. However, unlike the silly and sentimental *For Richer or Poorer, Witness* is an artistic film directed by a respected craftsman: Peter Weir, the Australian director who garnered attention for *The Last Wave* (1977) and *Gallipoli* (1981), and then admiration for *The Year of Living Dangerously* (1983), *The Dead Poets' Society* (1989), *The Truman Show* (1996), and the spectacular *Master and Commander* (2003). Impressive simply for the company it keeps, *Witness* (1985) also generated eight Academy Award nominations, winning Oscars for Best Original Screenplay and Best Film Editing.

Witness also generated an incredible amount of controversy—much more than did *For Richer or Poorer*—in part, I am sure, because it is a much better film. After all, one does not get offended by the performance of a poodle. Much of the outrage over *Witness* was elicited by its filming, Pennsylvanians protesting various invasions of Amish culture, as though in protection of the pastoral ideal. Ironically, failure to understand pastoral conventions contributed to one of the fundamental protests against the film after its release: its lack of accuracy.

Some critics, for example, pointed out that the Amish do not sing church songs at the end of a day's work as seen in *Witness* after the barn raising scene.[13] But if we consider that the film is not about the Amish so much as it is about the desire for Arcadia, we realize that the singing symbolizes harmony not only among rustics but also between them and the land. Significantly, inhabitants of Arcadia "were famous for their musical accomplishment as well as for their ancient lineage, rugged virtue, and rustic hospitality."[14] Thus, true to its pastoral antecedents, *Witness* sets up a contrast between the discordant chaos of the city and the harmony of rural community, eliciting contempt from film critic Pauline Kael, who naively attributes the inaccurate "split between good farmers and bad urban dwellers" to the history of film conventions.[15] She seems not to realize that a much larger history is invoked by the film, a tension between city and country dating back to Theocritus in the third century BCE.

In *Witness,* the city is Philadelphia, to which a recent Amish widow, Rachel Lapp (Kelly McGillis), and her young son, Samuel (Lucas Haas), travel by train. In the nineteenth-century American pastoral, writes Leo Marx, "the train stands for a more sophisticated, complex style of life," exposing "the pastoral ideal to the pressure of change—to an encroaching world of power and complexity or, in a word, to history."[16] Significantly, it is in the Philadelphia train station where Samuel witnesses a gruesome throat slashing from a bathroom stall. The camera employs shot/reverse shot to emphasize an assault not only on the victim but also on Samuel's psyche: the camera displays the antagonists at the bathroom sink, reverses to focus on Samuel's one wide eye peering through the door, the rest of his face cut off from view, then reverses back to the violent crime. As a member of a rural pacifist community, Samuel has witnessed an act inimical to his worldview—quite literally: Samuel's large eye has never before viewed anything like this in the world.

Witness emphasizes disjunction in perspective even before the violent assault on Samuel's eye. Prior to entering the restroom, the boy wanders around the station, stopping with a hopeful look behind a man wearing a hat just like his own. But when the man turns around with a quizzical look at the staring boy, it becomes clear that, rather than an Anabaptist plain person, the hatted man is an Orthodox Jew, an ethnic parallel addressed in Julia Spicher Kasdorf's essay below. In *Witness,* this brief incident initiates the theme of false appearances: John Book disguises himself as Amish in order to escape corrupt policemen, who, pretending to be honest, murder their fellow police officer in front of Samuel's eye. Significantly, as Book lies on his belly in an Amish bed, recuperating from a gunshot wound inflicted by one of the corrupt officers, a close-up shows us one open eye. A mirror reflection of Samuel's left eye in the city bathroom, Book's right eye witnesses an act of grace in the Amish bedroom: Rachel, asleep in a chair by his bed, has tended him all night.

What Samuel and Book witness, each with their one eye, has the potential to change them. This becomes clear the first time we see Samuel on screen after the long take of Book's eye. Eli, Samuel's grandfather, asks the boy whether he could "kill another man." Samuel replies "I would only kill a bad man," a problematic response for people who "believe it is wrong to take a life." Eli therefore challenges Samuel about the limitations of perspective: "Only the bad man. I see. And you know the bad men by sight? You are able to look into their hearts and see this badness?" When Samuel answers "I can see what they do; I *have* seen it," Eli replies, "And having seen, you become one of them." With this statement we are given an apologetic not only for Amish separatism but also for the pastoral genre: seeing the Other can transform the self.

Witness, then, is about the "seeing" of John Book—in both senses: Book's seeing of the Amish and their seeing of him. And as the film develops, we wonder if, having seen the Amish, Book will "become one of them." Book's "seeing" is most dramatically—and controversially—symbolized when he witnesses Rachel bathing. Noticing Book's eyes in a mirror, Rachel turns to show him her breasts. While critics describe this moment as uncharacteristic of an Amish woman, Rachel's simple offering is not uncharacteristic of Arcadia: "Though the pastoral world itself may be pure, it can also be erotically alluring. Simplicity may be so uncommon that it is provocative."[17] Thus experiencing the "conflicting temptations of honour and desire in love" often generated by pastoral retreats,[18] Book turns away. Later, he tells Rachel that if they had made love that night, either she would have to leave the Amish, or he would have to stay, as though in fulfillment of Eli's words: "And having seen, you become one of them."[19]

Book's potential union with Rachel, and hence with the Amish, is anticipated in the barn raising scene, which is played to the hilt—or perhaps I should say "to the grain"—as an example of the pastoral ideal. Book joins the members of the community, all of whom work together in the midst of bucolic beauty, creating something necessary to agrarian life. His unity with the Amish is symbolized with a lemonade glass. An earlier scene showed Rachel's Amish suitor, Daniel (Alexander Godunov), sipping from a glass of lemonade to alleviate the awkward silence he feels as he sits beside her on a porch swing. In the next scene, Rachel brings Book lemonade in a similar glass, her demeanor displaying more attraction to the city man than to Daniel, a proclivity Daniel seems to recognize. However, Daniel does not allow jealousy to sully Arcadia. Later during the barn raising, as he and Book stand on crossbeams high above the ground, Daniel offers his lemonade to Book, so that both of them drink out of the same glass. True to pastoral convention, rustic interdependence supersedes the competitive individualism one finds in the city.

Peter Weir elicits a sense of Arcadia from the very start, beginning the film with undulating waves of grain—shot with a low-angle lens so that green wheat fills two thirds of the screen. Soon we see people in plain dress appear above the grain, walking into the screen from the right, presumably on a road hidden behind the greenery. Next an Amish buggy enters from the left, appearing to sink into the grain due to the odd camera angle. Finally, a row of heads arises out of the grain in the center of the screen, apparently walking toward us as they grow taller and taller in the midst of the vegetation. Viewers who protested that Amish would never walk through a field in their formal attire missed the symbolism of the shot.[20] Like a scene from Virgil's *Bucolics,* the opening shots of *Witness* connect humans to humus, so that the Amish appear to grow up out of the land itself, like stalks of corn. Even Amish technology—a buggy—sinks into the land, nature swallowing up culture. Significantly, when the corrupt cops enter Arcadia, having finally tracked Book to the Lapp farm, we see them approach in a car. However, once they see the farm, they back the car up to get it out of sight. The camera once again films the shot with a low-angle lens, so that it looks like the reversing car is sinking into the land beneath the horizon. It is as though the film is tipping its Amish head coverings to Leo Marx's famous definition of the American pastoral: "The sudden appearance of the machine in the garden is an arresting, endlessly evocative image. It causes the instantaneous clash of opposed states of mind: a strong urge to believe in the rural myth along with an awareness of industrialization as counterforce to the myth."[21]

Repeatedly throughout *Witness,* when violence from the city invades peaceful Arcadia, we see agricultural products swallowing up urban corruption. After Eli warns the young Samuel about the evil of guns, Book asks Rachel to hide his bullets. Then, when he later needs the bullets, Rachel opens a flour tin and pours them out, coated with the bleached wheat. This humorous moment anticipates the most horrific scene of the entire film, when Book traps one of the corrupt cops in a flour-tin shaped silo and smothers him with corn. As tons of grain pour down on top of him, we see the criminal choking on the dust until his body is completely covered. Book then enters the silo and digs through the corn in search of his enemy's weapon—a scene reminiscent of the moment when he dusts off his flour-covered bullets. Finally, for the denouement of the film, the leader of the corrupt city contingent holds a gun to Rachel's head. But when Samuel rings the house bell, scores of Amish farmers rise up out of their fields and run to the Lapp house, their sheer numbers discouraging the criminal from taking violent action. In all these cases, that which originates in rural fields overpowers machines of violence.

Nevertheless, death cannot be kept out of Arcadia, dramatically symbolized when blood from one of the dishonest cops shot by Book stains a white wall of the Lapp barn. The acknowledgement of death in Arcadia is, in fact, part of the pastoral tradition, manifest in pastoral elegies written by the likes of Edmund Spenser, John Milton, and Percy Bysshe Shelley. However, it was the painter Nicolas Poussin who made famous death's pastoral statement—"Et in Arcadia Ego" (Even in Arcadia, there am I)—by placing it on a tomb in a 1645 painting, with rustics somberly contemplating the phrase.[22]

Significantly, *Witness* starts with rustics contemplating death, the Amish walking through grain on their way to a funeral. Their speechless communal bereavement, dozens of plain-dressed people quietly surrounding the coffin and then sitting wordlessly with the widow, operates in stark contrast to the loud and noisome murders of the criminals at the end of the film. It is the radical disjunction between these deaths in Arcadia that finally kills the incipient love between Rachel and Book. This time it is Rachel's horrified eyes that witness the gory results of Book's police training, and we recognize, along with her, the insurmountable barrier that divides their psyches.

To his credit, Weir refused to give viewers a generic Hollywood love story, whereby either Rachel runs off with Book to the city, or he decides to live with her among the Amish. Instead, after Book has murdered his foes, we see him standing on the Lapp porch, his body framed by the bright white clapboard. Next to him, on the left side of our screen, is the open door to the house, the inside entirely dark in contrast to the sunny outside. We see Rachel slowly emerge from the dark; however, she never steps out of the doorway onto the porch with Book, so that she remains framed in black while Book is framed in white. This, of course, symbolizes the separateness of their worlds, and as the camera takes Rachel's perspective to look at Book, we see a road that runs from behind his head off into the horizon. It is the road that Book must take—like visitors to Arcadia before him. Molded by the ways of the city, he must renounce Arcadia in order to return to his urban responsibility: promoting peace in a land of violence.[23] Having seen the Amish, he does not become one of them.

And neither do we. The film establishes a parallel between Book and its viewers, implying that, just as Book has entered into a pastoral community, we have entered into the pastoral genre—developed over the centuries in books. The correlation is made blatant during the bathing scene as the camera places viewers in the same position as the viewing Book: witnessing Rachel in a private moment from behind her back. The mirror by which Rachel witnesses Book faces out toward the audience; but instead of our own faces, we see Book in the mirror. It is as though the film acknowledges the concerns of John A. Hostetler, who denounced any film about the Amish because the "voyeuristic camera eye" turns "the intimate and sacred into public property."[24] Indeed, when Rachel turns toward the camera, she offers her breasts not just to Book but to us. However, like Book, we will turn away after our bit of voyeurism, returning at the end of the film to our (sub)urban lives. That, in fact, is what pastoral is all about: "In the best of pastoral literature, the writer will have taken the reader on a journey to be changed and charged upon return for more informed action in the present."[25]

The Amish as Witness

The pastoral, then, is inherently ethical—not in spite of its escapist impulses, but because of them—for it leads reflective readers/viewers to assess how they might ameliorate that which needs escaping. Terry Gifford believes that this is "the essential paradox of the pastoral":

> A retreat to a place apparently without the anxieties of the town, or the court, or the present, actually delivers insights into the culture from which it originates. Pastoral authors are inescapably of their own culture and its preoccupations. Thus the pastoral construct always reveals the preoccupations and tensions of its time. Even if it is an unintended reflection, the most determined escape returns something to its audience.[26]

Skeptics might respond that pastoral films merely use the Amish to receive financial returns from the "returns" experienced by their audiences, and I would have to agree. However, I would add that these latter "returns" might be more in harmony with Amish values than critics of *Witness* aver. For pastoral is inherently anti-Constantinian, exposing the dishonesty and violence that can corrupt the ruling class—even in so-called democratic societies. And though patriarchal legalism and stiff-necked intolerance similarly corrupt Old Order communities, the Amish nevertheless give witness to willed independence from the violence of life-destroying machines, both industrial and political.

However, it is this very witness that creates the ethical conundrum of *Witness*. Pastoral fictions arise from an intense desire for Arcadia to be "real." This pastoral impulse, however, is predicated on an authenticity no longer accessible to those who nostalgically seek to preserve it. In classical tradition, pastoral inaccessibility was geographical: the Greek poet Theocritus placed the pastoral ideal in Sicily, whereas the Latin poet Virgil placed it in Greece. While Renaissance resuscitators of Arcadia imagined it in the irretrievable past, Elizabethan dramatists attributed inaccessibility to a radical disjunction between levels in the social hierarchy: though urban dwellers can enter Arcadia and experience "a green refuge from the troubles and complication of ordinary life,"[27] their responsibility to uphold the social structure requires them to forgo attraction to swains and shepherdesses in order to properly return to their leadership positions—albeit refreshed by their bucolic encounters. In the seventeenth century, Europeans focused their pastoral dreams on America, an Arcadia made inaccessible by the Atlantic Ocean. Those who made it to the New World, however, encountered not bucolic landscapes but a "hideous wilderness" impeding agrarian bliss.[28] Once the land was cultivated, Arcadia was destroyed by the locomotive—to which Thoreau alludes in almost every chapter of *Walden*.[29] In other words, as soon as Arcadia is made accessible, whether by train or by some other technology, it can no longer be Arcadia.

It should come as no surprise, then, that the technology-resistant Amish have come to embody the pastoral ideal: "free and modest, honest and ingenuous."[30] And true to pastoral convention, outsiders can visit but not permanently access this idyllic life—because it is a fiction, perpetuated by its very inaccessibility. In the case of the Amish, of course, inaccessibility is due to the community's own sectarian ethic. "Be ye separate"—that famous statement of Amish self-definition—is, in fact, recited by the Amish grandfather in *Witness*. This separatist ideal explains why no "real" Amish appear in the film; all the roles are played by professional actors or local extras who—like John Book, as well as Brad and Carolyn in *For Richer or Poorer*—disguise themselves in Amish clothing to appear Amish. In other words, that which makes the Amish an icon of the American pastoral precludes the possibility of filming them. The Amish Arcadia is always already inaccessible.

Notes

Epigraph: Quoted in Donald B. Kraybill, *The Riddle of Amish Culture*, rev. ed. (Baltimore: Johns Hopkins University Press, 2001), 45.

1. See David Weaver-Zercher, *The Amish in the American Imagination* (Baltimore: Johns Hopkins University Press, 2001), 152–80, and David Walbert, *Garden Spot: Lancaster County, the Old Order Amish, and the Selling of Rural America* (New York: Oxford University Press, 2002), 173–77.

2. For a history of the pastoral genre in film, see Gerald C. Wood, "The Pastoral Tradition in American Film before World War II," *Markham Review* 12 (1983): 52–60.

3. Erwin Panofsky, "Et in Arcadia Ego: On the Conception of Transience in Poussin and Watteau," in *Philosophy and History: Essays Presented to Ernst Cassirer*, ed. Raymond Klibansky and H. J. Paton (New York: Harper & Row, 1963), 225.

4. Ibid. About Helen R. Martin's Pennsylvania Dutch novels, see Weaver-Zercher, *Amish in the American Imagination*, 34–46.

5. Andrew V. Ettin explains, "Like the terms *tragedy* and *comedy*, the term *pastoral* denotes experiences and ideas that are permanent parts of our thinking and writing" (*Literature and the Pastoral* [New Haven: Yale University Press, 1984], 1).

6. Quoted in Walbert, *Garden Spot*, 212.

7. Ettin, *Literature and the Pastoral*, 97.

8. William Rose Benét, "Pastoral," *The Reader's Encyclopedia*, 2nd ed. (New York: Crowell, 1965), 764.

9. Panofsky, "Et in Arcadia Ego," 229.

10. David M. Halperin, *Before Pastoral: Theocritus and the Ancient Tradition of Bucolic Poetry* (New Haven: Yale University Press, 1983), 76.

11. Glen A. Love, "*Et in Arcadia Ego:* Pastoral Theory Meets Ecocriticism," *Western American Literature* 27 (1992): 196.

12. John A. Hostetler and Donald B. Kraybill, "Hollywood Markets the Amish,"

in *Image Ethics: The Moral Rights of Subjects in Photographs, Film, and Television,* ed. Larry Gross, John Stuart Katz, and Jay Ruby (New York: Oxford University Press, 1988), 222.

13. See Paul W. Nisly, "*Witness:* A Film Directed by Peter Weir," *Conrad Grebel Review* 4 (1986): 294.

14. Erwin Panofsky, *Meaning in the Visual Arts* (Chicago: University of Chicago Press, 1982), 297.

15. Pauline Kael, "Plain and Simple," *New Yorker,* 25 February 1985, 78.

16. Leo Marx, *The Machine in the Garden: Technology and the Pastoral Ideal in America* (New York: Oxford University Press, 1964), 24.

17. Ettin, *Literature and the Pastoral,* 151.

18. Terry Gifford, *Pastoral* (New York: Routledge, 1999), 59.

19. For protests about Rachel's boldness, see Weaver-Zercher, *Amish in the American Imagination,* 161, and Nisly, "*Witness,*" 294–95. An interview with one of the film's screenwriters reveals that the bathing scene was originally meant to echo 2 Samuel 11 "in which David was aroused from his bed and walked upon the roof of the king's house and saw a beautiful woman washing herself" (Michael T. Marsden, "Evolution of the Academy Award–Winning Script for *Witness,*" in *In the Eye of the Beholder: Critical Perspectives in Popular Film and Television,* ed. Gary R. Edgerton, Michael T. Marsden, and Jack Nachbar [Bowling Green, OH: Bowling Green State University Popular Press, 1997], 51).

20. In his review of the film, Stanley Kauffman questions whether Amish would walk through the grain (*New Republic,* 18 February 1985, 24).

21. Marx, *Machine in the Garden,* 229.

22. Both Panofsky texts discuss the intriguing interpretive history of the Poussin painting.

23. Significantly, as Book drives away from Rachel, he passes his Amish rival, Daniel, who is walking toward the Lapp house.

24. Quoted in Nisly, "*Witness,*" 296.

25. Gifford, *Pastoral,* 80.

26. Ibid., 82.

27. M. H. Abrams, *A Glossary of Literary Terms,* 3rd ed. (New York: Holt, Rinehart & Winston, 1971), 121.

28. Marx, *Machine in the Garden,* 42.

29. Ibid., 260.

30. Paul Alpers, *What Is Pastoral?* (Chicago: University of Chicago Press, 1996), 17.

Devil's Playground, *a documentary funded by HBO, follows Faron Yoder and several youth from Amish communities as they experience* Rumspringa.
Photo by Steven Cantor; used by permission of Stick Figure Productions.

Chapter Two

Reel Amish

The Amish in Documentaries

Dirk Eitzen

No cameras please.
—sign in an Amish-owned business

Documentaries in America have always perched somewhat precariously on the divide between entertainment and reportage. Anthropologists use the word "liminal" to describe the boundary between two cultural categories. For example, in cultures like the Amish, in which entry into adulthood is marked by a rite of passage, an adolescent who is no longer a child but not yet an adult is said to be in a liminal state, caught up perforce in a kind of struggle for self-definition. The documentary has always occupied such a zone because of its peculiar niche between two thoroughly entrenched cultural imperatives: to make a buck, and to convey newsworthy or culturally significant information. The so-called social documentary—the exhortatory documentary tradition that dates back to the early 1930s and is carried forward in movies like Michael Moore's *Fahrenheit 9-11*—stems from a third time-honored cultural imperative: to preach. But as *Fahrenheit*

9-11 clearly demonstrates, this tradition too straddles the entertainment/information divide.

The first rule of documentary filmmaking is that telling a good story trumps getting across good information. While it is well and good to be passionate about social issues or deeply interested in some historical event, if a documentary filmmaker does not put the audience's interests first, his or her film will probably never be seen by more than a handful of people. The fact is, people watch movies, even nonfiction movies, for the *experience,* that is, for the emotional payoff. Information is, in a sense, irrelevant, except to the extent that it is emotionally loaded (like reports of a catastrophe), or utilitarian (like a television weather report), or cloaked in some sort of entertaining garb (such as a story). Moreover, to sustain interest for an hour or more, the promise of an emotional payoff has to be continually reinforced. A recital of facts, no matter how significant, is deadly.

On the other hand, in documentaries, entertainment value and information value are inextricably bound together. Woe to the documentary that appears to play fast and loose with facts. Seriousness, social relevance, intellectual enlightenment, moral edification—these are and have always been a big part of the cultural capital on which documentaries have traded.[1] Entertainment value per se does not jeopardize this capital. Documentaries have always been full of sensationalism, scenes contrived for dramatic effect, cheap pathos, and even humor. But if in a particular documentary any of these elements seem to be deliberately misleading, spectators can wind up questioning the whole film.

Sensational, yet with an aura of social import; the form of a story, yet one that does not appear to take liberties with the facts; the appearance of informativeness, but not cluttered up with too many boring details. That is a forty-word recipe for documentary success. Nonfiction filmmakers, from the earliest producers to the stars of today's documentary firmament like Errol Morris and Michael Moore, have always intuited this formula.

The perennial dance between sensationalism and seriousness, information and entertainment, factual accuracy and fictional form, making a buck and making a difference—this is what characterizes the documentary's liminal state. On one side is the magnet of Hollywood entertainment, with its well-established formulas for commercial success; on the other is the "just-the-facts-ma'am" tradition of news and historical reportage, which despite being itself very much the product of commercial forces, has longstanding and thoroughly institutionalized guidelines for what counts as legitimate reportage and what does not.

The Allure of the Other

Given this state of affairs, one can begin to understand the attraction that the Amish exercise on documentary filmmakers. On one hand, there is the established "entertainment value" of the exotic—the allure of the Other. In some respects, this is akin to simple curiosity: we wonder about people who are different from ourselves. This curiosity is part of our makeup and is one of the engines of narrative. But in the case of documentaries, this curiosity also has a sensational edge: it is bound up with surface differences—visible things like bonnets and buggies.[2]

On the other hand, the Amish are a "serious" subject: a religious group that has made deliberate lifestyle choices that cast the values of mainstream society into relief. Bonnets and buggies do not just represent difference to most Americans; they represent a clear alternative to cars, television commercials, and other modern headaches. As a result, they trigger a sentimental response—a kind of vague utopian longing that seems quite impervious to recognition of the "old-fashioned" headaches of horse manure, authoritarian church leaders, and no Internet.

Curiosity about people who are not like us is a natural human trait. Young children are fascinated by difference, by people in wheelchairs, for instance. In Africa, children want to feel straight blonde hair. In rural Iowa, children are curious about kinky black hair. Adults have the same curiosity, and documentaries about Others both indulge this curiosity and profit from it. There is a long history of such documentaries, from early actualities of "natives" to the National Geographic documentaries on television today.

The first feature film in this vein, Robert Flaherty's 1922 *Nanook of the North,* neatly illustrates several tendencies of the genre. *Nanook,* which tells of an Inuit tribesman struggling to eke out a living in "the mysterious Barren lands . . . which top the world," is first of all a story. Flaherty realized that to compete in movie theaters against popular melodramas and comedies he needed to have a narrative, for narrative is what sustains Hollywood movies. Narrative, in turn, is sustained by conflict. In *Nanook,* the conflict is the protagonist's struggle to stave off starvation and freezing. Flaherty deliberately set up this struggle with florid intertitles and escalated it by having the movie begin in the summer and end in the middle of winter.

There is truth to the claim that Inuit life in the 1920s was a struggle for survival. Even so, compared to fiction films of the era, *Nanook* is quite slow. The scenes are more a collection of loosely related activities than the connected series of goal-oriented actions that moves the typical story along. The problem is, of course, that documentary footage, even if it is somewhat contrived, does not lend itself to the kind of goal-driven emplotment that characterizes popular fiction films. Documentary footage inevitably leaves a whole lot of narrative gaps.

Nanook tries to compensate for this weakness in several ways. One of these ways is the sensationalism of the treatment: the aestheticization of the frozen landscape, the poetic language of many of the intertitles, and the deliberate use of harpoons for hunting when rifles were at hand. In addition, Flaherty worked hard to appeal to viewer sentiment through what might be called "the cuteness factor." For example, the first major scene opens with the deliberately funny shot of an astonishing number of children and dogs piling out of a kayak, like clowns from a VW bug. The scene continues to make much of fluffy puppies and cuddly children. In fact, Nanook himself is depicted as kind of a child: harmless, jovial, and naive—in a word, cute.[3] Nanook is nothing if not endearing.

There is still another subtler, deeper, and more pervasive appeal to sentiment throughout the movie: its mythic quality. Flaherty did not shoot *Nanook* because he was interested in the reality of Inuit life; he shot it because he was fascinated by his own idealization of Inuit life. Flaherty cherished a deep and abiding notion that the essence of humanity revealed itself in the battle against nature's elements.[4] This ideal shines through *Nanook* and helps explain the film's success. If *Nanook* were simply an assembly of actuality footage, we might be briefly intrigued, but there would be no point in watching it through. It is not the protagonist's actuality that is supposed to sustain viewers' interest, but his heroism. The movie is not just a story; it is a lesson about life.

Cultural theorists have observed that the Other is always a kind of projection—more a reflection of our own preoccupations than of the reality of the Other. That is as obviously true of popular views of the Amish as it is of Flaherty's view of the Inuit. The realities of Amish life—the lack of educational opportunities, the authoritarian social structures, and occasional domestic abuse—are not generally part of the popular image of the Amish. The Amish Other that fascinates people is an imaginary one—the "pastoral" one, as Crystal Downing notes in chapter 1—that fulfills a modern longing for an idyllic communitarian existence. It is not the idea of wearing black polyester button-up trousers that exercises the modern imagination. It is the idea of doing away with modern impediments to community such as cars, which enlarge the distances between us even more than they shrink them, and television, which isolates us even as it seems to expand our horizons. These are things we like to imagine as having no impact on Amish life, so that in looking at the Amish we can entertain pictures of how it might be if these things were not part of our own lives.

Of course, one can do this kind of imagining from the window of a car while driving through "Amish Country," but films and photographs may support it in a special way. Photographs and films always signify the "presence of an absence." That is, they indicate a real person or place that is quite literally not there and an actual moment in time that is past. Some theorists have therefore argued that the very nature of film triggers an unconscious yearning for what is depicted. This yearning, they say, explains much of the emotional power of movies.[5]

Myths about Others are also easier to sustain if there are visible differences to latch on to. Many of the things that set the Amish apart are outward and obvious: not just quiet farm living and a communitarian lifestyle, but horses and buggies, wide-brimmed hats, and colorful cape dresses. These differences are not just visible; they are downright picturesque. Without them, the popular myth of idyllic Amish communities would be much less salient. Conversely, without the myth, the visible differences would seem far less important.

In sum, the Amish seem to be a perfect subject for a modern-day Flaherty. They possess all of the same attractions as Nanook: sensational difference, sentimental appeal, and mythic significance for the modern viewer. It's just too bad they don't like to be filmed.

Shooting Amish

If you ask an Amish minister why the Amish are not allowed to have their pictures taken, he will probably point to the Bible's prohibition against "graven images" (Exodus 20:4). In fact, it is not the Bible that makes the rules for the Amish, but the bishops. The Bible does not say anything about cars, telephones, electricity, or even photography. Amish rules governing the use of these modern technologies are all church rules. They may be based on scriptures, but these scriptures are interpreted and enforced by church leaders on a district-by-district basis. Even when all the bishops supposedly agree, as they do about photography, the rules frequently get bent in lenient districts and progressive households.

Amish bishops may not be formally educated in the ways of biblical interpretation, but they have keen intuition about which practices promote community and which practices undermine it. Most Amish rules are ultimately concerned with keeping the community together. For example, horses and buggies naturally tend to keep people from straying too far, uniform dress discourages individualism and materialism, and television is forbidden because the Amish suppose that it undermines face-to-face relationships.

But how does photography undercut community? The answer here can be traced to the Amish emphasis on humility. Wearing makeup or showy clothes, spending money on non-necessities such as musical instruments, even exhibiting an unusual fondness for book learning—all of these are seen as showing off and are typically frowned upon. Similarly, posing for photographs, or even willingly allowing one's picture to be taken, is regarded as vain, individualistic, and self-indulgent—*hochmutig*. Although what the bishop doesn't know . . .

Several years ago, a successful Lancaster County Amish businessman consented to give an interview in a Swiss documentary about the Amish. He evidently felt that it would do some good to tell people about the Amish and that it would do no harm to his standing in the community, since nobody outside of his family would know. But the documentary was picked up for broadcast by a local PBS affiliate, and his appearance in it created quite a stir. As a result, the Amishman was disciplined, which amounted to sitting apart in church for six weeks and making a humiliating public confession. The news of this disciplining spread like wildfire through the Amish community. Although boundaries are often gray about what is permissible and what is not, one incident like this goes a long way to discourage risk taking.

On the other hand, an Amish woman in Lancaster County who has a successful quilt shop allowed me to videotape in her store for a documentary I was making. She did not set any boundaries (and I deliberately did not ask), so I casually filmed her selling her wares to tourists. She was obviously unusually progressive—a boundary pusher—and I was told that the district bishop was her father, which might have contributed to her willingness to take risks. Still, it is practically inconceivable that this woman would have let me film her in her home or consented to an on-camera interview, for her complicity with the filming would have then been undeniable, almost surely prompting disciplinary action. Even the marginal access to which this woman implicitly consented is exceedingly rare. I talked to dozens of Amish businesspersons in Lancaster County. A few said, "You can film my products, but not me." Most of them turned me away at the door.

For a filmmaker wishing to make a documentary about the Amish, this lack of openness presents a real problem, for the whole approach of *Nanook* hinges on the willing cooperation of the subject. Filmmakers, television crews, and still photographers have thus resorted to three strategies to shoot candid pictures of Amish life: pushiness (shooting without regard to Amish sensibilities); poaching (shooting discretely, from a distance, or surreptitiously); and shooting young adults and children in situations in which Amish adults are absent.

The pushy approach is characteristic of investigative journalism, like the series of reports on network television, over the years, on domestic abuse and rape among the Amish.[6] One of the rules of journalism is that, in situations that are deemed newsworthy, the "public's right to know" outweighs the privacy of citizens. This tends to be counterbalanced by the rule that, except in extraordinary circumstances, one cannot shoot private citizens or on private property if asked to refrain. Anyway, pushiness is more likely to result in images of angry or upset Amish than in an intimate picture of Amish life.

For this reason journalists tend to rely more on the second approach—photographic poaching—an approach the Amish prefer and, at least to some degree, accommodate. Because of the ubiquity of camera-toting tourists in Amish settlements and because of the growing economic reliance of many Amish communities on trade with tourists, Amish bishops have generally agreed that it is okay for Amish persons to let their pictures be taken, so long as they are going about their business and do not "pose." What this means for most Amish is that if someone takes a picture of you in a public place, you ignore him. Of course, the notion of "going about your business" requires some interpretation, leading a few unusually progressive Amish (like the quilt shop owner I mentioned earlier) to play the game of what might be called plausible deniability. Still, allowing an outsider to take pictures of you interacting with family members inside your home is strictly taboo.

What does this approach mean for the documentary filmmaker? As a practical matter, it means that it is possible to shoot the Amish in public places, at farmers' markets and around Amish businesses (as long as one is not too obvious about it), and outside Amish farms, homes, and church meetings (as long as one shoots from the street). If in any of these instances a photographer is too obvious or intrusive, Amish subjects may hide their faces or ask him to desist—which means a telephoto lens is often useful or necessary. Of course, using a telephoto lens is somewhat less than ideal for filmmakers: although it accommodates the "illustrated lecture" style of documentary filmmaking, it virtually precludes the kind of intimacy on display in *Nanook,* on which narratively structured documentary depends.

There is one notable exception to the Amish prohibition of photography. Young people who are not yet members of the church may agree to have their pictures taken. There is no rule against Amish children posing for photographs. Moreover, in some Amish communities unbaptized Amish teenagers are allowed a remarkable amount of freedom to experiment—

with cars, popular culture, alcohol, and sex—in a period known as *Rumspringa,* literally "running around."

In practice, however, the Amish are very protective of their children, discouraging them from interacting with outsiders. And most Amish young people do not care to involve themselves with documentary filmmakers. Indeed, the idea of "being on television" does not have the same appeal to them as it does to non-Amish youth. The makers of *Devil's Playground,* a 2002 Cinemax documentary on *Rumspringa,* tried for months to find Amish young people in Lancaster County willing to take part in their project, with no luck. They finally gave up and moved to an Amish community in northern Indiana, where they met with more success.

Despite these obstacles, sensitive filmmakers and photographers, knowing Amish rules about photography, have been somewhat less leery of shooting Amish children and youth than of shooting Amish adults. This has led to an unusually high proportion of images of children and youth in films and photographs of the Amish, which has had the perhaps unintended fringe benefit for the picture takers of enhancing the cuteness quotient of their pictures.

Revealing "Deep Truths"

Documentaries about Others do not just show pretty pictures or tell interesting stories; they purport to reveal deep truths. In addition to making documentaries relevant and worthwhile to viewers, deep truths serve to compensate for the fact that, as movies go, documentaries are inevitably pretty dull. *Nanook* purports to reveal deep truths both about the hardships of Inuit living and about the nature of humanity. Modern documentaries about groups of people like the Amish are supposed to lay bare deep truths in the same way, even though these truths are likely to be more subtle, more cautious, and more politically correct. Even postmodern documentaries that deliberately reject the notion of deep truths uphold that rejection as a kind of deep truth. If a documentary is supposed to fly, deep truths of one kind or another are practically inescapable. Of course, an appropriately skeptical scholar is wise to put that term in quotation marks—or better yet, to characterize such "truths" as ideologies or myths. For the sake of brevity, I will use the term *myth*.

The title of a documentary often reveals the myth beneath it. That is certainly true of the first two widely distributed documentaries about the Amish, *The Amish: A People of Preservation* (released in 1976 and expanded in 1991) and *The Amish: Not to Be Modern* (1985).[7] Contrast these two titles to the title of sociologist Donald B. Kraybill's book about Amish life: *The Riddle of Amish Culture*.[8] Against the background of the popular notion of the Amish as "the people of preservation," Kraybill's title suggests the Amish are instead "the people of the odd accommodation." Instead of remarking, "Isn't it odd that the Amish don't have electricity in their homes?" Kraybill asks, in effect, "Isn't it odd that the Amish don't have electricity in their homes while, at the same time, they have a generator in the barn to charge the car batteries that run cash registers in the shop?" Anything more than a superficial look at the Amish reveals dozens of such anomalies. That is the "riddle" to which Kraybill refers.

The obvious question to ask of documentaries about the Amish is, Do they penetrate the riddle of the Amish, or do they succumb to the myth? Do they dismantle the myth, embrace the myth, or start with the myth and qualify it? Of course, the "deep truths" of documentaries are seldom expressed outright. They lie as much in what is *not* said as in what *is* said: in the structure, the patterns of selection and ordering of materials, in the "spin" of the story or argument. Sometimes they are even evident in the mood or tone of a film.

The spin of *A People of Preservation* (1976) is first apparent in its soundtrack. The movie begins with more than a minute and a half of "silence": birdsong layered over in succession by the sounds of a passing horse and buggy, a distant Amish hymn, and the voices of Amish children playing. The film is replete with quiet moments like these. Except in a few scenes that deliberately show the intrusions of modernity on the Amish way of life, there is no sound of passing traffic, no hum of planes overhead, no babble of tourist commerce—very little unwanted "noise" whatsoever, successfully conveying closeness to nature, piety, community, and, above all, tranquility.

The film's images, too, are by and large pastoral and calm. They foreground nature, children, and quiet retreat. The narration is beautifully written, informative yet almost poetic, delivered in a voice that is quiet, measured, even languid. The tone of the whole movie is authoritative yet deeply reassuring, according perfectly with the film's interpretation of Amish life.

The odd accommodations to modernity and the stresses and strains of Amish life are by no means denied, but they are deliberately downplayed. For example, the narration acknowledges that the use of a gasoline engine on a horse-drawn bailer might seem like an inconsistency to an outsider. But "to the Amishman, it simply means that he will not let modern technology run away with his community or his family at its own pace." Explanations of the Amish lifestyle are, as in this instance, "simple," uncomplicated, and above all, the result of Amish *choices*. The lifestyle of the Amish is not a riddle at all, the film assures; it is a choice.

Moreover, *A People of Preservation* is extremely circumspect in its regard for the Amish way of life. In some cases, untidy facts (or possible interpretations) are deliberately swept under the rug. For example, of *Rumspringa,* the narration reports that Amish adults "wink at" transgressions like dressing up a horse's harness or turning up the brim of a hat; there is no mention of rock-'n'-roll parties, getting drunk, and driving a car. In another place, the narration describes the Amish practice of ending formal education at eighth grade—one of the essential means by which the Amish maintain their social order—as follows: "Learning and skills are seen as detrimental, since they do not prepare a person with the practical skills and tastes needed for life in an Amish community." This is true, but one could equally truthfully say, "Access to learning and skills are strictly controlled in order to assure that young people's opportunities to leave the Amish community are curtailed." The narration of this section continues: "By the time they are fourteen, most [Amish young people] *prefer* to leave school for practical vocational activity." It would be more accurate to say that most Amish young people do not see higher education as a real option. To call this a preference is not false, exactly, but it is clearly a kind of wishful thinking—a myth.

Anthropologists and sociologists recognize that lifestyles are very rarely a matter of deliberate choice, of "simple" beliefs. One might describe an accountant's suit and tie as a choice, but it is more than that: it is the product of peer pressure, advertising, job requirements, and a large measure of unconscious habit reinforced by cultural conventions. To reduce dress to a matter of choice is to oversimplify it as much for the Amish as for anybody else. But because the Amish are "different," we buy the idea more readily.

That is the overarching myth of *A People of Preservation:* the myth of a tranquil lifestyle governed by deliberate choices and beliefs. In fact, individual Amish are, by and large, far less aware of the roots of their cultural practices than is the author of this documentary. That is shown quite clearly (albeit unintentionally) by the second widely distributed documentary about the Amish, *Not to Be Modern.*

Not to Be Modern begins, "In *this* film, the Amish speak for themselves; they tell their own story." This is a clear dig at *A People of Preservation,* in which the filmmaker, John Ruth, speaks for the Amish. But there is a real irony here. John Ruth is a Mennonite minister, writer, and historian, deeply familiar with Anabaptist theology and Amish traditions. He speaks with clarity and vision and illuminates Amish beliefs and practices much more clearly than most Amish persons can do themselves. With their eighth-grade educations and their suspicion of intellectualism, most Amish are simply not capable of putting these beliefs into words in a way that conveys their real substance. That takes a scholar like John Ruth. If Ruth is overzealous in describing these as choices, he is at least correct in his understanding of the underlying principles that govern Amish life and *Ordnung.* Those principles are what order *A People of Preservation.*

Not to Be Modern, in eschewing such broad claims, winds up getting stuck on the superficial, even while purporting to give greater access to the Amish. The lack of focus, the absence of any guiding "deep truth" in this film, is particularly apparent in some of the longer interviews. In one long story, told over images of youths working in the fields, a father tells about promising his kids a trip to McDonald's because they really like french fries, which his wife does not make because they take too much oil. When the family got there, the place was full of college kids out cruising, so they went to Burger King instead. "It had real good food and good service," the story concludes. This anecdote may be somewhat amusing, but its inclusion reveals nothing of substance except perhaps the filmmaker's own preoccupation with the "peculiarities" of the Amish.

In this way and others, *Not to Be Modern* appears to have been made by an outsider who is fascinated by the Amish lifestyle but never really "gets it." The Amish interviewees do not express their beliefs particularly well, and the filmmaker does not presume to try to explain them. The result is arguably a less-illuminating and less-interesting film than *A People of Preservation*. It is without question a less-coherent film. What happens when "deep truths" go missing is that a documentary can wind up skittering over the surface of interesting and profound riddles. That is what happens in this case.

Debunking "Deep Truths"

Scholarly works also have myths, although we do not call them myths; we call them "paradigms." David Weaver-Zercher has written, for example, about the way Amish-born sociologist John A. Hostetler's personal vision of what the Amish *should be* occasionally colored his representations of what they *were*.[9] Similarly, the foremost contemporary scholar of the Amish, sociologist Donald Kraybill, the author of *The Riddle of Amish Culture*, is a Mennonite and a well-known advocate of Anabaptist theology.[10] Kraybill's solution to the "riddle" of Amish culture is that, despite the continual negotiations between tradition and modernity on practical matters, the Amish have maintained a way of life informed by key theological principles. These same principles characterize Kraybill's own theology.

In the interest of full disclosure, I too am a Mennonite—and a documentary filmmaker to boot. That means I have a personal stake in the subject matter I am dealing with here. But academics *always* have a personal stake in what they write about. My own myths, which without doubt lurk between the lines of this essay, are also evident in a public television documentary I produced about the impact of tourism on the Amish of Lancaster County, *The Amish & Us* (1998).[11]

The Amish & Us starts from the premise that there is something just as curious about the folks who flock to "Amish Country" to gawk at the Amish as there is about the Amish themselves. The film deliberately performs a kind of bait-and-switch. It hints at images of the Amish but actually serves up more pictures of tourists, with the aim of making viewers self-conscious about their own fascination with the Amish. The point is not to set up some new myth, or even to debunk old myths. It is rather to dangle the myths in plain view for people to look at and be aware of. It reflects a postmodern sensibility: not merely self-consciousness, but *ironic* self-consciousness. Much of the film is deliberately tongue-in-cheek. In this regard, it is diametrically opposed to *A People of Preservation;* it is about as *un*-Amish as a documentary about the Amish can be.

But despite purporting to be above myths, *The Amish & Us* does insinuate a single guiding myth that pokes through in lots of places in the film. One example is in the last section, "What's in Store?" This section shows the same series of images three times, with three different narrations, each entirely true but suggesting vastly different points of view. For example, over an image of tourists buying quilts at an Amish shop, the first narration says, "The constant contact with outsiders and the appeal of tourist cash lure Amish young people away from traditional practices and beliefs." The second says, "For those who prefer to stay on the farm, the millions of dollars tourists spend every year on quilts and crafts provide the extra income to make ends meet." The third says, "The real danger isn't change itself, but the erosion of the spiritual values that are the foundation of the Amish way of life."

If you line up the three parallel sequences side by side, you discover a discrepancy. One image in the third version does not fit. It is an add-on that breaks with the deliberate parallels, a crack in the film's ironic facade. This image shows a crowd of tourists buying sticky buns at a bakeshop. The narration that accompanies it declares, "Tourism represents a completely different set of values: self-gratification, accumulation, the pursuit of private pleasures."

The myth revealed here is that Amish values and tourist values are diametric opposites. It perceives Amish culture as a rare holdout against consumer culture, against what I call the Coca-Cola regime. The reason the Amish have been so successful in resisting this regime is not (or not just) that their belief in firm principles has led to the persistence of a certain lifestyle (as *A People of Preservation* suggests), but the reverse: that sticking to a certain lifestyle, regardless of the reasons, has created a culture that, because it has no room for television and the Internet, has to some extent inoculated itself against Coca-Cola values. But I recognize that this involves a large measure of wishful thinking. The fact is that Amish people drink Coke, too—more and more of it, I daresay.

In its structure and style, *The Amish & Us* is deliberately postmodern. The goal of high modernism (good old-fashioned pre-postmodernism, that is) was to smash myths and get to the underlying "reality" of things. One critique of contemporary *post*modernism is that this ideal has washed out of modernism, leaving behind only a smug blanket of irony. If "deep truths" are just myths and myths are inescapable, why bother with them? Despite the postmodern style of *The Amish & Us,* this is not the attitude that the film seeks to convey. I believe that if "deep truths" are just myths and myths are inescapable, it behooves us to pick and choose among them carefully. So beneath the ironic facade of *The Amish & Us* lies another purported "deep truth"—that Amish-style community represents a way out of the excesses of consumerism.

The mark of a truly myth-busting documentary is that it discovers things that surprise even the filmmakers. Nothing surprised John Ruth in making *A People of Preservation,* for the film communicated things he already knew. The little revelations of *Not to Be Modern* are more odd and quaint than surprising. And I knew what I was out to get in *The Amish & Us,* so there were no real surprises for me there, either.

In contrast, the makers of the recent documentary *Devil's Playground* encountered a great many surprises.[12] *Devil's Playground* is a truly extraordinary work in that director Lucy Walker really manages to get beneath the surface of Amish life, or at least a little corner of it, in spite of the walls the Amish throw up against outsiders. The filmmakers knew more or less what they wanted—a movie about the Amish practice of *Rumspringa* that conformed to the shape of a story, with a main character who undergoes real changes—but they did not know how or even if they would get it. That they did get it in the end was the result of incredible perseverance: more than three years of labor and three hundred hours of videotaping. And because of their immersion in the lives of their Amish subjects, they were genuinely and repeatedly surprised along the way.[13]

Perhaps their biggest surprise was to discover that not all Amish lead the quiet pastoral life depicted in *Witness.* In fact, in northern Indiana, many of them work at grinding, tedious factory jobs. Another surprise was that, for most Amish youth, heaven and hell are as real as New York and Los Angeles. Still another was that, after sixteen years of restrictions, Amish youth in *Rumspringa* soaked up the modern like sponges. The boys did not want to drive horses and buggies on camera; they wanted to show off their cars instead.

None of these insights comes as a big surprise to anyone familiar with the Amish, of course. The point is that the filmmakers, in search of a story rather than a lesson or a report, were getting to know their subjects as individuals, not just observing them as exemplars of a group.

The filmmakers follow the story where it leads, unencumbered by the need to be diplomatic or discrete. Their sensitivity to the Amish takes a different form from the other documentaries described here: genuine interest in getting to know *individual* Amish people, whatever their struggles may be. And this, in turn, leads to the biggest surprise of all: the most charming and articulate of the Amish young people, a youth named Faron (arguably the "star" of the film) is a heavy crystal methamphetamine user. This is shown on camera.

All of these surprises are, in a happy but somewhat bewildering irony, ultimately the product of commercial pressures on the filmmakers. *A People of Preservation* and *Not to Be Modern* and even *The Amish & Us* were all produced on a shoestring, for some noble-minded purpose. In contrast, *Devil's Playground* was produced with substantial up-front funding from cable heavyweight HBO. That means the filmmakers' objective, first and foremost, was to tell an engaging story. That objective *required* them to focus on individuals. It *required* that they show these individuals in intimate and dramatic circumstances—hanging out with friends and partying, for instance. It *required,* above all, a central character with a dramatic trajectory to his life.

Devil's Playground was produced in the wake of a nationally publicized drug bust in Lancaster County's Amish community, so there was a certain amount of sensational interest in the subject matter.[14] But the filmmakers also realized that *Rumspringa* was an ideal topic for a narrative documentary because of its intrinsic drama. For sixteen years, Amish children live tame, obedient lives under the close supervision of their parents and church. They are then allowed to kick the traces, and in some Amish communities, they do this in some pretty dramatic ways (the boys, in particular). Then, after several years, they start thinking about marriage, and they either decide to join to the church and settle down—which the vast majority do—or they drift away from the church. *Rumspringa* is a truly liminal moment in the life of an Amish person, and liminal moments tend to be the stuff of high drama.

Still, the story structure of *Devil's Playground* was not just "found." It was deliberately sought for and crafted. The filmmakers set out to follow four Amish young people: a boy and a girl who eventually join the church, and a boy and a girl who leave it. This turned out to be impossible, partly because Amish youth on their way to joining the church often did not wish to be filmed, but more importantly, because even in *Rumspringa* most of the kids led pretty uneventful lives. It was not until Faron turned up, well into the filming, that the movie began to take shape. "Until that point," the producer says in the DVD commentary, "I don't think we thought we really had a film."

Faron was picked as the central subject of the film, not because he was representative (to the contrary), nor because he was particularly smart and outgoing (which he was), but because he was particularly troubled (remember, trouble or "conflict" is the main ingredient of narrative). Partly on account of his drug use, Faron's life, Walker says, was "like a five-act drama." He dealt drugs. He was arrested and cooperated with police. He received death threats and returned to the farm to lay low. His dad kicked him out of the house. He fell in love with a model-pretty Amish girl, Emma, and followed her to Florida. He had no money and then crashed his uninsured car. He broke up with Emma, returned home, and eventually (an epilogue informs us) landed in prison.

This is precisely what the filmmakers were looking for. Faron's troubled life gave the film its "through line." What *Devil's Playground* does not tell you, of course, and what the typical viewer may not recognize, is that Faron's story is also highly unusual. In fact, when Walker first met Faron at an Amish party, he acted so differently from the other kids that she assumed he was not even Amish. When she spoke with him later, he was much more forthcoming than the typical Amish youth, even "chatty." It turns out he was high.

So in the end, one could dismiss *Devil's Playground* as just another Hollywood-style treatment of Amish life. After all, Faron was singled out by the filmmakers, not because his life is typical of Amish youth, but because it is typical of Hollywood movies—a fact that led some critics to complain that *Devil's Playground* conveyed the false impression that lots of Amish young people are into crystal meth.

It is true that there is nothing in the movie that specifically dispels this impression. Still, I think that the film's treatment of its subjects *as individuals* leads viewers to draw a different "deep truth" from the film: namely, that Amish youth have special problems—problems that stem from their authoritarian upbringing, their lack of education, and the way independence is discouraged in the Amish community. This implicit conclusion is the movie's ultimate surprise. It is by no means flattering, but it is accurate, and it provides an important corrective to the popular idealization of Amish life. It shows the other side of the coin, a side seldom imagined and never before shown on film.

Devil's Playground is, in short, a real myth-buster. That is the power and the good of the film, and it derives largely, ironically, from the filmmakers' search for a "story." Myths are static. Although one myth may challenge another (as indicated in the multiple endings of *The Amish & Us*), the presentation of a myth involves no intrinsic change in perspective. Stories, on the other hand, are dynamic. Stories revolve around changes in perspective. That is part of their power. Good stories always involve surprises—the unexpected. That is their reward. And *Devil's Playground* is full of surprises.

That said, *Devil's Playground* would be an incomplete film—it *is* an incomplete film—without the filmmakers' commentary on the DVD. *A People of Preservation* requires no commentary. Its narration *is* a commentary. An extra director's voice-over track would be redundant, except perhaps to discuss technical details. No back-story is needed because there is no story.

But *Devil's Playground* does tell a story. To put this story into perspective, it is crucial to recognize that the filmmakers were, on one hand, thinking like filmmakers—actively hunting for "characters" and "stories"—and, on the other hand, actively involved in the lives of their subjects. The commentary track on the DVD explicitly acknowledges this, but the film itself does not. Indeed, the filmmakers' push to achieve a kind of narrative transparence tends to paper over these stresses and strains. (For example, when Faron is involved in a car accident, the film makes no mention of the fact that the videographer who was riding with him was badly injured.) Since viewers rarely bring this kind of critical awareness to documentaries they see on television, the filmmakers' commentary is a very important part of the documentary's myth-busting potential. More of it might easily have been included in the television version of the film.

Because of the level of trust the makers of *Devil's Playground* won from their Amish subjects, the film penetrates the "riddle" of Amish culture in a way that the other documentaries do not. But there is a potential downside to this for the Amish. In an essay written upon completion of *Devil's Playground,* Lucy Walker confesses,

> I'm ambivalent about having documented a community that didn't want to be documented. One of the Bible passages often quoted by the Amish is 2 Corinthians 6:14: "Be ye not unequally yoked together with unbelievers: for what fellowship hath righteousness with unrighteousness. . . ." Filming the Amish is a painfully unequal yoke and I'm relieved to stop. And I wanted to promote understanding, but I didn't want to ensnare people in worldly media when their life's work is to remove themselves from it.[15]

I myself do not think Faron and Emma are going to suffer from having taken part in Walker's documentary. But "ensnarement" affects the whole community, not just individuals. When an Amish businessman is disciplined for taking part in a documentary, it is a reminder to the larger community of the dangers of *Hochmut.* The very opposite happens when Amish young people see themselves or others like them making a splash on cable television—and there is no question that lots of Amish young people watched *Devil's Playground.* I suspect that many of them were impressed by Faron, who, despite his drug problems, exudes charisma and charm. I can imagine them thinking, "Perhaps I, too, could be on television." Indeed, when UPN launched its reality television series *Amish in the City* a couple years after the release of *Devil's Playground,* more than a dozen Lancaster County Amish youth called the local affiliate asking how they could get a part in the show.[16] Willing participation in photographic projects *can* undermine community. Once again, the instincts of Amish elders in these matters seem remarkably sound.

Epilogue

After this essay was completed, another hour-long documentary about the Amish was released on DVD, this one entitled *The Amish: How They Survive* (2006).[17] I was intrigued to see that the faces of non-Amish bystanders who appear in that film were carefully blurred out, while none of the Amish faces were. This illustrates a double standard that is implicit in virtually every ethnographic film, even if it is rarely so obvious. Our presumption is that something is revealed in films about cultures outside the mainstream that warrants unusual intrusions by filmmakers. But is this true?

Documentary filmmaking is by nature an exploitative enterprise. When a fiction film like the comedy *Kingpin* (1996) depicts Amish people, the portrayal may be erroneous, stereotyped, and even offensive to some, but it is still just actors acting. In contrast, a documentary about the Amish, no matter how respectful, builds stories and arguments on the backs of real Amish people. This raises a host of ethical questions. Is it ever justified to surreptitiously film Amish people? Is it acceptable to photograph Amish children without the express consent of their parents? Is it disrespectful to lure Amish merchants into sly complicity with filmmakers or Amish youth into open involvement with them, knowing that the Amish faith frowns upon photography? Although questions like these are not explicitly addressed in this essay, it is important to remember them.

Lucy Walker describes the dilemma of everyone who presents images of real Amish people to the public: "I wanted to promote understanding, but I didn't want to ensnare people in worldly media when their life's work is to remove themselves from it." The problem is that the interests of the public (in stories, sensations, and the satisfaction of curiosity) are in many ways completely at odds with the interests of the Amish (privacy and preservation of their communities). It is not so much a matter of striking a balance between the two as it is of choosing one over the other. And when it comes to such a choice, the Amish are severely disadvantaged. For one thing, filmmakers serve the public, not the Amish, for the public pays their bills. Even when a negotiated balance is struck, when Amish people like Faron willingly take part in a documentary, they do not really understand what they are getting involved in. The filmmaker holds all the cards.

There is an even deeper problem. Walker's dilemma requires a cost-benefit analysis. When does a documentary promote genuine understanding? What is the value of such understanding? What harm is there in exposing a culture that resists exposure? The answers to these questions are so murky that a meaningful cost-benefit analysis is just about impossible. And yet, in view of the recent trend in documentaries toward sensationalistic entertainment, led by reality television shows (including *Amish in the City*), such analysis seems increasingly urgent. We at least need to try to be clear about what the stakes are. What the stakes are for the Amish is a question that needs to be addressed by sociologists and anthropologists—and ultimately, by the Amish themselves. What the stakes are for the rest of us is a question I hope I have at least begun to answer in this essay. I pursue it further in "Hollywood *Rumspringa*," an essay on *Amish in the City* (chapter 6).

Notes

1. In *Representing Reality: Issues and Concepts in Documentary* (Bloomington: Indiana University Press, 1991), film theorist Bill Nichols characterizes documentaries as "discourses of sobriety."

2. In the case of so-called cultural tourism, which draws "visitors" to Amish settlements by the millions, the same fascination with sensations extends to buyable things, like quilts, and edible things, like shoo-fly pie. And it explains the ubiquitous camera. Snapshots are mementos of an "experience." The same is true of tourist trinkets, which is why it does not matter that so many of them are plastic and made in China.

3. William Rothman writes about the patronizing quality of scenes like this in "The Filmmaker as Hunter: Robert Flaherty's *Nanook of the North*," in *Documenting the Documentary: Close Readings of Documentary Film and Video*, ed. Barry Keith Grant and Jeannette Sloniowski (Detroit, MI: Wayne State University Press, 1998), 23–39.

4. Richard Barsam, *The Vision of Robert Flaherty: The Artist as Myth and Filmmaker* (Bloomington: Indiana University Press, 1988).

5. This line of reasoning stems from Christian Metz, *The Imaginary Signifier:*

Psychoanalysis and the Cinema (Bloomington: Indiana University Press, 1982). As a causal explanation of the emotional impact of movies generally, it has been rather thoroughly debunked in Noël Carroll, *Mystifying Movies: Fads and Fallacies in Contemporary Film Theory* (New York: Columbia University Press, 1988) and elsewhere. It still seems illuminating, however, as a phenomenological description of the power of nonfiction films.

6. The most recent of these aired on ABC's *20/20* on December 10, 2004. News shows like *20/20* are not documentaries in the sense that I discuss in this essay, since they focus on particular incidents, not a "way of life." Because they are firmly on the information side of the information/entertainment divide that I described in the first part of this essay, I do not treat them here.

7. *The Amish: A People of Preservation* was produced, written, and directed by John L. Ruth, with the assistance of Amish-born scholar John A. Hostetler. *The Amish: Not to Be Modern* was produced by Michael Taylor and directed by Victoria Larimore.

8. Donald B. Kraybill, *The Riddle of Amish Culture* (Baltimore: Johns Hopkins University Press, 1989; rev. ed., 2001).

9. David Weaver-Zercher, *The Amish in the American Imagination* (Baltimore: Johns Hopkins University Press, 2001), 172–80.

10. Kraybill's theological writing includes *The Upside-Down Kingdom*, 2nd ed. (Scottdale, PA: Herald Press, 2003).

11. The film was produced by Dirk Eitzen and co-written and directed with David Tetzlaff.

12. Directed by Lucy Walker, shot with Daniel Kern, produced by Steven Cantor with Stick Figure Productions, and edited by Pax Wasserman.

13. Everything reported in this essay about the production of the film was gleaned from the filmmakers' commentary on the DVD.

14. For a consideration of the media coverage of the 1998 drug bust, see chapter 10 of this volume.

15. "Notes on Completing *Devil's Playground*," in the undated webzine, *21c* at www.21cmagazine.com/issue1/devils_playground.html (accessed 27 February 2005).

16. I learned this in a conversation with Matt Uhl, general manager of Clear Channel Television (UPN 15, Harrisburg, PA) in July 2004, when *Amish in the City* aired.

17. Produced by Burton Buller, who shot John Ruth's *A People of Preservation* thirty years earlier.

In this Associated Press photo from 1973, two Indiana Amish couples exchange greetings with a southern California surfer.
© Larry Armstrong; used by permission.

CHAPTER THREE

"Why We Fear the Amish"

Whiter-than-White Figures in Contemporary American Poetry

Julia Spicher Kasdorf

If they think so much of us, why don't they live like us?
—an Amish woman in Mifflin County, Pennsylvania

Several years ago, I was talking with my dad about death threats received by African American athletes and student leaders at Penn State University and the resulting protests, which included an extended occupation of the student union by the Black Student Caucus and their white student allies. My father, who grew up just over the mountains from State College, Pennsylvania, said he was not surprised by bigotry in that area. When he was a boy, he never saw a black person around there, ever. "Back then," he said, "it was Amish people they went after."

My father spoke from experience, for he was one of those Amish targets. In the 1940s, at his one-room public school, bullies pulled his long hair, called him "dumb Dutch," and once threw his black hat down the outhouse hole. Now a Mennonite, who worked most of his professional life in a corporate research laboratory, he finds it ironic and even a little humorous to think about the past in light of the present. "These days," he laughed, "people hang pictures of Amish children up in their living rooms."

I notice an assumption that there must always be someone to pick on and ponder the way this observation may make race analogous with ethnicity. As maligned outsiders, it suggests, Amish people of the 1940s were the black people of today—as if racial stratification were not a distinct problem, and as if integration were as simple as European immigrants' assimilation into the American mainstream. At the risk of "playing the white ethnic card," I have to think that those idealized photographs are the other side of the bullying coin, because both impulses cast Amish people as Other—either threatening or exotic.[1] And given that difference in America is obsessively traced along racial lines, I am interested in thinking of Amish people in racial terms, to see what can be learned about their place in the mainstream imagination.

Whiteness as "We"

Amish ethnic tourism in areas of Pennsylvania, Ohio, and Indiana, and the allure of all things Amish, are manifestations of the kinds of us/them attitudes that sustain racism and bigotry. Social scientist Dean MacCannell, whose work on tourism is discussed by Susan Biesecker in chapter 5, locates ethnicity as a category of Otherness somewhere between biological descriptions of race and sociological and anthropological ideas of culture. First used by Europeans to refer to non-Jewish groups of Others, the term *ethnic* had come to mean, by the time of Columbus, any group of people who were neither Christian nor Jewish. By the time of Darwin and Marx, it was recognized that some ethnic groups—like today's Amish—had as much at stake as the Europeans in keeping the us/them distinction clear, with Europeans or whites designated as "them."[2]

Just as signs of Amish identity like plain dress and the use of the Pennsylvania German language function as rhetorical gestures to consolidate Amish identity (us) and to set Amish people apart from contemporary secular culture (them), so "whiteness"—the unselfconscious center or mainstream (we)—depends on the definition and designation of nonwhite Others (them). The difference is that whiteness in America operates *as if* it were a freestanding norm that does not need nonwhite and ethnic Others to keep power aligned with whiteness, as if countless advantages still tied to race were simply natural entitlements.[3]

Physically, Amish communities exist as internal colonies amid whiteness; and as a group, the Amish occupy a unique and somewhat unstable position in the American imagination. On the one hand, they are raced as white—that is, of European origin and Christian. In fact, with their extensive genealogies and seemingly closed communities, the Amish might even embody the myth of white racial purity. (White racial purity is always a myth, of course, even in the remote Amish community of Mifflin County, Pennsylvania, where it is recalled that at least one early family included Native Americans.) On the other hand, America is deeply invested in positioning Amish people outside the mainstream, as Other—if not racially Other, then as some kind of extra-ethnic, nonimmigrant, anachronistic ideal. In terms of the racial binary, the Amish must then be figured nonwhite or, as I temporarily claim for the sake of this essay, *whiter than white:* innocent, pure, plain—Puritans but without their unhappy edge. Scholars working in whiteness studies have identified the need for whiteness to project its undesirable or uncontrollable qualities onto nonwhite Others, as expressed in table 3.1. I believe that both nonwhite and ultra-white aspects must be projected outside to maintain the illusion of neutrality and rationality associated with the normalized "we" that is whiteness.

Media portrayals of the Amish can serve both purposes, reflecting contradictory attempts to either whitewash or expose the dark sides of Amish society—to paint them either as saints or as fallen angels, as David Weaver-Zercher has observed.[4] Relationships between these poles become clear when I place the stereotypical qualities associated with Amish people on a continuum beside the embedded and often invisible characteristics associated with whiteness and those qualities associated with nonwhite Others.

Table 3.1 The continuum of stereotypical qualities associated with Amish people

Whiter than White	*White*	*Nonwhite*
silent, controlled, patriarchal and authoritarian, dour and withdrawn	reserved, true, transparent, justice ensuring equal access for all who deserve it	loud, rhetorical, spontaneous, emotional, wild, anarchic
traditional, ritualistic, dogmatic, religious rules being trivial and legalistic	modern, rational, analytical, technological	primitive, natural, pagan
innocent, childlike, humanity before the Fall *or* super ego, repressed	mature, reasonable, moral ego, balanced	impulsive, childish, overly sexual, immoral id uncontrolled
plain, ascetic, severe	tasteful, neutral, beige	excessive, ornamental, colorful, attractive
self-sufficient, frugal, penny-pinching and stingy to the point of dishonesty or deprivation	financially responsible and secure, independent, planning ahead but enjoying life	dependant, spendthrift, unwise
skillful, ingenious craftsmen, work horses, perfectionistic, honest workers, punctual, clean	capable, standard	need supervision, may be sloppy, lazy or dirty, late, cutting corners, clever or sneaky
beyond white (absence of all color)	white (presence of all color)	black or colorful

Amish People in Contemporary American Poetry

In this essay, I trace contours of the whiter-than-white type in a handful of representative contemporary poems that depict Amish people. Mostly published during the last fifteen years, these poems were written by poets who work as university and college professors and who happen to have lived near Amish settlements but who have no close familial ties with Anabaptist culture. Mindful that negative attitudes persist in some areas—and Amish people still suffer from bias and even physical violence from their rural, white neighbors—I am nonetheless most interested in the subtle stereotypes I found in the work of these educated authors. Through some swift readings of these poems, I find traits of the contradictory whiter-than-white outsider who is at once more trivial and more spiritual; more connected (to God, community, and the earth) and more separatist; more legalistic, hardworking, and more free; more gracious, pure, and more punishing than "we" are.

Why We Fear the Amish

Because they are secretly Jewish and eat matzoh on Saturday.
Because they smell us in fellowship with the dead works
of darkness and technology. Because we doubt ourselves.
We find their clothing remorseless; we find their beards unsanitary.
Who among us is not ashamed, speeding, to come upon a poor
horse pulling a cart uphill, everyone dressed the same?
We believe in the state and they believe in the button.

With their fellow Pennsylvanians, the Quakers, they hold noisy pep rallies.
They know the quilting bee, the honey bee and the husking bee
are the only proper activities for women.
Even their horses are thrifty and willing to starve for Christ.
In the Poconos, the men vacation with Hassidim and try on
each other's coats. Back home, no tractors with pneumatic tires.
Pity the child who wants a radio and must settle for a thermos.

When the world shifts to Daylight Savings Time, there's no time
like slow time, to stay out of step. In Standard Time
their horses trot faster than ours, for the Amish
set their clocks ahead. In January, they slaughter the animals.
In March, they go to sales. In April, they plant potatoes.
In June, they cut alfalfa. In August, they cut alfalfa again.
In October they dig potatoes. In December they butcher and marry.

They modify the milk machine to suit the church, they change
the church to fit the chassis, amending their lives with hooks-and-eyes.
Their dress is a leisurely protest against chairmindedness.
We know their frugality in our corpulence. We know their sacrifice
for the group in our love for the individual. Our gods are
cross-dressers, nerds, beach-bums, and poets. They know it.
By their pure walk and practice do they eye us from their carts.[5]

"Why We Fear the Amish," by my Penn State University colleague Robin Becker, initially set me on this inquiry. When another Mennonite poet complained to me about the poem after it appeared on a full page of *American Poetry Review,* I sent a copy to a friend who teaches Mennonite literature and who had recently studied postcolonial literature and theory in Britain. His one-line e-mail response amused me: "Have you ever seen an Amish person riding in a cart?" (a wagon or a buggy, but usually not a cart, as this poem says—twice). Put off, and despite his sophisticated critical background, that reader's first instinct was to dismiss the poem by discrediting the outsider author's knowledge of the subculture. This is a fairly typical gut response from those close to the Amish community who search for the detail that enables them to write off a source as inauthentic—although this dismissal fails to make an adequate critique. Initially, I sought to defend the poet, whom I consider a friend, eager to grasp what an outsider could see that we miss from nearby. But when I heard the poem read to considerable comic effect on my own campus one evening, I began to feel otherwise.

To begin with, there is the troublesome title, which positions one group as "we" in relation to another, "the Amish." It assumes that readers share the powerful, white—neutral, rational, literate—perspective of the poet, and perhaps of published poetry in general. "The Amish," like "the Chinese," are an undifferentiated mass and the object of fear. Maybe "the Amish" as a group are no less diverse than "we" readers, but the poem depends on, and derives its humor from, stereotype and a simple us/them opposition in which "we" are the norm. In that sense, it functions like an ethnic joke. The title tells us to expect a list of reasons we should fear the Amish, but humor must be the intent, for who could possibly fear a group of quiet pacifists plowing with horses, so apparently harmless on the pastoral landscape?

"Because," the first line surprises us, "they are secretly Jewish and eat matzoh on Saturday." In other words, the title is not so outrageous when you consider this other ethnic group, "the Jews," and remember that "we" have been quite capable of projecting menace onto them. (Elsewhere in her book, readers may infer that Becker is herself Jewish and deeply concerned with the problem of anti-Semitism.) The Amish may be America's pet minority group, and the Jewish immigrants of stereotype have prospered in this country, but both groups still encounter bias. And, she reminds us, the orthodox sorts can look an awful lot alike, too. As seen in movies like *Witness* and *The Frisco Kid,* Amish men dress like Hasidic Jews, and that comparison seems to never wear out. If you type "Amish" into "EthnicNews Watch," the electronic database for American ethnic publications, several citations come from Jewish newspapers, where Hasidim are described as "urban Amish." In one piece, a Jewish professor, considering a job in Shippensburg, Pennsylvania, feared the "right-wing, born-again Christians" in that area but figured that "the hippest folks around were Amish."[6] Maybe that was a throwaway line, as clever as Becker's "In the Poconos, the men vacation with Hassidim and try on / each other's coats," yet it hints at a felt affinity. What the groups share beyond the cut of their black frock coats is a sense of being outsiders in America—west of the Hudson, at least—white, but not quite.

The poem is driven by a relentless and sometimes contradictory us/them opposition, an analogue of the white/nonwhite construct. "We" feel ashamed in the presence of Amish people because they seem pure and certain, whereas "we" "doubt ourselves" and assume that they judge us from a holier-than-thou, whiter-than-white stance. (Does it follow that *they* make *us* nonwhite, smelling in us "fellowship with the dead works of darkness and technology"?) Nevertheless, they are the objects of our scrutiny and pronouncements: we find their clothing remorseless and their beards unsanitary. We feel ashamed speeding past their buggies and believe in "the state" (i.e., grant authority to secular, civil systems), whereas they all dress the same, "believe in the button" (i.e., grant authority to the sect and its rules), are silent, oppress women, are thrifty and self-sacrificial, are overly utilitarian, and willfully segregate themselves from the world. Their worldview is fraught with irrational contradiction: while their labors and lives are ruled by the seasons, their religion is an inconsistent negotiation with technology. In the last four lines, diction follows the poem's logic, admitting that our knowledge of them is based only on ourselves; they are our opposite, our Other. The last line projects judgment or at least some kind of knowledge of and curiosity about the world onto the Amish people in the buggy, even as the entire poem seems a jokey liberal screed against the limits imposed by tradition and religious orthodoxy—whether it be Jewish, Quaker, or Anabaptist.

Who is watching whom, after all? Who is finally more secure in the us/them binary? Maybe the poem is more aware of itself than it seems. As with homophobia, anxiety about the orthodox Other in this piece masks similarity and eliminates any possibility for solidarity. The final opposing of Amish attributes against our own (frugality/corpulence, sacrifice/individuality, pure walk and practice/cross-dressers, nerds, beach bums, and poets) may enact a self-critique by performing an outrageous amplification of what "we" need in order to feel safe. Likely the buggy's occupants hardly notice the speaker passing in her car, but their difference and indifference as well as their visible marks of piety call forth a detailed and tonally complex response.

Contrast the way Becker's "Amish" are constructed through the speaker's anxieties projected onto broader culture with the way one Amish person touches off an individual's personal anxieties in "Uneven Light," a narrative in six parts by Ohio poet Roger Mitchell.

Uneven Light

I.
Four Amish, one man and three women,
enter the Greyhound depot in Columbus, Ohio,
at three in the morning.
They sit apart.

II.
Outside, the street gives back a watery,
uneven light.
After ten minutes of being stared at,
one of the women blossoms into a girl.

She spins on one foot, throws out an arm,
neither motion dislodging her bonnet board.
III.
Every dream I have hugged to myself comes back to me,
every dream I have held down to the floor
as it went berserk, murmuring, my knee on its back.
IV.
My mother telling me at age twelve—
had she told me before?—about Santa Claus,
or her dismantling, at the last possible moment,
the last hope of living in a world of pure thought.
V.
And my father, the same year, telling me
I was too old now to kiss him goodnight.
I went up to bed and never gave it a thought.
I went upstairs and put it away so carefully
even the wreckers couldn't find it
when they came looking for it thirty years later.
"Goodnight, Dad." I said. Though I see now
how he must have waited for weeks, maybe months,
phrasing it one way, phrasing it another,
the secret weeping in his bloodstream,
like the death of his father when he was twelve
stirring, sliding a few if its fine, sharp grains
downstream.
VI.
                    Where I sit resting from broken sleep
in a strange town, in a plastic chair,
in a depot locked against drifters and drunks,
on the way to visit children I still call
mine.
        Watching these Amish, sitting apart.[7]

The speaker begins by looking at "four Amish"—once again the collective noun—who "sit apart" in a Columbus bus station at three o'clock in the morning. He notices how they attract the interest of others, including himself. Observing that "after ten minutes of being stared at," one of the women "blossoms into a girl. / She spins on one foot, throws out an arm, / neither motion dislodging her bonnet board." She performs this possibly exhibitionistic, but spontaneous, childlike stunt—all without disturbing the order of her ritualized costume, its rigidity captured in Mitchell's own term, "bonnet board"—like mortar board?—coined to name the black, helmet-like cap that plain-dressed women wear away from home.

The speaker's astonishment at this gesture—an Amish woman dancing freely like a child—sends him into a reverie on his own life: its broken dreams, loss of innocence, and failures of faith and intimacy. What he sees in this Amish woman—unselfconscious play within constraint—suggests that the whiter-than-white strictures of Amish tradition may protect one from the ravages of time and experience, the idyll of childhood somehow preserved through community discipline. In the next to last line, we learn that the speaker is traveling to visit children he no longer lives with, underscoring another presumed difference between himself and these people, who are believed to live in unbroken extended families and communities. The details of that stanza point to other fallen features of contemporary life: he rests from "broken sleep" (a troubled mind but also prefiguring the "broken" family), in a "strange town" (transience), in a "plastic chair" (unnatural, man-made world), in a depot "locked against drifters and drunks" (a society that drives individuals to dislocation and addiction, and that is incapable of caring for these most fragile members). By the final line, "Watching these Amish, sitting apart," he continues to look at them, but now it is the speaker—not they—who sits apart, estranged. They have become a point of reference—a moral or cultural norm, whiter than white in relation to the unsettled speaker, who now judges his own position as slightly off-center. (The shifting of positions is signaled visually by the staggered positions of the final line in the first section and the first and last lines in the final section.)

That the sight of another could trigger an epiphany or inspire insight about one's self is very common in the first-person poems of everyday life that take objects in the world as catalysts for self-discovery and articulation. This type of poem became the dominant mode in American poetry during the latter half of the twentieth century. And not incidentally, this habit of mind parallels the social construction of mainstream identity: I know I am white because I see that others are not white. For this reason, this type of first-person narrative poetry has become vulnerable to critique on political grounds, despite its persistence in contemporary literature. Among such autobiographical poems is "June," by Denise Duhamel, who taught for a few years during the 1980s at Lycoming College in Williamsport, Pennsylvania:

June

The blue forest, chilled and blue, like the lips of the dead
if the lips were gone. The year has been cut in half
with dull scissors, the solstice still looking for its square
on the calendar. Perhaps the scissors were really
lawn mowers or hoes. Perhaps God's calendar is Chinese.
As first I didn't understand those burlap dolls
slouched in Central Pennsylvania craft stores.
Where were the button eyes, the tiny pearl nostrils?
the smudgy pink watercolor cheeks?

I enter the woods—part Gretel, part Little Red.
Such a small patch of sun makes it to the ground
through the leaves. The tree trunks are all elbows and knees,
all arthritis and gripes. The Amish think it's wrong
to render nature, quilts abstracting each pattern's name
of tree, buggy, corn, horse, farm.
My uncle, not Amish but superstitious, holds his palm
to the camera in a Christmas photo. Before she died
my grandmother ripped up all the pictures of herself.
She liked a novel with mystery, magazines without nudity.

The boy was killed by a drunk driver. My Amish neighbors
forgive. I prefer seeing it all, the snot, the optical nerve, the liver
behind the belly's skin. I prefer a good fight,
a wailing of grief. The Farmers' Market sells apples
as red as tricycles. The dolls without faces

want it silent. The forest, all anger and yesterday,
newspapers blank as white cotton sheets.
the branches, the teeth, the awful vees.[8]

The occasion of the poem is the speaker's meditation on the death of an Amish neighbor boy killed by a drunk driver and the speaker's inability to understand his parents' insistence on responding with forgiveness. To enact the speaker's bewilderment and disorientation—at the tragedy, at living in the hinterlands of Central Pennsylvania?—the details of the story are slightly fragmented and embedded within the fairy tale convention of a child lost in the forest.

The speaker recalls the perplexing blank-faced dolls she has seen in local crafts stores. (Created largely for the tourist trade, these dolls are sold as authentic products of Amish humble style.) Also using the collective noun, she attributes the dolls' featureless faces to an aesthetic and ethical principle associated with devout Muslims: "The Amish think it's wrong / to render nature, quilts abstracting each pattern's name." And as if to draw her subjects closer, she adds that her uncle, "not Amish but superstitious" also refused to be photographed, and a grandmother destroyed pictures of herself before her death. These comparisons seem to be honest attempts to understand unfathomable beliefs and practices, and in the end the speaker can only delineate distinctions between herself (significantly "I" rather than "we") and her Amish neighbors.

In contrast to the Amish and her own iconoclastic relatives, the speaker insists in the poem's climax, "I prefer seeing it all, the snot, the optical nerve, the liver / behind the belly's skin. I prefer a good fight, / a wailing grief." She must see, name, and render the things of the world and express feelings about them—as poets often do—unlike the dolls who "want it silent," the quilts "abstracting each pattern's name," or the people who seem to stifle their grief and rage because their beliefs oblige them to forgive. Like "blank cotton sheets," these pious people are whiter than the speaker—featureless and so restrained as to be voiceless, inarticulate, emotionally repressed, or in denial. By meditating on their beliefs and differences, the speaker is able to discover and say something important about herself and the world, but in order for her to do so, the Amish subjects must remain flat, ideological, and dispassionate.

If outsiders looking at plain people mostly learn something about themselves, it is no wonder that we fear the Amish. Consider a story told to me as true by an acquaintance who lives in Lancaster, Pennsylvania: an Amish woman went down to Rehoboth Beach and waded into the ocean, but as her long skirts grew heavy, she became weighted down and was swept out to sea in the undertow and drowned. When I first heard it, I could not believe it. (How heavy can a wet summer dress get?) Later, when I saw it retold in a slightly different form in a poem by Philadelphia poet Deborah Burnham, I felt even more certain that the story had the feel of legend, a tale that may not be entirely factual but that may be truthful in the sense that it reveals some truth about the tellers and their values. This story says that plain dress is a burden and that the weight of tradition can reach up, drag down, and destroy a body, even as the individual takes a step toward freedom. Embedded in it are America's twin fears of history and tradition (the Old World), and of entrapment and enclosure within family or community (loss of individual liberty), and those fears are projected onto a peculiar, communitarian people.[9]

Ocean City

fills with Methodists in summertime. Their hymns
at breakfast scrub and sanctify the air,
so they weren't surprised to see, one day
on the broad beach, an Amish family, their blue
and violet shirts glowing like hydrangeas
amid the salty, oiled skins. After the first
stares, no one paid them mind; the sea's the largest
miracle we have, and why should everyone
not want to see it? They found scraps of shell
which glowed inside their pockets, reminding them
that soon they'd bend into the green and yellow
fields they'd sown, heaping corn and squash in baskets
like Peter, Andrew, James and John who plucked

fish from the sea's ripe garden. They set
their boots and sneakers in neat rows and stepped
into the ocean, shy at first, but soon trusting
the smooth waves. They sang while cold salt water
rinsed the stains of weariness from their clothes
and hands, rejoicing as the water held them
up, off their tired feet. The oldest woman
floated past them, feeling the water ease
her life of weeding corn and scrubbing walls.
She felt her skirts grow heavy as the woolen
blankets she'd wrung out for sixty years;
she floated farther and began to sink,
pulled by the weight of tasks she could not finish,
her pockets full of clicking shells.[10]

Burnham's narrative poem is infused with white piety and Christian imagery; Methodists sing hymns at the old New Jersey Protestant enclave to "scrub and sanctify the air" making it fit for the arrival of an Amish family that represents a more immediate and natural kind of spirituality. Their "glowing" blue and violet shirts are compared to flowers—hydrangeas—in contrast to the nearly nude bathers' bodies on the beach. They get some stares at first as they gather sea shells, an activity that is compared to the biblical tropes of harvest and the work of the fishermen apostles. They arrange their shoes in a neat row on the sand, and singing, they wade like innocent children into the sea, "shy at first, but soon trusting." The waves, like the waters of baptism, rinse "the stains of weariness" and lift them "off their tired feet," redeeming them, not from sin, but from obedient lives of overwork.

The oldest woman feels the water "ease / her life of weeding corn and scrubbing walls." As her skirts grow heavy, she begins to sink, "pulled by the weight of tasks she could not finish, / her pockets full of clicking shells." This poem may see Amish people as mules—more hardworking than we—at a vacation site, but there is also great sympathy for their imagined lives of ceaseless labor, and an insistence on their humanity. (The poem cannot imagine that hard work—because it is esteemed and usually shared with others—might be joyful.) When the other bathers gawk, the speaker gathers "everyone"—Amish and non-Amish people—together into one visual sweep down the beach, locating the miraculous in the natural rather than spiritual world: "the sea's the largest / miracle we have, and why should everyone / not want to see it?"

I am especially interested that the old woman drowns—either metaphorically or actually—with shells in her pocket, like Virginia Woolf, who drowned with stones in her pockets. Indeed, both were "pulled by the weight of tasks [they] could not finish"—tasks heavier than stones or shells or skirts. This final image links the Amish woman to a host of female figures in literature and film who self-destruct in order to escape nonnegotiable circumstances, as in the final scenes of the novel *The Awakening* or the film *Thelma and Louise*. Her plight, then, is less the plight of an Amish person than the plight of an oppressed female whose only free choice is a fatal assertion of self-determination. In this way she carries the freight of an entire world's trouble; for surely patriarchy is not limited to Amish people, although whiteness may project an extreme and archaic sense of that system onto them.

Finally, I turn to Mary Swander, who of all these poets has the most intimate and complex understanding of her Amish subjects, largely due to her life circumstances. In 1983 Swander was given an allergy vaccine fifty times the correct dosage, which destroyed her immune system and gave her environmental illness. At first she was unable to eat anything or survive outside sanitary hospital conditions. In the course of her recovery, she bought organic vegetables and meat from Amish farmers and learned to raise and preserve food herself. In 1987 she moved into what had been the last functioning one-room public schoolhouse in Iowa, near Kalona. So in her story, whiter-than-white Amish purity is actual and stands in contrast to pollution and the deadly toxins of modern life. A 1995 work of nonfiction significantly titled *Out of This World* describes her illness, healing, and rural life, and several of the poems in *Heaven-and-Earth House* deal directly with her Amish neighbors. In an interview, Swander summarized her view of Amish people, mindful of the stereotypes that "we" may assume, even as she implies that "we" belong to a single, neutral group with common problems and values: "They're surprising, wonderful people. They've got a great sense of humor. Of course, they've been stereotyped as dour and withdrawn; they don't want to have anything to do with you. Yet, they are quite friendly, warm, smart, and innovative. They have all the problems we have. They just have them on a different scale." Continuing, Swander describes Amish culture as Other or even opposed to the pressures and values of whiteness, alluding to standard notions of other idyllic, earthy (primitive?) cultures, and comparing her Iowa experiences with ethnic tourism:

> I get these cards from my friends telling me that they've gone to Kenya for the summer. They've gone to this or that place and they're having some kind of multi-cultural experience. And I think: I'm having one right here. The Amish speak a different language, have a different culture. Their society truly is the closest in America to the non-competitive culture of the Native Americans. Even though it is Germanic, the Amish society is more circular than linear. There isn't the constant striving. For the Amish, once you've got the farm, you've arrived. That's the good life. In contrast, we usually feel if you're born on the farm, you work to get off it.[11]

Swander's poems nonetheless reflect the perspective of a respectful and intimate outsider. For instance, her "Amish Phone Booth" takes up a technology taboo that most outsiders find inconsistent and amusing or hypocritical.

Amish Phone Booth

The letter of the law is: no lines in from
the outside world. But this phone in a garage
down the road is fine, and a trip across
the field on foot enough to make you think twice
before a call. Above the receiver—chiropractor,

vet, weather report, all numbers penciled
on the wall. Below—a doodle of a stallion
with the caption STUD. *Bareback and buckboard,*

the gallop in at night for help with a fire
in Chester Yoder's barn, the hay put up too wet,

or aid with a stuck calf who must be sawed
in half to get out. Doc, I'm not sure what to do.
This little room holds in all the pain for miles,
and the joy that doesn't travel by buggy or bonnets
nodding together after church. The Bontragers

had another. After thirteen boys, a girl!
After thirteen years, the thin line that runs out
to the transformer still ices, sways in the winter wind,
goes down with any little spring storm.
A person could depend upon that thing too much.

More reliable, the fence wire, that runs from
Swander to Yoder to Miller, is never busy,
charges nothing extra, leaves no gap in between.
Better to walk out and tap a message that will
hum from post to post, a party line for everyone

to overhear. Better to ring your alarms out there
in the pasture where the cattle, the sheep,
the nanny goat, their cries bleating across
the grass, will listen, and pass the word.
Please come, and bring the others this time.[12]

The poem insightfully plays on the culture's internal tension between law and grace, as manifest in community phone practices. She reveals both the phone's purpose as well as the community's concerns by showing that the numbers of "chiropractor, vet, weather report" are written on the booth's wall. Hereby help comes for Chester Yoder's barn fire or the tragedy of "a stuck calf who must be sawed / in half to get out." She artfully summarizes the difficulty of phone use for Amish people; it is a technology or nonhuman medium, for transmitting human news: "This little room holds in all the pain for miles, / and the joy that doesn't travel by buggy or bonnets / nodding together after church."

Amish people speak in italicized lines in this poem, not as silent subjects of an articulate poet's gaze. In the phone booth, we hear pain ("Doc, I'm not sure what to do") and joy ("The Bontragers / had another. After thirteen boys, a girl!"). Then, concerning the phone itself, when its delicate lines are downed in a storm, someone says, "A person could depend on that thing too much." The Amish depend on one another and on God, not on technology; so, the speaker playfully suggests, they might instead tap messages like Morse code on the fence lines that run "Swander to Yoder to Miller," her outsider's name falling in rhythm and rhyme with the names of her Amish neighbors. The poem concludes with a final line spoken by an Amish person that shows characteristic Amish hospitality and a desire to entertain strangers in this seemingly closed community: "Please come, and bring the *others* this time" (my emphasis).

In the hand of one less skillful or empathetic, quotation could seem false and wrongly appropriating, but Swander has done the spiritual work of a poet, what Keats called "negative capability"; that is, she has listened deeply and imagined her way into these other lives. "Shunning" takes this move of imagination and empathy one more step, because the entire poem is spoken in the first person plural, "we," so that the "them" of the Amish community becomes "us," her readers.

Shunning

The doors are always closed to those we know
too well. The well brings up our deepest sin.
To those who stray so far, we must say no.

Amish store: suspenders, hook and eye.
We cannot sell our wares to half our kin,
for the doors are always closed to those we know.

We cannot wave or stop and say hello
to ones who go beyond the daily norm.
To those who stray so far, we must say no.

To some we may seem hard, or mean, or more,
to lock our families out in such a storm,
but we hang on to ours in rain or snow.

Without rules, where would we be now?
Lost souls, by the masses taken in,
like men who hold the sword and not the plow.

A knock. Oh, no, we mustn't even go.
The pain of holding out, is holding in.
The doors are always closed to those we know,
and we leave nothing, no one in the cold.[13]

Although Swander typically writes in free verse, she chose for this poem a highly structured traditional European verse form, the villanelle, which depends on excessive repetition and rhyme. Forms like this are called "obsessional" because they create spaces for brooding on troublesome subjects that will never be resolved. Technically, she demonstrates that in art, as in life, tradition lends form to chaos, and that without conventions, culture would have no shape. Thus, she explains a community discipline practice that may seem cruel or archaic to some as a basis for the community's identity and cohesion: "Without rules, where would we be now? / Lost souls, by the masses taken in, / like men who hold the sword and not the plow." Paradoxically, shunning preserves the community's peaceful and separate ways even as it appears to perpetrate another form of violence: "To some we may seem hard, or mean, or more."

Swander counts the cost of the practice, recognizing that it is painful for those on both sides of the rule. And later in the poem, the wrenching of relationship becomes more immediate: "A knock. Oh, no, we mustn't even go. / The pain of holding out, is holding in." Ambivalent at most, the poem neither defends nor condemns the practice, but worries over its rationale and weighs the emotional consequences of faithfulness to a practice, "holding out," and self-restraint, "holding in."

In addition to these two, there are numerous other poems in Swander's collection in which Amish people appear but are not necessarily the primary subjects. What becomes clear in her poetry as well as her prose is that she neither reveres nor fears her Amish neighbors because, perhaps, familiarity casts away those distancing and simplifying responses.

Coda: To Write Birds in Flight

In response to America's whiter-than-white esteem for Amish people and things, my now-deceased great-aunt, Annie Spicher, once scoffed, "If [they] think so much of us, why don't [they] live like us?" Annie had lived long enough to see Amish people both persecuted and praised, and she remained unimpressed. (Her remark felt particularly pointed on a rare visit to her farm, when I sought information for my own research and publication: Was I there as a niece or yet another tedious seeker?) I also hear in her voice a frustration with "them": others gawking from their cars like the first poet in this essay, or passing through the bus station like the second, or browsing in a gift shop like the third, who do not take time to stop and "visit," let alone learn, as Mary Swander has. Who among us (them) finds time to visit with our own neighbors, let alone the Amish figures on the outskirts of our busy lives, strangers who clearly display their outsider status, which may disguise a genuine spirit of hospitality?

Of course, Amish identity is never as intrinsic or static as it seems to be when it is fixed in written form as a foil for self-discovery; I know this as much from my own writing as from my reading of others' work. Ethnic tourism assumes a mobile subject and a static object on exhibit in its natural habitat. In these poems, however, Amish people are also on the move, tourists themselves, spotted like exotic birds outside their cages, dancing in the bus station in the middle of the night or blazing blue and purple on the beach. A latent thread in my reading of several of these poems follows my own preoccupations with mobility and with the ways that place can shape one's sense of self. The poems may not be so much about Amish stereotypes or even the poets, as I have often suggested in this essay, as they are about those fleeting moments of contact between the speakers and their Amish subjects, time and place granting at least as much meaning to the individual lives as the static categories and types that culture constructs.

Notes

I am indebted to Peter Kerry Powers and Jane Juffer for conversations and suggestions that helped me to refine the argument in this paper, and also to David Weaver-Zercher for his kind encouragement and evenhanded editorial remarks.

1. In white America, ethnicity is often merely "symbolic" and does not influence the professional and personal choices and everyday lives of most people. It nonetheless serves as a potent, often unrealized means of denying the realities of racism and racial stratification. See Charles A. Gallager, "Playing the White Ethnic Card: Using Ethnicity to Deny Contemporary Racism," in *White Out: The Continuing Significance of Racism,* ed. Ashley "Woody" Doane and Eduardo Bonilla-Silva (New York and London: Routledge, 2003), 145–58.

2. Dean MacCannell, "Reconstructed Ethnicity: Tourism and Cultural Identity in Third World Communities," in MacCannell, *Empty Meeting Grounds: The Tourist Papers* (London and New York: Routledge, 1992), 159.

3. These thoughts follow some basic assumptions of whiteness studies, an interdisciplinary area of investigation that includes research in legal studies, history, cultural studies, anthropology, education, and sociology. Unlike previous work in ethnicity and race relations that focused on studying the cultures of "marginal" and "minority" groups, this approach shifts the focus of study to the dominant group and locates the problems of racial stratification and injustice in the practices and beliefs of the mainstream. For a broad survey of the literature and key concepts, see Woody Doane, "Rethinking Whiteness Studies," in *White Out,* 3–18.

4. Stereotypes typically consist of extreme contradictions, for example, woman as virgin or whore, black man as incompetent bungler or fearful threat. David Weaver-Zercher notes that, especially during the years following the release of the film *Witness,* representations of the Amish have flourished in America along contradictory lines he characterizes as "saving remnant" and "fallen saints" (*The Amish in the American Imagination* [Baltimore: Johns Hopkins University Press, 2001], 181–96).

5. Robin Becker, *The Horse Fair: Poems* (Pittsburgh: University of Pittsburgh Press, 2000), 80.

6. Nicole Bokat, "Bar-Mitzvah Boy Leads 'Lapsed' Parents Back to Shul," *Forward,* 19 January 2001, 1.

7. Roger Mitchell, *A Clear Space on a Cold Day* (Cleveland: Cleveland State University Press, 1986), 22–23.

8. "June" was originally printed in *Third Coast,* Winter 1996, and can be found at www.wmich.edu/thirdcoast/Poetry/duhamel_june.html.

9. When I contacted Burnham to find out where she had come across the story that inspired her poem, she told me, in the spirit of all urban legends, that a friend insisted it "really happened." I later learned that a Lancaster newspaper reported that an Amish girl, caught in the undertow and unable to swim, did drown at Ocean City, New Jersey. For details, see Andrea Fishman, *Amish Literacy: What and How It Means* (Portsmouth, NH: Heinemann Educational Books, 1988), 42–43. It is

the teller's focus on the girl's garments and the persistence of the tale in people's minds, rather than the accuracy of the story, that most interests me.

10. Deborah Burnham, *Anna and the Steel Mill* (Lubbock: Texas Tech University Press, 1995), 27.

11. James Grove and Steven Horowitz, "Mary Swander," *Iowa Woman,* Winter 1993, 15. See also Joyce Dyer, "Portrait of an Iowa Poet," *Iowa Woman,* Autumn 1995, 22–26.

12. Mary Swander, *Heaven-and-Earth House* (New York: Knopf, 1994), 5–6.

13. Ibid., 52.

In the eyes of many outsiders, Amish quilts reflect the simplicity of Amish life.
Photo by Dennis Hughes; used by permission.

Chapter Four

Pursuing Paradise

Nonfiction Narratives of Life with the Amish

David L. Weaver-Zercher

You painted the "English" too bad and the Amish too good. . . . Life doesn't come in black and white but subtle shades and hues of gray.

—an Amish woman, responding to Randy-Michael Testa's *After the Fire*

Each fall I teach a seminar for first-semester college students entitled "An Amish Paradise?" The course, the title of which is a take-off on Weird Al Yankovic's musical parody of Amish life, introduces students to the theological and sociological underpinnings of Amish culture.[1] About halfway through the semester, we take a break from traditional classroom learning and become tourists, traveling to Lancaster County, where we visit a produce auction and at least one Amish-theme tourist venue. But the highlight of the field trip, both for my students and for me, is our noontime meal in an Amish home. The food—baked chicken, boiled potatoes, green beans, applesauce, homemade bread, and two or three choices for dessert—is always plentiful, and it is invariably downed amid comments like, "Just think—we'd be eating in the *college cafeteria* right now." Even more impressive to my students is our Amish host: a cheerful, articulate, and attractive thirty-something woman who, along with serving our meal, tells us about her former life as an Amish schoolteacher and her current life as a dairy farmer and mother of six children under the age of thirteen.

It is usually at this point in the course—sometimes when we are eating our meal, sometimes on the return drive to campus—that one of my students tells me that she would like to live with an Amish family. Is that possible, she asks? How might she arrange it? I typically respond by mentioning a cross-cultural course taught by one of my faculty colleagues, a course that includes a weeklong stay with an Amish family. That satisfies some who inquire, but not others. College courses are better than nothing, but what most of these students want is something more authentic, something less mediated.

What they really want is what they encounter a few weeks later in two of my required course texts: Sue Bender's *Plain and Simple: A Woman's Journey to the Amish,* and Randy-Michael Testa's *After the Fire: The Destruction of the Lancaster County Amish.*[2] Published in 1989 and 1992 respectively, these books record their non-Amish authors' emergent interest in the Old Order Amish, an interest that compels them to seek out Amish families for lengthy home stays. Bender, a middle-aged artist and therapist who, in her words, had a long-standing "obsession with the Amish," finally succeeds in finding Amish hosts for two relatively short summer stays, first in Iowa and then in Ohio. Testa, a Harvard graduate student who hopes to write a doctoral dissertation on Amish education, locates his host family in Lancaster County, Pennsylvania, where he soon becomes involved in a variety of public issues (e.g., farmland development) affecting the Amish community. In some ways, the two books and the authors who wrote them could hardly be more different, but at their core they are very much alike: both are autobiographical accounts of white, economically privileged Americans who, troubled by certain aspects of their mainstream American lives, find something redemptive in their journeys to the Amish.

To say that Bender and Testa find something redemptive in their journeys to the Amish raises two important questions. First, what is that *something?* Second, to what degree (and in what ways) are Bender and Testa *redeemed?* As we shall see, both authors testify to living less-than-satisfying lives that demand remedies from beyond themselves, remedies that in their view are delivered to them in the course of their journeys. In that sense, traveling to Amish Country assumes for both authors elements of spiritual pilgrimage. Nonetheless, given their radically different starting points—that is, given their respective social locations and the existential afflictions they hope to remedy—their journeys take radically different forms. Not surprisingly, "the Amish" they discover, learn from, and write about assume different forms as well.

Pilgrimage, Tourism, and the Old Order Amish

The practice of pilgrimage tracks a long history in many of the world's religious traditions, so much so that it has received prominent attention in the field of comparative religion. The most influential of these treatments has been Victor and Edith Turner's *Image and Pilgrimage in Christian Culture,* which describes pilgrimage as "a liminoid phenomenon."[3] According to the Turners, most ritual processes are characterized by three phases. In the first phase, called "separation," the ritual subject detaches from a "relatively stable set of cultural conditions." This process of detachment moves the ritual subject into the second stage, called the "liminal stage." Here the subject finds him- or herself in a realm that shares few attributes with both the former and future stages; the subject, according to the Turners, now exists "betwixt and between all familiar lines of classification." Eventually, however, the ritual subject moves into the third stage ("aggregation"), assuming once again a stable state, albeit a different state from the initial one (2). So, for instance, fraternity members go through rites of passage as they move from their lives as non-Greeks to their lives as Greeks. During the pledging period, when their lives are filled with hazing activities and high anxiety, they are neither Greeks nor non-Greeks. They are liminal subjects occupying a liminoid state, betwixt and between, where the rules and expectations are different from before but are not yet what they will be.

What does this have to do with religious pilgrimage? According to the

Turners, the notion of liminality provides a useful heuristic device for considering all sorts of social change "in which previous orderings of thought and behavior are subject to revision and criticism" (2). Examples abound in this regard, including the experience of pilgrimage to a sacred site at some distance from the pilgrim's home. On such a journey, write the Turners, the pilgrim "gets away from the reiterated 'occasions of sin' which make up so much of the human experience of social structure" (7). The roads traveled may be difficult and the experience lonely, but "these fresh and unpredictable troubles represent . . . a release from the ingrown ills of home" (7). Moreover, the troubles one experiences on the way pale in light of the ultimate goal: "release from the sins and evils of the structural world, in preparation for participation in an afterlife of pure bliss" (8).

More recently, some anthropologists and sociologists have made connections between religious pilgrimage and modern tourism, which, like pilgrimage, involves geographical displacement from one's place of residence. In addition to citing *historical* connections (noting, for instance, that medieval religious pilgrimage and its commercial accoutrements paved the way for mass tourism), some scholars have argued for a *structural* relationship between the two experiences, averring that tourism provides for modern travelers what pilgrimage provides for religious pilgrims: the opportunity to enter a liminal state that affects the subject, who then returns to his or her place of departure transformed.[4] Accordingly, souvenirs have been described as "messengers of the extraordinary" that "freeze in time a fleeting, transitory existence," messengers that "bring back into ordinary experience something of the quality of an extraordinary experience."[5] In this line of thinking, souvenirs are more than material objects by which to flaunt one's travels. Rather, they are potent signs that remind the traveler of a "particular heightened reality," signs that can sustain the existential change that was wrought in the liminal experience.[6]

Some scholars have cautioned against making a simple identification between religious pilgrimage and modern tourism, and rightly so. These critics, many of whom stress a divergence between the two forms of travel, point to the superficial, frivolous nature of tourism when compared to pilgrimage. Even travelers who engage in cultural tourism, traveling to places where they can observe local "peasants" and learn about their culture (e.g.,

Amish Country tourism), find numerous opportunities to engage in the sort of frivolous activities that historian Daniel Boorstin famously labeled "pseudo-events" (e.g., the Disneyesque Dutch Wonderland amusement park east of Lancaster city).[7] But while critics like Boorstin provide a helpful caution, they too have drawn the lines too simply, underestimating the depth of the quest that some tourists undertake.

The solution to this impasse, best summarized by Erik Cohen, is to recognize that different people engage in different modes of tourism that vary according to the magnitude of their existential quests. Cohen identifies five tourist modes, ranging from "recreational" at the one extreme to "existential" at the other.[8] *Recreational tourism,* writes Cohen, is the most culturally conformed version of tourism. In other words, recreational tourists adhere closely to their home society's core values, embarking on their tourist forays only as a means to restitute themselves in order to perform once again their culturally sanctioned roles (53). On the other end of the spectrum lie *existential tourists,* who find themselves significantly alienated from the values and expectations of their home cultures. These tourists, says Cohen, search for and ultimately commit themselves to an alternative that becomes "a new, 'elective' center" in their lives (55). Lying between these two extremes, at the midpoint of Cohen's five-point continuum, is *experiential tourism,* which "consists of the conscious quest for the vicarious experience of the authentic life of others." In contrast to the recreational tourist, experiential tourists quest for something other than rest and relaxation. Unlike existential tourists, however, experiential tourists wish only to "observe the authenticity of the life of others"; they do not "seek to live it [themselves]" (54). In sum, Cohen's modes of tourism correlate to the degree of existential alienation felt by the tourist in his or her home culture. The more alienated a potential tourist feels, the more likely he or she is to use tourism as a tool to engage in a serious existential quest.

Here, then, we see that even existential tourism both converges with and diverges from true religious pilgrimage. According to Cohen, the existential tourist's ideal—a mystical experience, living only in the present, with no thought of past or future—is most homologous with that of the pilgrim (55). At the same time, their structural positions diverge sharply. Whereas the existential tourist seeks a center of meaning that is far removed from his or her home culture, the religious pilgrim's center remains in conformity with his or her society. In other words, the religious pilgrim travels to a place (e.g., Mecca) that is considered legitimate—indeed, is considered the sacred Center—by his or her home culture.[9] Existential tourists, on the other hand, engage in a quest that is considered semi-legitimate at best. They follow their "own lights," find an elective center at their society's periphery, and "transform the Other into their center" (59).

As Susan Biesecker's essay in this volume attests, the vast majority of tourists who make their way to Ohio's Amish Country are *recreational* tourists. In other words, they are *not* alienated from the core values of middle-class American society whatsoever. In fact, as Biesecker suggests, they are heavily invested in a form of tourism that avoids challenging the givenness of their middle-class American lives. Traveling to Amish Country in SUVs and minivans, they spend their time eating in air-conditioned restaurants and gazing on Walnut Creek's Victorian homes, only occasionally encountering Amish people along the way, almost always from a distance. Of course, the tourists who make their way to Mount Hope—where Amish people are more immediate, the architecture is less Victorian-themed, and the tourist accoutrements are minimal—are more likely to fall into Cohen's *experiential* mode, vicariously experiencing the lives of local Amish residents. Few tourists, however, can be found in Cohen's *existential* mode. The relatively shallow samplings of the experiential mode (e.g., riding in an Amish-like buggy, eating Pennsylvania Dutch food, and attending an auction where Amish people gather) constitute the experiential limit of most Amish Country tourists. Anything beyond these mild undertakings is too unsettling, too Other.

Occasionally, however, Amish Country becomes more than a setting for a few vicarious experiences. Occasionally Amish Country becomes a destination for visitors in a more radical tourist mode, visitors who find themselves significantly alienated from their home cultures. In their popular narratives, Sue Bender and Randy-Michael Testa both begin by describing the alienation they feel in their home cultures and then proceed to chronicle the personal transformations they undergo while living among the Amish. Significantly, however, the alienation they describe diverges sharply in their two accounts. Correspondingly, the transformation they experience among the Amish reveals itself in markedly different conceptions of Amish life.

A (Wealthy) Woman's Journey

In the first few pages of *Plain and Simple,* Sue Bender describes the occasion of her attraction to the Old Order Amish: in 1967 she was thirty-three years old when she first spied some Amish quilts hanging in a Long Island gift shop. The quilts "spoke directly to me," Bender remembers, going "straight to my heart." Soon, she says, visiting the quilts became a part of her routine, "something like a spiritual practice," which eventually broadened to include gazing on Amish-made dolls. Powerful though they were, these material relics from Amish culture ultimately proved insufficient to sustain Bender's spirit. In the summer of 1981, she decided to travel to Lancaster County to visit the Amish themselves.[10]

Bender's initial journey to the Amish is less than satisfying. Traveling through the most tourist-oriented Amish settlement, Bender finds the "neon signs flashing 'Plain and Fancy'" distracting (19).[11] Worse yet, Bender finds that the industry created to cater to recreational tourists constrains her from becoming anything more than a frustrated experiential tourist. Realizing that Lancaster County's tourist culture would inhibit rather than advance her existential search, Bender and her husband extend their road trip to eastern Ohio where, they are told, the Amish live in more secluded communities. There Bender succeeds in making a more immediate connection to an Amish person, venturing to an Amish home and conversing at length with an Amish woman. A year later, Bender's existential journey begins in earnest when she moves to Iowa, where she has made advance arrangements to live with an Amish family for a few weeks. Two years later, in the summer of 1984, she journeys to the Amish once again, this time spending the bulk of her summer with an Ohio Amish couple and their nine children.

Before we consider the effects of Bender's touristic experiences, it is important to consider the way she describes her prior self: a frazzled, frantic, fragmented person, stretched to the breaking point by culturally imposed but now internalized messages. "My life was like a crazy quilt," she writes of her home life, "hundreds of scattered, unrelated, stimulating fragments, each going off in its own direction" (4). There was, she writes, a "tug-of-war" raging inside of her between "creative" things and "boring, everyday things," a conflict that was only exacerbated by her multiple roles as wife, mother, artist, and therapist (4–5). Bender ticks off the things that she had learned to value most highly—accomplishments, the sense of being special, and results—even as she acknowledges that the drivenness needed to achieve these things wrought mostly frustration. Some of this pathology she pins on her upbringing, which taught her to believe "the more choices I had, the better." The ultimate result, she concludes, was a "tyranny of lists" that "created the illusion that my life was full" (6).

It is significant to note here that Bender subtitles her book, "A Woman's Journey to the Amish." In her telling, the pilgrimages she takes are attempts to escape, and perhaps ameliorate, the "quiet desperation" that was part and parcel of her life *as a woman* (8). She therefore trains her lenses on her female hosts, seeking to find in their lives the antidote she needs. For instance, in contrast to Bender's own sense of franticness, the Amish women "moved through the day unhurried" (48); in contrast to her own sense of fragmentation, "their life was all one piece" (51); and in contrast to her need to be special, the Amish women somehow found "meaning in work itself" (61). Bender does not devote explicit attention to social critique, and theorizing about gender is noticeably absent from her narrative. But her use of the phrase "a woman's journey" parallels the argument of some recent feminist scholars who contend that women like Bender—well-educated, suburban, professional mothers—experience a malaise that rivals, and perhaps exceeds, the malaise experienced by the stay-at-home mothers Betty Friedan wrote about in the 1960s.[12] These Bender-like professional women, brought up to value choice and accomplishment, frequently discover that the choices dangled in front of them are mutually exclusive, more so for them than for their male counterparts. Unlike well-educated men, for example, for whom being a "good dad" is rarely pitted against being a successful professional, women frequently find that demanding careers undercut their ability to meet broader social expectations for "good motherhood."

It is not surprising, then, that Bender's narrative has resonated more fully with female readers than with men. Still, we must also recognize that her existential dilemma has as much to do with her economic class as it does with her gender. Passing comments in her narrative about homes in northern California and Long Island, graduate degrees from Berkeley and Harvard, a Volvo in the driveway, and dinner parties in the Hamptons add up to an obvious conclusion: Bender has achieved the consumer capitalist definition of the good life. That life, filled with all sorts of economically enabled choices, fails to satisfy her; but despite a few gestures to the contrary, she never really questions the assumptions that fuel her dilemma. In fact, she routinely operates from those assumptions in order to resolve that dilemma, visiting trendy Long Island gift shops to glimpse Amish quilts, buying Amish dolls to sit on her mantle, and at one particularly anxious moment in her life, remodeling her entire kitchen in Amish chic, "simple and white" (89).

Indeed, Bender's journeys to the Amish must themselves be seen as consumeristic attempts to transform herself. Bender is clearly frustrated with certain aspects of her life, but she is not significantly alienated from the assumptions that undergird it. She is less a seeker than a shopper, thereby coming closer to Cohen's description of an experiential tourist than an existential tourist, seeking a transportable experience/lesson that she can carry back and plug into life-as-usual.[13] For her part, Bender identifies that lesson as "self-forgetfulness." Comparing the Amish to Zen Buddhists, Bender suggests that, unlike Zen masters who work for years to achieve self-forgetfulness, the Amish "seem to have that quality in their genes," each person knowing that he or she is "a necessary part in a larger universe" (77). Contentment, therefore, has nothing to do with being deemed extraordinary by one's contemporaries. Rather, it comes from recognizing the constraints of time, space, and culture; accepting those limits; and working purposefully within them. Although Amish women may be better suited to recognize these constraints than she is, Bender is optimistic that this lesson is fundamentally transportable—with the tangible assistance, of course, of her newly installed Amish kitchen and some strategically hung Amish quilts.

Bender may be unique in her dependence on white Formica cabinets and Corian countertops to sustain her portable Amishness, but she is not unique in identifying this sort of lesson from the Amish. In "What Good Are the Amish?" sociologist Marc Olshan argues that the value of the Amish to outsiders lies, not in the particular lifestyle choices the Amish make, but rather in the way they testify to "the need for limits."[14] Invoking Durkheim, Olshan argues that modern American society suffers from "the malady of infiniteness," which exhibits itself in "morbid restlessness" and "insatiable appetites," phrases that closely parallel Bender's observations about herself.[15] Olshan dismisses the idea that the Amish provide a broadly applicable pattern for solving this problem, but in a somewhat Bender-like move, he suggests that individuals suffering from a sense of fragmentation might benefit from establishing a "personal *Ordnung*" that draws clear limits and thereby resists the tyranny of mainstream American life.[16] As a student of Amish life, Olshan surely recognizes the incongruity of modifying the word *Ordnung* with the word "personal," for the Amish *Ordnung* is by definition a communally sanctioned set of expectations. Still, for people committed to the conventions of a liberal society, the notion of a personal *Ordnung* is the best Olshan has to offer. On that level, at least, he has little to say beyond what Bender has already said.

Olshan's analysis does, however, offer something more—two things, in fact. First, Olshan more clearly recognizes that Bender's malady—restlessness, fragmentation, insatiability—is integrally connected to the basic assumption of consumer capitalism: more money means more choice, both of which are "good." Second, Olshan reminds his readers that the Amish not only provide real-life examples of resisting limitlessness, but they also reveal that the "imposition of limits" comes with "enormous costs" to those who embrace those limits.[17] Bender writes relatively little about the costs of setting limits. More specifically, she says little about the painful self-denial that is an integral part of being Amish and therefore of *enjoying* the benefits of Amish living. For instance, when Bender talks of Amish disciplinary practices, she speaks with a sense of horror, as she also does when she describes the humility she encounters in some Amish women (77). In other words, even though Bender *notices* the costs of setting limits in Amish society, she describes them as pathological elements in an otherwise rich culture or, alternatively, downplays the costs' impact by suggesting the Amish have an almost genetic ability to live the way they do—as if being Amish were not a series of hard choices to deny oneself for the sake of the community. Not surprisingly, Bender gives scant attention to the theological underpinnings of Amish life, which assure those who deny themselves and embrace the church's *Ordnung* that they will find friendship with God in eternity. In the end, it is entirely unclear whether Bender has more than a surface understanding of the way Amish life functions.

Of course, one could argue that Bender's subtitle tells us that we should not expect too much. The book is not about the Amish per se; it is rather about "a woman's journey to the Amish" and the ways in which that particular woman was affected by Amish quilts, dolls, and people. On that level, Bender's book succeeds quite well; only the most cynical reader would conclude that Bender's journey to the Amish did not transform her patterns of self-reflection. Still, her glossing over of Amish religious commitments results in a book filled with heroic but cardboard Amish figures. These figures need not sacrifice themselves, because they have no egos to sacrifice. Historical and social forces have little effect on them and their enlightened ways, for they stand outside of history, beyond the social forces that history entails, beyond the pain other human beings experience, happily "freed from the necessity to make choices" (76). It is this very assumption that Randy-Michael Testa wishes to challenge in his narrative, *After the Fire.*

An Activist's Journey

Whereas the larger society in which the Amish exist is distinctly absent in *Plain and Simple,* it looms large and powerful in *After the Fire.* Some of this contrast can be attributed to the narratives' different settings: whereas Bender's Amish hosts live in relatively undeveloped regions of Iowa and Ohio, Testa's hosts live in teeming, crowded Lancaster County. More important than their respective settings, however, is the nature of the two narratives. Bender's journey to the Amish is largely internal, an endeavor to fix herself by "letting the spirit of the Amish take over" (136). Testa's journey is likewise spiritual. Initially a research trip for his Harvard dissertation on Amish educational practices, his stay in Amish Country comes to focus less on writing his dissertation than on rescuing his tired soul. Significantly, however, Testa's journey pushes him outward in a way that Bender's did not. He becomes an activist, challenging what he believes are the corrupt forces in mainstream America that imperil Amish life.

In one sense, Testa finds himself responding to the same problem that plagues Bender: the social fragmentation of modern American life. For Testa, however, this fragmentation is largely external to himself, exhibiting itself most acutely in the social pathologies he has encountered as a school teacher in Denver, Colorado. In his book's first chapter, Testa describes his pre-Harvard experience as a third-grade teacher in a private Denver school. After five years of teaching, he writes, "I was tired, morally tired." Testa links his exhaustion to his participation in a materially rich but spiritually bereft community, describing the desolate home lives of his seemingly privileged students and concluding with a question of pastoral concern: "How could the children of such parents know what to do with the darkness they beheld?" More importantly, he asks, "How could I?" Unable to answer these questions, Testa leaves the classroom for a doctoral program in moral education at Harvard University. Later, at the encouragement of his professors, he determines to study Amish educational practices, hoping to learn something from the Amish that was unbeknownst to him in Denver.[18]

What Testa learns from his hosts goes far beyond pedagogical theory. Although claiming that he did not travel to Lancaster County as a religious seeker (22), he becomes increasingly enamored with Amish life and eventually attests to something like a conversion, not in the sense of joining the Amish church—Testa declares that he has neither the desire nor the will to become an Amish church member (176)—but in the sense of being transformed by his encounters with Amish people. Even though Testa criticizes "the hordes of souls" who visit the Amish "to fill an unfillable void in their own lives," he himself invokes Christian language to describe his touristic experience, calling his interactions with the Amish a "journey into grace" (22, xii). Later, as he recounts his various experiences among the Amish, Testa tells how his former worldview becomes increasingly problematic, whereas the Amish view becomes increasingly sensible and satisfying. At one point, after unsuccessfully explaining to his befuddled Amish hosts the need for college philosophy courses, Testa confesses that he is "ashamed of the culture I am being asked to interpret" (93). Shortly thereafter, upon being challenged to explain the point of youth soccer camps, he observes that "among these people, life makes perfect sense," but "the outside world does not" (97). Convinced that mainstream Americans have much to learn from the Amish worldview, Testa decides to become a "witness" on behalf of the Amish, living and writing in ways that "would not make sense if God did not exist" (96).[19]

Testa's explicit Christian language at this point not only reveals his theological distance from the amorphously spiritual Bender, but it also points to their contrasting interpretations of the alienation they feel. For Bender, this sense of alienation derives from internalized social expectations that had fractured her life. Except for bemoaning societal emphases on achievement, she does little social criticism and consequently looks for personal therapeutic resources to resist these pressures. Testa, on the other hand, finds within Amish culture a ready-made worldview by which to contest many of the fundamental values of mainstream American life. The Amish not only school their children differently, he discovers, they do almost everything differently, for they start from radically different assumptions about what constitutes the good life. Of course, Bender notices these different assumptions as well, but rather than granting them morally privileged status, she takes pains to note that the Amish way is not *the* way, but rather "*one* way—a way that works for them."[20] Testa responds to this sort of relativism with a resounding no. From his perspective, the Amish way of life is *the* way, the best way, to pursue the good life. To drive home this point, he advances a thoroughly dualistic view of Lancaster County life, repeatedly contrasting the Amish with their English neighbors, noting the superiority of the Amish moral vision at almost every turn.[21]

Testa illustrates his moral argument by telling about "the destruction of the Lancaster County Amish." This destruction takes various forms in Testa's narrative, though his most prominent villains are farmland development and mass tourism, two industries that, in his view, exhibit most clearly the money-grubbing nature of mainstream American life. The fallout from this turpitude spreads in all directions, Testa says. First, it ruins the lives of those who pursue economic prosperity at all costs, a lesson he claims first to have learned when teaching his privileged Denver schoolchildren. Second, it harms the social fabric of entire communities, even those segments that refuse to embrace the gospel of prosperity. In Lancaster County in particular, development and tourism push Amish people off their land "one family at a time" (180). As a result, the entire Amish community is "on the verge of conflagration," and there is precious little time to save it (xiv). Concluding that he cannot remain passive in the face of this crisis, Testa throws himself into the fray, protesting farmland development and helping Amish people navigate disputes with local authorities. Still, Testa's tone is not a hopeful one. Even the politicians are incapable of helping the Amish, he says, for to do so would mean to defy the forces of mammon, which in turn would mean "political suicide" (179).

What are we to make of Testa's journey to the Amish and the morality play he weaves from his experience? Does Testa's journey ultimately fit into Cohen's mode of the existential tourist who searches for and embraces a new elective center? Clearly not. Although Testa finds himself unsettled by his foray into Amish life, he is never so unsettled by it that he is willing to forgo the privileges of a Harvard education (which arguably gained him access into the Amish community in the first place),[22] the technological conveniences of mainstream American life, and the many choices that a good education and ample money can buy. Testa recognizes that unwillingness in himself, noting that to *really* convert to the Amish faith would require a much greater sacrifice than he is willing to make (176). It is hard to find fault with that sort of conclusion; indeed, most outside observers would attest to finding features of Amish life attractive but would nonetheless be unwilling to become fully Amish. What *is* problematic, however, is Testa's cover-to-cover valorization of Amish life as morally supreme, a valorization that, given his unwillingness to embrace it, rings hollow. In that respect, Bender's narrative, as much as it misses the point about Amish religious commitments, is the more honest personal memoir. Testa, who understands better than Bender the way consumer capitalism contributes to personal and social fragmentation, would likely be critical of Bender's bald attempts to buy into Amish life. At the same time, his one-armed embrace of Amish life ultimately reveals that he is basically the same sort of traveler, seeking portable lessons to help him navigate his life back home.

Even more problematic is Testa's proclivity to cast Lancaster County in a starkly dualistic light—good versus evil, Amish saints versus English devils. Despite the editorial counsel of an Amish woman who warned that he "painted the 'English' too bad and the Amish too good," Testa deliberately forgoes nuance in his book for the sake of moral argument (xiii). It is not that Testa is *unaware* of his tendency to draw his lines too sharply; it is rather that he believes advocacy and nuance are incompatible.[23] Convinced that the English world had become blind to its own moral decay, Testa determines that his witness on behalf of Amish life must be painted in black and white with nary a shade of gray. In that respect it is helpful to understand Testa's narrative, not just as a personal memoir, but as apocalyptic literature much like the New Testament book of Revelation. With stark distinctions between good and evil, and pitched battles with eternal consequences, *After the Fire* aims to do more than tell an interesting story. It aims to evoke changes in its readers, encouraging the faithful (who value people over money and status) and shaming the wicked (who do just the opposite).

Ultimately, however, Testa's choice to recount his journey in apocalyptic form dishonors the Amish struggle to resist the hegemonic forces of American life. That is not his intent, of course. Unlike Bender's Amish, whose self-forgetfulness allows them to hover above history in the timeless present, dispensing nuggets of wisdom from their egoless souls, Testa's Amish are embedded in and affected by an array of socioeconomic forces. Accordingly, Testa rightly underscores the fact that living the Amish life is a constant struggle against larger forces that fray their community fabric. But even as Testa is right to underscore the struggles inherent in Amish life, his investment in the outcome of that struggle belittles the agency of Amish people as they navigate their lives. Fully convinced that true Amishness means agrarianism, Testa is quick to brand Amish persons who participate in certain nonfarming endeavors as faux Amish. According to Testa, these faux Amish persons—for instance, Amish who host tourists for home-cooked dinners—have been seduced by the world's material comforts. They have "chosen to squeeze themselves out of their own society, . . . becoming ever more English, ever more worldly" (180). Could it not be, however, that these Amish entrepreneurs have more than material comforts in mind when they treat English consumers as consumers? Might not these exchanges also serve the function of keeping essential Amish life inaccessible, even as they offer outsiders the illusion of access?[24] Testa does not consider this possibility. Rather than seeing these entrepreneurial Amish men and women as historical agents making their own measured choices, Testa sanctifies an ahistorical, agrarian ideal that, by the time he arrived in Lancaster County in 1988, had already been jettisoned by many Amish people who resided there.

Of course, Testa's investment in a static, pastoral view of Amish life is hardly unique. In Crystal Downing's analysis of the films *Witness* and *For Richer or Poorer* (chapter 1), we see just how strong this investment is for storytellers who wish to offer narratives that are both emotionally gripping and morally engaged. More than just serving a narrative function for English storytellers, however, this agrarian bias continues to hold sway in most Amish communities, where even those who have left their farms voice the conviction that the farm is the best place to pursue faithful living. Still, it is one thing to view the farm as the best incubator of traditional Amish values; it is another to dismiss Amish persons who have left the farm and/or become involved in Lancaster's tourist industry as having fallen prey to the materialistic English world. It is this sort of distinction that Testa's apocalyptic narrative too easily elides, but one that my first-year students vigorously wish to make, especially after our tourist-like meal with an Amish host whom Testa would construe as not *really* Amish.

The Value of Personal Narratives

The first-semester college students I teach are almost all eighteen years old. They are almost all white, middle-class, politically conservative Christians. The men and women are equally dismissive of feminist concerns about the nature of American life (at least at this point in their undergraduate careers). Unlike Bender and Testa, they do not think of themselves as significantly alienated from mainstream society. Indeed, most of them are eager to compete, succeed, and eventually "make a good living." On the surface, at least, they display relatively little existential angst.

Still, they quickly become fascinated with Amish life, a fascination that turns to enchantment for at least a few of them, often when we take our mid-October field trip to Lancaster County. We drive country roads past little schoolhouses and cornfields full of pumpkins, eventually winding up at the home of our Amish host, where, as I stated at the outset, at least one of my students always asks whether it would be possible to live with an Amish family.

It may be telling that my inquirer is almost always a woman. Could it be, six weeks into college life—with the pressure to make new friends, heightened competition to achieve good grades, and perhaps a nascent recognition that motherhood and professional advancement do not make an easy match—that this young woman is experiencing anxieties that she had not experienced before? Then again, perhaps it is simply homesickness, an emotion not restricted to my female students. Our Amish host, who tells us about her former life as a schoolteacher and her current life as a dairy cow–milking mother of six, provides an attractive alternative to the stresses of college life. Her oldest children walk to and from school, and they see their grandparents, who live right across the road, each and every day. That our host is bright, articulate, and from all indications content with her lot and restful in her faith, only adds to my students' enchantment. Far removed from the text-messaging lives my students live, our Amish host strikes us as centered, whole, and fully at home. She has seemingly found her calling, and without needing to take organic chemistry.

What Bender and Testa do for my students is extend their touristic experience and, at least to some degree, give them words for what they felt that day. Although not without their flaws, *Plain and Simple* and *After the Fire* enable my students to weigh the costs and benefits of being Amish more deliberately than our fact-filled sociological texts can do on their own. They also enable my students to see that their own way of living, though sanctioned by their parents, their churches, and the executives who think up reality shows and advertising campaigns, is not the only way to live in contemporary America. What Bender and Testa do, in a word, is *relativize* my students' lives, unsettling some of their previous assumptions about living the good life in twenty-first-century America. That, of course, is not the end of the process. In fact, it is only the beginning, to be followed by questions I want them to ponder long after the semester ends: Would you want to become Amish? What would you gain, and what would you lose? Is it possible to transplant the most attractive features of Amish life into your own life? The last question is the hardest one, and I warn my students not to be sanguine about it. Finding paradise, like being Amish, is much harder than it first appears.

Notes

1. Yankovic's lyrics are at www.azlyrics.com/lyrics/weirdalyankovic/amishparadise.html.

2. Sue Bender, *Plain and Simple: A Woman's Journey to the Amish* (San Francisco: HarperSanFrancisco, 1989), and Randy-Michael Testa, *After the Fire: The Destruction of the Lancaster County Amish* (Hanover, NH: University Press of New England, 1992).

3. Victor Turner and Edith Turner, *Image and Pilgrimage in Christian Culture* (New York: Columbia University Press, 1978), 1–39. Page numbers of quotations are given parenthetically in the text.

4. "[W]e are *not* ourselves. We are a new person who has gone through re-creation and, if we do not feel renewed, the whole point of tourism has been missed" (Nelson H. H. Graburn, "Tourism: The Sacred Journey," in *Hosts and Guests: The Anthropology of Tourism,* ed. Valene L. Smith [Philadelphia: University of Pennsylvania Press, 1989], 27).

5. Beverly Gordon, "The Souvenir: Messenger of the Extraordinary," *Journal of Popular Culture* 20 (1986): 135.

6. Ibid., 144.

7. Daniel Boorstin, *The Image: A Guide to Pseudo-Events in American Society* (New York: Harper & Row, 1964).

8. The five modes are recreational, diversionary, experiential, experimental, and existential. Erik Cohen, "Pilgrimage and Tourism: Convergence and Divergence," in *Sacred Journeys: The Anthropology of Pilgrimage,* ed. Alan Morinis (Westport, CT: Greenwood Press, 1992), 47–61. Hereafter cited parenthetically in the text.

9. Cohen draws on the work of Mircea Eliade and Victor Turner to argue that pilgrimage moves toward the Center, "the most sacred place on earth, the meeting point of the heavenly and the earthly planes." The Center, Cohen writes, attracts pilgrims "as the source of religious merit, divine blessings, and 'the inward transformation of spirit and personality' " and the pilgrimage is thus "an experience of re-creation, revitalization, grace, and exultation" (51).

10. Bender, *Plain and Simple,* 1–2. Page numbers of quotations are given parenthetically in the text.

11. Bender laments that she and her husband were "tourists like everyone else. . . . This was their world, and we were voyeurs, looking at them with the same curiosity we might look at someone in a freak show" (18–19).

12. See Ann Crittenden, *The Price of Motherhood: Why the Most Important Job in the World Is Still the Least Valued* (New York: Henry Holt, 2001), and Judith Warner, *Perfect Madness: Motherhood in the Age of Anxiety* (New York: Riverhead Books, 2005).

13. In fact, Cohen's five-point scale includes another tourist mode that falls between the experiential tourist and the existential tourist: the *experimental* tourist, who "tries out various alternative life-styles" in an effort to "find" herself. Bender may in fact most closely adhere to that touristic mode. See Cohen, "Pilgrimage and Tourism," 54.

14. Marc A. Olshan, "What Good Are the Amish?" in *The Amish Struggle with Modernity*, ed. Donald B. Kraybill and Marc A. Olshan (Hanover, NH: University Press of New England, 1994), 239.

15. Ibid., 237. Olshan takes those phrases from Stjepan G. Mestrovic and Helene M. Brown, "Durkheim's Concept of Anomie as *Dérèglement*," *Social Problems* 33 (1985): 81–99.

16. Olshan, "What Good Are the Amish?" 240–41.

17. Ibid., 242.

18. Testa, *After the Fire*, 1, 4. Page numbers of quotations are given parenthetically in the text.

19. Testa borrows this definition of witness from Dorothy Day.

20. Bender, *Plain and Simple*, 145; emphasis added.

21. In this way, Testa echoes the assumptions of his mentor, Amish scholar John A. Hostetler, who paints a similarly dualistic portrait of Lancaster County in his foreword to the *After the Fire*. "Two ways of life are competing for fulfillment," wrote Hostetler. "The one is maximizing material prosperity, comforts, protection, and status [whereas] the other way looks upon the maximization of prosperity as a disease, deeply destructive of the way humankind was intended to live" (foreword to *After the Fire*, ix). Hostetler became Testa's mentor when Testa contacted Hostetler for help to find an Amish host family.

22. Testa gained access into an Amish home via John A. Hostetler, the leading scholar of Amish life from 1960 to 1985. In his initial inquiry to Hostetler, who often refused access to researchers and others interested in Amish life, Testa noted that he was a Harvard student who studied under Harvey Cox and Robert Coles, an introduction that clearly impressed Hostetler. See *After the Fire*, viii.

23. "To the hard of hearing you shout, and for the almost-blind you draw large and startling figures," Testa writes in his book's introduction, quoting Flannery O'Connor (xiv).

24. I am indebted to Julia Spicher Kasdorf for this observation. See also Donald B. Kraybill, *The Riddle of Amish Society*, rev. ed. (Baltimore: Johns Hopkins University Press, 2001), 290–91.

With its wrap-around porch, extensive spindle work, and asymmetrical design, Carlisle Village Inn sets the ornate Victorian theme in Walnut Creek.
Photo by Gerald J. Mast; used by permission.

CHAPTER FIVE

Heritage versus History

Amish Tourism in Two Ohio Towns

Susan Biesecker

I think we should show a kind, friendly, and meek spirit so that they will want to serve the same God we do. Maybe we can be a good witness and example to them.
—letter from an Amish writer in *Young Companion*

Home to the largest Amish settlement in the world, Ohio's Amish Country is visited by over a million tourists a year.[1] Only Cedar Point amusement park rivals Amish Country in its ability to attract tourists to an Ohio destination. Located in the northwest quadrant of the state about ninety miles southwest of Cleveland, Ohio's Amish Country attracts most of its tourists from elsewhere in Ohio.[2] However, as options for overnight lodging in the area have increased over the last decade, so too has the area's ability to draw tourists from neighboring and distant states.[3] Wherever they come from, tourists to Ohio's Amish Country are a rather homogenous group. Although African American and Asian American tourists are sometimes seen in the area, the vast majority of tourists of Ohio's Amish Country are white, middle-aged (or more), middle Americans who typically drive late-model domestic SUVs or minivans and relax in modestly priced sportswear often featuring American flags and Harley Davidson motorcycles.[4]

Ohio's Amish Country is blessed with a number of aesthetic advantages, including rolling hills, lush valleys, and clear streams, but the Amish serve as the distinctive draw for the area. As the introduction to this volume points out, the term "Amish" refers to a collection of ethnic-religious sects that take seriously the call not to be conformed to this world (Romans 12:1–2). Seeking to live in obedience to the teachings of Jesus, the Amish have developed a host of countercultural practices—from conscientious objection to war, to untrimmed beards, to four-hour worship services, to horse-drawn buggies—that distinguish them, often very visibly, from the broader culture in which they live.[5] Their visibility as a plain, humble, and simple people is a primary reason that they have become a major attraction for twenty-first-century high-tech, patriotic, style-conscious tourists.

The way that tourists see the Amish, however, is not uniform throughout Ohio's Amish Country. This is because the contexts in which the Amish appear vary throughout the area. In some towns the Amish appear in the context of a great deal of mediation by the tourist industry. These "touristy" towns typically have many shops and restaurants that cater to tourists, offering them Amish-style food, Amish-made furniture, and images of Amish people and culture on everything from coffee mugs to T-shirts to shot glasses. In less touristy towns, the Amish appear in a context that caters to them more than to tourists. Generally, these towns are smaller and include fewer shops, restaurants, and trinkets.

Judging from the relative number of tourists who visit these two sorts of towns, tourists appear to prefer views of the Amish that are provided by more rather than less touristy venues. In this essay, I compare the views of Amish offered by two towns in Ohio's Amish Country. One town, Walnut Creek, is very popular among tourists; the other town, Mount Hope, is significantly less popular. Ultimately, I argue that Mount Hope is less popular than Walnut Creek largely because its representation of the Amish constitutes the tourist in ways that are less reassuring for middle Americans. But before I offer my readings of Walnut Creek and Mount Hope, I turn first to some theoretical work on tourism that addresses the question of "authenticity," which is the apparent draw among tourists to the Amish.

Authenticity as Tourist Attraction

In his seminal work *The Tourist,* Dean MacCannell seeks to explain the dynamic of tourist attractions. To understand tourism, he argues, we must first recognize that tourism is always about contemporary culture, and more specifically, it is about the dominant mode of consciousness of that culture. Even when tourism focuses on the past, as in a museum of natural history or rock-'n'-roll, its attraction to visitors lies in the way it constructs and relates that past to the present and to the tourists of that present. For MacCannell, tourism is central to the experience and consciousness of modern people because it tells them about the cultural moment in which they live and who they are as subjects of that moment.[6] It does so through a process of "differentiation" in which tourists are shown who they are by the ways that tourist attractions show them who they are not.[7] That is, whenever tourists confront "the exotic," often in the form of persons of another culture, they learn something about who they are as "un-exotic," which is to say, "normal."

What counts as exotic within tourism is that which is most different from what is modern. A key characteristic of modern Western cultures, says MacCannell, is their relationship to reality, which is different from the relationship that premodern cultures have to reality. According to MacCannell, premoderns simply take things as they are. By contrast, moderns assume that there is always more than what meets the eye. Whereas premoderns are content to accept what they perceive on the surface of things, moderns are always looking underneath the surface for the deep structure or meaning of any phenomenon. For instance, while a premodern would be inclined to accept the words of another as a statement of, say, their intentions, a modern would tend to look beneath the explicit text of their speech for hidden motives, whether of conscious or unconscious origin. In this way, MacCannell argues, moderns have lost a simple relationship to the real. For moderns the real is always obscured by some mediation—words, an image, a set of behaviors, and so forth.

What tourism always offers, MacCannell argues, is a kind of return to that premodern relationship to the real through what he calls "the authentic." For MacCannell, the authentic is some phenomenon to which a modern can imagine having an unmediated relationship. In other words, the authentic is some person or thing that appears to present itself in a manner that hides nothing. So-called native peoples are often seen in this way—as authentic because they do not attempt to appear as other than they really are.[8] According to MacCannell, then, what attracts modern tourists is the promise that a tourist site will provide what modern times cannot—namely, an unmediated experience of the real.

We might imagine a tourist experiencing unease in the face of the authentic, since the authentic could evoke dissatisfaction with modern life. But this is not so, says MacCannell, because tourism always *mediates* the authentic. Like all meaning-making systems, tourism never simply presents the authentic. Instead, it always re-presents the authentic in some particular manner.[9] In modern times, tourism represents the authentic as always developmentally inferior to the modern.[10] Compared to the modern subject who "knows" that reality never simply exists, the authentic is always represented as primitive, naive, or childlike. This representation of the authentic is reassuring for the modern tourist since it positions that tourist as more civilized, worldly, or mature.[11] Thus, the tourist's encounter with authenticity is rendered safe and pleasurable.[12]

If MacCannell's theory of tourism holds for Ohio's Amish Country, then the following would seem to be true. First, millions of middle Americans visit Ohio's Amish Country in order to see Amish who are visibly different so that they can better understand themselves. Second, when these modern middle Americans encounter the seemingly premodern Amish as exotic, they come to understand themselves as normal. Finally, in the context of tourism's representation of Amish as authentic (primitive), these middle Americans are confirmed in their self-understanding as comparatively advanced. Again, if MacCannell's theory is correct, then middle Americans who visit Ohio's Amish Country experience a pleasing reassurance about the superior character of their own lives.

MacCannell's explanation for the pleasure visitors experience at tourist sites is helpful for at least two reasons. First, it teaches us that we should approach tourism as a complex system of signs that is significant for human beings insofar as it makes meaning of their world for them. Second, it alerts us to the value of studying tourism as a way to understand what makes sense or what shapes consciousness in contemporary culture. If we can understand the dynamics of tourism, MacCannell shows, we can better understand ourselves, our culture, and our world. With respect to tourism in Ohio's Amish Country, MacCannell's insights help us understand why the towns that appear to be most authentic (e.g., Mount Hope) are actually less popular with tourists than towns that offer the most obviously mediated experience, Walnut Creek being a prime example.

Walnut Creek's Victorian Theme

Walnut Creek, located just off the main east-west highway through Ohio's Amish Country, is one of the most popular tourist destinations in Ohio's Amish Country.[13] Throughout the spring, summer, and fall, tourists can be seen waiting in long lines for a table at the "Amish-style" restaurant, filling up large parking lots with their vehicles, and keeping shopkeepers busy with their purchases.[14] In addition to its popularity among tourists, Walnut Creek is distinguished by another feature: its Victorian theme. A bit like Main Street in Disney World, Walnut Creek has taken on a "look" that calls to mind a late-nineteenth-century Victorian-American town.[15] Through architecture, interior design, landscaping, and merchandise, an environment has been constructed in Walnut Creek that invites the tourist to experience a selective memory of another time. In a book-length study of three popular tourist towns in Ohio's Amish Country, I write extensively about the construction of Walnut Creek's theme, the story it tells, and how that story may resolve key anxieties in the lives of middle-American tourists.[16] For the purposes of this essay, what is needed is only a general sense of the theme and how that theme constructs Amish and positions tourists.

In the last decade or so, buildings in Walnut Creek have been demolished, constructed, expanded, and renovated so that a Victorian style has emerged throughout the town. Now nearly all of the buildings that house tourist businesses, whether they be inns, restaurants, or shops, display architectural features typical of the Queen Anne Victorian style that was popular during the last two decades of the nineteenth century in the United States.[17] Thus, throughout the town can be seen asymmetrical building designs, walls set on angles, large gables, wraparound porches, and extensive spindle work. The interiors of these buildings further develop the theme, featuring saturated wall colors, floral wallpaper patterns, crown and dentil molding, lace window treatments, wicker furniture, and silk flowers. The prominence of flowers continues outdoors in extensive gardens through which curving footpaths meander around white gazebos. Finally, merchandise sold throughout the town includes elaborate tea and china sets; lace tablecloths, table runners, and valences; silk flower arrangements; garden statues; Thomas Kinkade framed pictures, calendars, and throws depicting romantic village and garden scenes; and reproduction "Oriental" rugs. Thus, nearly everything that a tourist may see, smell, or touch around Walnut Creek, whether indoors or out, contributes to an experience of a Victorian-American setting.

Mount Hope's Jarring Juxtapositions

Mount Hope, which is located six miles north of the main east-west highway in Ohio's Amish Country, is not as popular among tourists as is Walnut Creek.[18] Although the food is excellent at Mrs. Yoder's Kitchen, a line is rarely seen extending outside.[19] In addition, Mount Hope has only two moderately sized parking lots at the restaurant as compared to the multiple large parking lots in Walnut Creek that were constructed to accommodate tourist buses and recreational vehicles. Moreover, unlike Walnut Creek, which supports two inns, Mount Hope offers only a few rooms for overnight lodging. Given the difference in tourist traffic between Walnut Creek and Mount Hope, it is not surprising that Walnut Creek recently installed a new traffic light to manage tourist traffic, whereas in Mount Hope a few stop signs at the main intersection continue to do the job.

Mount Hope differs from Walnut Creek not only in its lower volume of tourists but also in the fact that it does not convey a theme. Unlike Walnut Creek, Mount Hope displays no unifying architectural style. Although the architecture in the town is generally attractive and sometimes even award-winning, it does not call to mind a particular historical period as does Wal-

The Mt. Hope Fabrics and Gift Shoppe, which largely serves Amish customers, features a combination of colonial architecture and Victorian details.
Photo by Gerald J. Mast; used by permission.

nut Creek's.[20] Instead, Mount Hope features a wide variety of styles, the juxtaposition of which is sometimes jarring.

At the central intersection of the town sits a large, two-story building that is home to Mt. Hope Hardware. This vinyl- and cedar-sided building has a partial drop porch, a few small windows on the second floor, and two large display windows on the first floor. Catercorner from the hardware store sits a Victorian-style building that houses the Mt. Hope Fabrics and Gift Shoppe. Built in 1995, this two-story building features red brick and white siding as well as shutters, dentil molding, bay windows, dormers, and spindle work. By contrast, the post office across the street is housed in a simple nineteenth-century folk house that is painted white and has a drop porch.

About a block off the main intersection sits the distinctive Country Mart with its Swiss chalet-style white trim on the front gable and balcony. Just behind the Country Mart is the Mt. Hope Auction, which consists of a col-

Suggesting a Swiss chalet style, the Country Mart caters to Amish customers, offering basic groceries and an ice cream shop.
Photo by Gerald J. Mast; used by permission.

Mrs. Yoder's Kitchen displays relatively simple architecture—one story and cross-gabled, with shuttered windows and brick accents.
Photo by Gerald J. Mast; used by permission.

Some of the older buildings of the Mt. Hope Auction, like these stables through which animals are received for auction, are of simple wood construction.
Photo by Gerald J. Mast; used by permission.

lection of early-twentieth-century wooden barns and mid-century cement-block storage buildings. Across the street from the Auction is Mrs. Yoder's Kitchen, the "Amish-style" restaurant in town. First opened in 1994, this large, one-story, cross-gabled structure appears to mediate the differences between folk-style buildings and the Victorian-style fabric store with its beige vinyl siding accented with a bit of red brick, large windows, and gray shutters.

In sharp contrast to all of the other buildings in Mount Hope is the postmodern structure that is home to the corporate offices of Wayne-Dalton, a manufacturer of overhead garage doors.[21] Constructed in 1992 of white panels manufactured in the plant next door, this 50,000-square-foot, three-story building consists of two large rectangular structures reminiscent of modern architecture that are disrupted by a two-story cutout in the back of the building and an almost cylindrical, three-plus-story entrance in the front. Like the cutout in the back, the entrance suggests both

Set in the context of a predominantly Amish community, the corporate headquarters of Wayne-Dalton provide a surprising example of postmodern architecture.

Photo by Gerald J. Mast; used by permission.

the solidity typical of modern architecture and the play of absence in post-modern structures as three-story columns break into the cylinder to create open space, and walls of windows suggest absence. As if to raise a question about its own identity, the structure's reflective windows mirror images of the houses, barns, and horses of Wayne-Dalton's Amish neighbors.[22]

The diversity that characterizes the architectural styles in Mount Hope is echoed in the interiors of these buildings and the merchandise sold within them. The interior of the hardware store consists of large, brightly lit rooms. But the feeling of the store is cozy, with fairly narrow aisles of merchandise (including everything from kitchen utensils, to gas lamps, to hand-crank ice cream makers, to nuts and bolts) breaking up the space. The interior of the Mt. Hope Fabrics and Gift Shoppe is similarly spacious yet full and displays a mix of Victorian and modern features including dark cherry woodwork, floral print wallpaper, fluorescent ceiling fixtures, and modular shelving. True to its name, the store offers many bolts of solid-color fabrics. In addition, it serves as a general store to the Amish, who can buy prayer coverings, felt hats, locally made broadfall trousers, and black bonnets there.

Just off that main intersection sits Marty's Shoes, which is housed in a simple two-story building that is lit internally by only the occasional bare light bulb powered by an outside generator. This store is tightly packed, with shoe and boot boxes stacked from floor to ceiling. Mrs. Yoder's Kitchen, which sits next to Marty's Shoes, seems huge by comparison, with its two large dining rooms separated by a long salad bar. Warmly lit with ceiling fixtures and decorated with floral prints, this restaurant offers hearty meals consisting of baked ham, roasted chicken, roast beef, real mashed potatoes, egg noodles, warm bread, and fresh-baked pie. Also just off the main intersection, but on the other side of the hardware store, sits the Mt. Hope Country Health Food Store, which is housed in another simple, one-story structure. The simplicity of its exterior is repeated in its interior, which is clean and plain, with its white ceiling tiles, fluorescent lighting, white metal modular shelving, and white vinyl floors. Inside can be found not only a wide variety of bulk foods such as flour, breakfast cereal, and nuts, but also aisles of vitamins and every sort of dried seed, leaf, and root.

Going beyond plain to almost primitive is the Mt. Hope Auction, which includes four areas: the livestock barn, the livestock auction room, a produce and egg auction room, and a diner. Throughout these spaces, interiors consist of a great deal of well-worn wood that was long ago fashioned into stalls, stepped seating areas, and walls. Little appears on the interior walls of the Mt. Hope Auction except a few advertisements for local businesses. Within these walls auctioneers sell a wide variety of animals—from horses, to calves, to camels—as well as produce, eggs, and baked goods.[23]

In dramatic contrast to the livestock auction, the interior of the Wayne-Dalton corporate headquarters is sun-drenched, immaculately clean, and contemporary in style. The three-story entry space, for instance, consists of two three-story walls of windows at the front and the back of the building. On the ground floor, low-slung contemporary furniture forms a seating area, and indoor trees offer a bit of shade. Unlike the Mt. Hope Auction, which sells a mode of transportation from another era—namely, the horse—Wayne-Dalton manufactures state-of-the-art garage doors and openers for residential and commercial customers.

Heritage versus History

With a sense of Walnut Creek's theme, on the one hand, and the preceding "virtual tour" of Mount Hope, on the other, a crucial difference between these two towns comes into view. Not only does Walnut Creek offer tourists a theme, but it also gives them a reassuring heritage. By contrast, Mount Hope offers no theme, instead providing indications of the complexities of history. In the remainder of this essay I want to explore the significance of this difference for the relative popularity of these two towns, for the way these towns are perceived as more or less authentic, for the way these towns figure the Amish, and finally, for the manner in which they position the tourist.

To say that Walnut Creek presents tourists with a theme is not only to say that it offers a unified look or style but also that it represents an alternative time and culture. Indeed, to move around Walnut Creek amid the restaurants, shops, inns, and gardens is to enter a well-planned and beautifully executed cultural memory of an era. All cultural memories are selective about what they include from the past, and Walnut Creek is no exception.[24] What is "remembered" in Walnut Creek about late-nineteenth-century American life is what is most pleasing, not just to the noses, eyes, fingers, and mouths of twenty-first-century tourists, but also to the psyches of those tourists. Thus, Walnut Creek's theme "remembers" charming architecture, quaint interiors, shaded porches, homemade food, and a slower pace. It does not "remember" other characteristics of late-nineteenth-century American life like labor disputes, mob lynchings, or war. Moreover, because Walnut Creek offers a cultural memory of an earlier time within American culture, it offers its middle-American tourists "a heritage." That is, it gives middle-American tourists a coherent and beautiful way to think about where they came from and thus who they are. As a people of such a beautiful and good past, middle-American tourists may be reassured of their own goodness.

In the context of Walnut Creek's theme, the Amish are figured as part of this heritage. Many Amish work and live within or near Walnut Creek, so they regularly appear in town. Amish women can be seen waiting on or busing tables at the "Amish-style" restaurant; selling bread, pies, and cookies at the restaurant's attached bakery; or hand-dipping chocolates at the chocolate shop. Amish men can be seen passing through town on tractors hauling hay or in vans on their way to work. Amish families are often seen pulling their buggies up to the hitching post outside the local general store. Thus, Amish are seen in Walnut Creek doing the kinds of things that late-nineteenth-century Victorian Americans might have done—serving up comfort food, baking bread and pies, engaging in agricultural work, and riding around in horses and buggies. Figured by the context of Walnut Creek's theme, then, Amish appear to confirm the cultural memory that is constructed by the theme. If this is so, then the Amish people that move about Walnut Creek may appear to tourists more as cultural relics of a bygone America than as living contemporaries. Indeed, tourist comments confirm this possibility when they say that the Amish in Walnut Creek do not seem real.[25] Of course, Amish people in Walnut Creek *are* perfectly real. But figured in the context of an American heritage, they primarily signify as historically prior versions of middle-American tourists.

In contrast, although the various shops in Mount Hope offer tourists pleasant sights, interesting merchandise, and tasty food, they do not come together to form either a unifying theme or a heritage. They do not convey anything like a coherent sense about some prior cultural moment. They do not coalesce into a "memory" of who Americans used to be that may transport the tourist from the uncertainties of their everyday lives to a memory of a wonderful bygone era. To the contrary, the architecture, interiors, and merchandise of Mount Hope constitute a hodgepodge of visual references to nineteenth-, twentieth-, and twenty-first-century architectural styles; to agricultural, industrial, and post-industrial economies; to Swiss, Amish, and Victorian-American identities; to primitive, low, and high technology. To move through Mount Hope is not to enter into an experience of a coherent, beautiful, prior kind of life. Instead, it is to pass through a collage of contrasting cultural moments and styles that are not only different but perhaps even opposed to one another.

What tourists experience in Mount Hope, then, are the vivid signs of a variety of human responses to the contingencies of history. For instance, they see efforts to sustain agricultural life alongside strategies for attracting tourists to "Amish Country," both of them nearby a successful enterprise in post-industrial manufacturing. In this way, Mount Hope's jarring juxtapositions signify, not as a memory of a shared heritage, but instead as reminders that the present is defined by tensions between older and newer ways of doing things that are responses to ever-changing exigencies. Importantly, then, what Mount Hope makes available for tourists are signs that, in fact, U.S. culture is not on a progressive trajectory from a primitive past to a developed present. Rather, it consists in a complex mix of economic and cultural factors that we all are obliged to negotiate. In sum, Mount Hope may be less popular among tourists because it has no unifying look, charming theme, or well-executed cultural memory and offers instead vivid references to a multiplicity of contrasting cultural moments. To put it another way, Mount Hope may see fewer visitors because it offers tourists precisely what they are *not* looking for: the contingency of history instead of the reassurance of heritage.

Many Amish live in and around Mount Hope, just as they do in Walnut Creek. Moreover, they can be seen doing many of the same sorts of activities in Mount Hope as in Walnut Creek, such as serving "Amish-style" food, selling bread and pies, and riding around in buggies pulled by horses.[26] But they may also be seen doing a fair number of other things like taking their livestock to auction, walking to a manufacturing or management job at Wayne-Dalton, picking out herbs and roots at the health food store, selling cowboy boots at Marty's Shoes, selecting a pair of broadfall pants at the fabric store, getting a slice of pizza at the Country Mart, and hauling their fruits and vegetables to a produce auction just outside of town.[27] In Mount Hope, then, it is not merely the case that there is no theme, no cultural memory, no heritage. Moreover, it is not just the case that the town offers visible indications of cultural tensions in the present. In addition, Amish seem to confirm those complexities as they are seen involved in activities associated with those many complexities. They are seen participating in tourism as they wait on tables, in agriculture as they auction their livestock and produce, and in post-industrial manufacturing as they go to work at Wayne-Dalton. Furthermore, throughout all this they are seen maintaining an alternative lifestyle that involves buying prayer coverings, running generators, and driving horse-drawn buggies. Engaging in activities like these in a context that underscores the contingencies of the present, Amish people in Mount Hope do not signify as cultural relics. Instead, they figure as living contemporaries who, amid the exigencies of the present, are nevertheless living otherwise than middle Americans. This may explain why tourists are heard to say that the Amish in Mount Hope seem real—or at least more authentic.[28] Again, Amish people in Mount Hope are no more real than those in Walnut Creek. However, in a context that conveys a strong sense of the contingencies of history, which is to say, the conditions of the present, Amish people moving about Mount Hope may seem more authentic in the sense that they signify as a contemporary alternative to the lifestyles of middle-American tourists.

To confront a living alternative rather than a past relic may be less reassuring for middle-American tourists. Again, in Walnut Creek the differences of Amish life signify as part of a larger "memory" of middle-American heritage. Thus, the Otherness of Amish in Walnut Creek's context is apt to represent a prior stage in the development of middle-American life. If this is so, then tourists may understand themselves as superior to Amish people, who are different only because they have not come as far along the road of cultural development. But Mount Hope does not offer a larger "memory" or story in which to situate both Amish and tourist. Instead, what tourists see in Mount Hope are their contemporaries, who are responding to the same exigencies of the present that middle Americans face but do so in markedly different ways. Thus, rather than reassuring tourists that they are not only normal but superior to the authentic Other, Mount Hope seems to offer a visibly viable alternative to middle-American life. Such an alternative may raise disconcerting questions for tourists as to whether their lifestyles are good by comparison. That may be especially true as tourists of Mount Hope enjoy themselves while observing an auction underway, browsing the hardware store, or eating a piece of fresh fruit pie. It is possible to live otherwise and with pleasure, Mount Hope seems to say. In the context of a seemingly intractable middle-American life, in which we are increasingly hard-pressed to get through the day without our mobile phones, this proposition may be unsettling indeed.[29]

Conclusion

As I noted at the beginning of this essay, MacCannell argues that modern tourists want access to authenticity because the unmediated real is precisely what modern culture renders unavailable. To the extent that MacCannell remains right on this point, he helps us to understand that Ohio's Amish Country is such a popular destination for middle-American tourists because it offers authenticity, albeit mediated. But authenticity is not simple. Walnut Creek and Mount Hope attest to the fact that there are multiple versions of authenticity. Moreover, as we have seen, the differences between these two versions of authenticity are constructed by the context in which tourists encounter the Amish. In the case of Walnut Creek, tourists encounter Amish people as their predecessors from a past heritage. By contrast, in Mount Hope tourists encounter them as their contemporaries in a present alternative.

However premodern Amish people may appear, whenever they intersect with tourism they are mediated by the systems of signs that construct the tourist environment. Whether amid Walnut Creek's Victorian theme, or Mount Hope's jarring juxtapositions, or some other more or less touristy town in Ohio's Amish Country, Amish cannot help but be figured by the specific content of those environments. Thus, tourists never encounter Amish *as such* but only ever come into contact with *particular mediations* of Amish for the present.

This being so, we might be tempted to conclude that within tourism, the Amish are merely objects represented by others (like tourist business owners) to others (tourists) and never subjects in their own right, shaping the manner in which they will be understood or challenging the way middle Americans receive them. Tempting as such a conclusion may be, I think it is far too simplistic. I think that the Amish do signify beyond the figurations of tourist environments even within those environments. I argue that the Amish witness to an important alternative to middle-American life even within the context of tourism, especially when tourist environments encourage tourists to see Amish as contemporaries. When tourist environments allow tourists to see Amish people negotiating their particular commitments to community, humility, defenselessness, and discipleship within the complex dynamics of contemporary culture, then the Amish speak to middle Americans out of their witness to the present reign of God. Such witness is, in fact, possible, even in environments that are a good deal more touristy than Walnut Creek. To be sure, such witness will be harder to see or hear whenever Amish are figured largely as relics from the past. Thus, the challenge to tourist business owners, many of whom share similar religious commitments with the Amish, is to construct tourist contexts that encourage the visibility and audibility of that witness—that enable tourists to see Amish people as living out a contemporary alternative.

If we think of the Amish only as objects constructed by a tourist environment, then we cannot see their potential for witness within tourism. Similarly, if we think of tourists only as passive receivers of the representations that tourism offers, then we oversimplify the relationship between tourists and that witness. It is all too easy to imagine that the middle-American tourist of Ohio's Amish Country happily and unwittingly accepts the representation of the Amish as a quaint and primitive sect. Moreover, it is all too easy to think that the Amish within the context of tourism can only remind us of the fine origins of mainstream American culture and help us to see that middle Americans are developmentally and culturally superior to those origins and are thus on a progressive historical trajectory. To be sure, this reception of a common representation of the Amish in Ohio's Amish Country occurs and may even be dominant. However, I think it is also the case, as media theorists have argued, that popular representations of American cultural life—whether they appear in a television show, an advertising campaign, or a tourist environment—only connect with an audience to the extent that they touch on some tension within the cultural experience of that audience.[30] If this is so, then even the tourist puzzled by the "peculiarities" of the Amish may be seen as available to the witness of the Amish—a witness that proclaims through daily visible actions the possibility of living in the contemporary world as a nonconformist people following Jesus' way of humble and defenseless service to one another.

Notes

Epigraph: "Let's Talk It Over," *Young Companion*, September 1978, 257. *Young Companion* is published for an Amish readership by the Pathway Publishing Corporation in Aylmer, Ontario. For more information about Pathway, see chapter 9.

1. Estimates vary on the numbers of tourists that visit Ohio's Amish Country annually. According to one 1997 article, over a million tourists visit the Holmes County area every year, and tourist traffic increases by about 13 percent a year (George M. Kreps et al., "The Impact of Tourism on the Amish Subculture: A Case Study," *Community Development Journal* 32 [1997]: 360). However, based on a 1998 unpublished study of tourist traffic conducted on behalf of the Holmes County Chamber of Commerce, Pat Brown, executive director, estimates that around four million tourists visit the area annually; see George Kreps and Shirley Lunsford, "1998 Holmes County Traffic Count Survey" (1998). For purposes of comparison, I note that the Lancaster County, Pennsylvania, settlement, which has a smaller Amish population but a longer history of tourism, sees about four million tourists annually. See Donald B. Kraybill, *The Riddle of Amish Culture,* rev. ed. (Baltimore: Johns Hopkins University Press, 2001), 10.

2. Of all the cars that pass through Holmes County that are not from either Holmes or Wayne counties (two adjacent counties considered to be part of the Ohio Amish settlement), 88 percent are from other Ohio counties. See Kreps and Lunsford, "1998 Holmes County Traffic Count Survey."

3. License plates indicate that visitors come from Pennsylvania, Florida, Michigan, West Virginia, and Indiana.

4. By "middle American" I mean Americans who are probably middle class, but might also be working class, and who think of themselves as belonging to the large group of Americans who, to borrow from Bill Clinton's rhetoric, "work hard and play by the rules."

5. For an account of Amish theology as lived in daily practice, see John S. Oyer, "Is There an Amish Theology? Some Reflections on Amish Religious Thought and Practice," in *The Amish: Origin and Characteristics, 1693–1993,* ed. Lydie Hege and Christoph Wiebe (Ingersheim: Association Francaise d'Histoire Anabaptiste-Mennonite, 1996), 278–99.

6. In this sentence I use "modern" to designate people of the contemporary moment—twenty-first-century people. I am not trying to mark a distinction between, say, modern and postmodern people. As indicated in his introduction to the 1989 edition of *The Tourist,* MacCannell was theorizing tourism for the modern subject—that is, the subject of modernity specifically. More recently, John Urry and others have sought to theorize tourism for postmodern subjects. Both MacCannell's theorizations about the modern and Urry's and others' postmodern revisions come into play in this essay since postmodernity includes modern features. See Dean MacCannell, *The Tourist: A New Theory of the Leisure Class* (New York: Schocken Books, 1989), ix–xx. See also John Urry, *The Tourist Gaze: Leisure and Travel in Contemporary Societies* (London: Sage Publications, 1990), and Jonathan Culler, "Semiotics of Tourism," *American Journal of Semiotics* 1 (1981): 127–40.

7. See MacCannell, *The Tourist,* 13.

8. As Dirk Eitzen shows in chapter 2 of this volume, this distinction between premodern and modern consciousness may be easier theorized than seen. Although this distinction may not ultimately hold, it remains helpful for thinking

about tourism because it clarifies what draws many tourists: the promise of an unmediated relationship to the real.

9. Of course, as MacCannell notes, inherent in tourism is a paradox: tourism promises what it cannot deliver (unmediated access to the real). This is a paradox, since tourism is, precisely, mediation. Nevertheless, that is the promise and that, according to MacCannell, is what attracts the tourist (*The Tourist*, 105–106).

10. Ibid., 83.

11. Ibid., 7–9.

12. Ibid., 3.

13. According to the traffic study, on a spring day in 1998, 1,872 cars, 16 buses, and 11 recreational vehicles moved through Walnut Creek. Those numbers are second only to those of Berlin, a town just west of Walnut Creek (1,924, 17, and 10). See Kreps and Lunsford, "1998 Holmes County Traffic Count Survey."

14. Der Dutchman can seat five hundred people in the restaurant and another five hundred in dining facilities located in the lower level of the nearby inn. At the peak of the season on a Saturday, Der Dutchman serves between 3,500 and 4,000 customers in a day, according to the office manager of Der Dutchman (interview with author, 18 January 2005).

15. For scholarly treatments of Walt Disney World's themes, see Project on Disney, *Inside the Mouse: Work and Play at Disney World* (Durham, NC: Duke University Press, 1995).

16. I am describing a work that is nearing completion and that is tentatively titled Tourist Attraction: The Visual Rhetorics of Tourism in Ohio's Amish Country.

17. For a description of the Queen Anne style of Victorian architecture popular in late-nineteenth-century America, see Virginia and Lee McAlester, *A Field Guide to American Houses* (New York: Alfred A. Knopf, 2002), 262–87.

18. The traffic study indicated that only 683 cars, 10 buses, and no RVs passed through Mount Hope—about one third of Walnut Creek's numbers. Interestingly, the traffic study also indicates that about three and a half times as many buggies pass through Mount Hope as pass through Walnut Creek. See Kreps and Lunsford, "1998 Holmes County Traffic Count Survey."

19. Mrs. Yoder's Kitchen can serve up to 225 people at a time, and on a Saturday during the peak of the season, about 2,000 customers are served in a day. This is obviously a large number, but it is only about half the number served at Der Dutchman in Walnut Creek on a similar Saturday (Gloria Yoder, interview with author, 3 January 2005). Gloria Yoder is owner of Mrs. Yoder's Kitchen.

20. Wayne-Dalton, a manufacturer of garage doors, won an award for the architectural design of its corporate headquarters located just a block off the square. See Eli H. Bowman, *Mt. Hope: A Pictorial History, 1824–1999* (Walnut Creek, OH: Carlisle, 1996), 319–20.

21. Bowman, *Mt. Hope: A Pictorial History*, 320. See also Wayne-Dalton, *Tradition* [web page] (2005 [accessed January 4, 2005]); available from www.wayne-dalton.com/AboutUs.asp. For a description and analysis of postmodern architecture, see Robert Venturi, Denise Scott Brown, and Steven Izenour, *Learning from Las Vegas:*

The Forgotten Symbolism of Architectural Form, rev. ed. (Cambridge, MA: MIT Press, 1994).

22. For photographs of postmodern architecture displaying these characteristics, see Mary Ann Sullivan, *Digital Imaging Project: Art Historical Images of Sculpture and Architecture from Pre-Historic to Post-Modern* (2004); available from www.bluffton.edu/~sullivanm/index3.html (accessed January 17, 2005).

23. The animals sold at the weekly Wednesday auction include the more typical horses, calves, and rabbits. At regular exotic animal auctions, camels, llamas, and ostriches are also sold, according to Steve Mullet, owner of the Mt. Hope Auction (interview with author, 30 December 2004).

24. See Kendall R. Phillips, *Framing Public Memory: Rhetoric, Culture, and Social Critique* (Tuscaloosa: University of Alabama Press, 2004).

25. Gloria Yoder, interview with author, 3 January 2005.

26. According to Gloria Yoder, the town is not centered on tourists but focuses on serving local customers, most of whom are Amish.

27. A longtime Amish employee of Wayne-Dalton informed me that while most Amish employed at Wayne-Dalton are involved in manufacturing, some are in management (Amish informant, interview with author, 30 December 2004).

28. Gloria Yoder, interview with author, 3 January 2005.

29. To be sure, there are multiple causes for the relative popularity of Walnut Creek and Mount Hope. The fact that Walnut Creek sits just a stone's throw from State Route 39 is one of the more obvious explanations. In this chapter I have offered an additional explanation—one that pays close attention to the dynamics of cultural representation in the context of tourism.

30. For an example of this theoretical view, see John Fiske, *Media Matters: Everyday Culture and Political Change* (Minneapolis: University of Minnesota Press, 1994).

Five Amish-raised participants joined six "city kids" in the Amish in the City *television program (2004).*
Photo by Tony Esparza, CBS Photo Archive; used by permission of Getty Images.

Chapter Six

Hollywood *Rumspringa*

Amish in the City

Dirk Eitzen

I have to make a choice between my family and the outside world. It's very hard.

—Mose, in *Amish in the City*

At the end of a two-week-long press junket in January 2004, Leslie Moonves, CEO of CBS and its sister cable network UPN, announced the creation of a new reality television series, *Amish in the City*. He described it as a fish-out-of-water series: the "fish" being Amish youth on *Rumspringa*, and the "out-of-water" being a glamorous Los Angeles condo with limousine outings to clubs, resorts, and so on. In anticipation of almost certain criticism, Moonves insisted that the show would be respectful, since it was being produced with members of the same team that produced the acclaimed Cinemax documentary *Devil's Playground*.[1]

When a reporter asked Moonves why he would allow television producers to manipulate a rite of passage that shapes Amish kids' lives, he replied, sardonically, "Because we couldn't do *The Beverly Hillbillies*." He was referring to *The Real-Life Beverly Hillbillies,* a reality television show he had announced a year and a half earlier, in which a poor family from Appalachia would have been transported to an opulent Beverly Hills mansion. So strong were the objections to that idea, led by the Kentucky-based Center for Rural Strategies, that the network dropped it. The difference with this show, Moonves joked, is that "the Amish don't have as good a lobbying group."

As if to prove him wrong, a month later, in Lancaster County, Pennsylvania, U.S. Representative Joe Pitts held a press conference denouncing the show. He had collected the signatures of fifty other members of Congress on a blistering condemnation of the proposed program. "We know of no other reality show that singles out the beliefs and practices of a specific group of people as a subject for humor. We find it hard to imagine that anyone would single out five Native American teenagers in a similar fashion, making light of the process of defining their personal and religious identity in a world often at odds with their own culture. In fact, no reasonable person would subject any minority community to that."[2] Despite such protestations, Moonves and UPN pressed ahead with production, and six months later the show was ready for broadcast.

Surprisingly, reviews of the show turned out to be quite positive. "Relax," quipped the entertainment newspaper *Variety,* "No Amish were harmed in the making of this show." *Variety*'s critic continued, "The only cringing generated by the show comes from six total jackass city kids the Amish are forced to live with in the mansion. From the vegan who thinks cows are extraterrestrials to the flamboyantly gay club promoter, they're straight out of reality show central casting—except quite possibly more moronic."[3] *Christian Science Monitor* went so far as to hail the show as a turn for the better for reality television.[4] Even a Mennonite newspaper praised the series for calling attention to Christian values.[5]

To be sure, some critics continued to express qualms. "My concern is that the show will breed more distortion than education," asserted Amish expert Donald B. Kraybill.[6] "I really don't see any good coming from this."[7] Nevertheless, for all of the principals, this story had a happy ending. The Amish young people professed to be pleased to have taken part in the show (and reportedly received twenty to thirty thousand dollars each for their trouble). The politicians got their names in the papers, the pundits got something to natter about, and Moonves got his hit: on its first night, *Amish in the City* attracted 5.4 million viewers, catapulting UPN from the bottom of the ratings to second place, its best performance in nearly three years.

In retrospect, one can hardly blame Moonves for bankrolling the show or the producers for making it. If there is any harm in the series—if it exploited Amish young people or belittles Amish culture and religion, for example—the blame must ultimately lie with the millions of television viewers who evidently have an insatiable appetite for that sort of thing.

Exploitation Television

Reality television is really exploitation television. There is no question about it. For one thing, the purpose of watching people bicker with housemates, get voted off an island, and gag on live worms is obviously not edification. It is sensation. For another, the so-called reality of these shows is contrived to the core. Transparently so.

Take, for example, the scene in the second episode of *Amish in the City* in which the Amish lad Mose, on a visit to the seashore, supposedly nearly drowns in the surf. The biggest contrivance was taking a group of Amish young people to the beach for the purpose of filming their behavior in this unfamiliar environment. But this contrivance occasioned an unanticipated "accident," to what must have been the filmmakers' unutterable delight: Mose got in over his head and began to founder in the waves.

When this is presented on television, we see Mose, from a camera just a few feet away, dog-paddling in the choppy surf; we hear suspenseful music; then, in quick succession, we see a lifeguard dive into the surf (shot later and cut in), a wave wash over Mose in slow motion (shot from just feet away), and one of the city girls swimming toward the camera (as though to rescue Mose). Even a columnist for the Amish newspaper *The Budget* commented on the artifice in this scene, calling it "an attempt to pep up the otherwise boring show."[8]

Pep it up, it does. That Mose was never really in any danger is clear, but that is beside the point. Mose *was* genuinely afraid, and the record of his fear is a sensational television moment—even if its occasion is wholly artificial and its presentation highly manipulated. Back on the beach, Mose cries, prays, and talks about how he might have died and gone to hell. The hell talk is revealing but incidental. What makes the scene engaging is Mose's display of emotions.

The purpose of this scene, as of reality television in general, is not to film reality; it is to record raw reactions to novel or stressful situations. In that respect, the "stars" of these shows are little more than subjects of the producers' social experiments—television lab rats. The experiment in the scene described above is, "Let's see what happens when we take Mose, who doesn't swim very well, and put him in the ocean." A big part of viewers' incentive for watching the scene is curiosity. How will Mose react? A big part of the payoff for viewers is that Mose becomes stressed and emotional. Happy emotions can produce a similar payoff, by the way. Earlier in this same episode, one of the Amish girls, Ruth, is moved to tears when she sees the ocean for the first time. A number of reviewers cite this as a rare and touching example of the positive potential of reality television. It is, however, no less the product of an experiment—an experiment designed to be videotaped, edited, and broadcast on television for the purpose of entertaining viewers and, ultimately, for securing advertising dollars. In other words, in both social and economic terms, exploitation is the name of the game.

Interestingly, the main problem that television critics had with *Amish in the City* was not that there is too much of this sort of thing, but rather that it is derivative, repetitive, and, for the most part, not particularly exciting. "What you get," wrote *USA Today*'s reviewer, "is just *The Real World* with Amish kids. Once they change clothes, there's very little here you haven't seen a thousand times before."[9]

Recipes for "Reality"

Amish in the City clearly follows the formula of *The Real World,* which has aired on MTV since 1992: throw together young people from a variety of backgrounds, typically in an upscale urban apartment, and film them as they negotiate common living. The social mix is set up to provoke both conflict (by pairing up a fundamentalist Christian and an openly gay man, for example) and romance (by having young men and women sleep together in the same room). It is much like a soap opera, except that the protagonists are younger—less established and more hormonal—and the entertainment of the show is generated by the thrill of observing unscripted and unpredictable behavior.

The downside of unscripted behavior is that it is often pretty boring. *The Real World* tries to compensate for this with two strategies. The first is to set up "activities," like dividing the participants into couples for "dates" or sending them as a group on various outings, often to exotic or expensive places. The second strategy is the on-camera confessional. Protagonists are encouraged to report their feelings directly to a camera, providing a glimpse into their "secret" and "private" affairs and an opportunity for them to chew over stresses and social conflict.

Amish in the City employs these same devices, but as *USA Today*'s reviewer notes, we've seen these tricks a thousand times before. The first one in particular—going on outings—seems shopworn. Transporting Amish youth to a sushi bar, to a mud spa, and to Hollywood Boulevard tells us nothing about Amish culture or values. These scenes may imply that the Amish lead sheltered lives, but their real purpose is to allow viewers to witness somebody (anybody) in a moment of "adventure" or "discovery." In *Amish in the City,* this wears thin. By episode four, Ruth's response to an aquarium visit, "It was cool; I never seen that before," has become almost routine.

Which brings us to the tell-all technique. It never works particularly well with the Amish in *Amish in the City,* perhaps because they are unaccustomed to navel-gazing, perhaps because they are unfamiliar with the conventions of reality television. Of all the Amish youth, only Mose is a talker, and he does not dwell on small upsets and petty disagreements. He speaks a little bit about his beliefs, as after his drowning scare, but not in any depth. He does enjoy talking about the little wooden toys he makes, but that is hardly the stuff of scintillating television. In televisual terms, the shortcomings of *Amish in the City* are pretty much the same as the shortcomings of *The Real World:* once the novelty wears off, the producers need to strain to find enough drama to sustain viewers' interest.

There are two additional techniques for trumping up the drama in reality television, pioneered brilliantly by the series *Survivor,* which debuted on CBS in 2000. One is to put cast members into open competition with each other by adding game show elements, often with physical challenges like relay races. *Amish in the City* does some of this, with a treasure hunt in Hollywood, for example. Collectively, the Amish kids perform no differently than the city kids. The purpose of these little competitions, as with putting Mose in the ocean, is to record people's raw reactions to unusual or stressful situations. Apart from the novelty of seeing Amish people in such situations, the fact that some of the participants are Amish is utterly irrelevant.

The second technique is to add the element of elimination: at the end of every episode of *Survivor,* one of the characters/competitors is "voted off the island." The person who remains at the end of the season gets a huge cash prize, and therefore a major part of every episode involves determining who will get cut. The elimination strategy amplifies the drama enormously because it exacerbates the interpersonal tensions and encourages scheming.

Amish in the City does not draw on *Survivor*'s elimination formula, but producer Jon Kroll thought the show's religious soul-searching theme might provide a good alternative to it. "The decisions these people are making in their lives help bring the viewer along," he said, "giving it the drive of an elimination show, keeping the action and the drama propelling it forward."[10] Every episode begins with a narrator intoning, portentously, "Will they choose to return to the only life they've ever known, or choose to remain . . . Amish in the city?" Kroll's assumption was that Amish young people's decision whether or not to join the church would be at least as compelling, in dramatic terms, as the decision of whether or not to kick somebody off the island.

It turns out Kroll was mistaken, for two reasons. The first is that the decision is not as urgent. Not only is there no deadline—even in the series' last episode, the Amish participants are all very noncommittal about their future—but the Amish youth in this show are, as one wag puts it, "pretty rumspringaed from the get-go."[11] Randy has a pierced ear, Ruth has dyed hair and smokes, Jonas is a self-described bad boy, and so on. Even though they all purport to entertain the option of returning to the Amish church, it is a long shot, as Mose admits in a pre-screening press conference.[12]

The second and even more basic reason is that the kinds of things that can easily be shown on television are not the kinds of things that have a bearing on Amish young people's decision to join the church. In other words, a treasure hunt *can* help determine who is going to get kicked off *Survivor*'s island, but it has no real connection to a young person's decision whether or not to remain Amish. In fairness, *Amish in the City* does include outings that are supposed to aid the Amish in their "quest": worship in a Baptist church, a talk with a seminary professor, even a trip to a Hare Krishna convention. In contrast to some of their city peers, the Amish youth are courteous, curious, and even (during the Baptist service) moved. Still, these scenes have nothing to do with the way Amish young people—even ones who agree to take part in a television show—choose whether or not to join their church. What these scenes are really about is reality television entertainment.

There is another kind of reality television show worth mentioning here because, even though it is nothing like *Amish in the City*, it most frankly addresses the fundamental appeal of most reality television shows. Its prototypical embodiment is *Jackass* (MTV, 2000–2002), in which the "stars" of the show drove down steep hills in shopping carts and engaged in other such stunts. *Jackass* brought to the surface something that is apparent, albeit less obvious, in most reality television shows: the "reality" of reality television is not real life. The "reality" of reality television is *risk*—risk of stress, conflict, embarrassment—or, in the case of *Jackass*, physical harm. If, in a "real" or "unpredictable" situation, a character goes off to have a nap, that obviously is not good television. So people are filmed in situations that are as far from napping as can be arranged—like fighting, or eating worms, or riding down steep hills in shopping carts. The situations in *Amish in the City* are tamer—bickering, eating sushi, and going parasailing—but they are still clearly designed to produce the thrill of exposing participants to unfamiliar and therefore stressful situations.

The typical reality television formula of today has gone beyond the uncomfortable social mix of *The Real World*'s early days to include competitions, elimination contests, deliberate embarrassment, and overt physical and social risks. Even *The Real World* has changed. In recent years, the mix of social types has proved nonessential, since the show's veneer of sociological discovery has given way to straight-up salaciousness (i.e., sex, violence, and bad behavior). One of the reasons this works is that participants in reality television shows have learned, by watching lots of reality television, that they are *supposed* to behave badly, since that makes for more interesting television. One sees some evidence of this in the behavior of the city kids in *Amish in the City,* starting with their rude "Oh my gawd!" reaction when the Amish appear on the doorstep in the first episode. On the whole, however, for better (sociological high-mindedness) and for worse (a relatively high tedium quotient), *Amish in the City* hews to the formula of *The Real World* of a decade ago.

Interestingly, this backward step led some reviewers to opine that *Amish in the City* was in fact a step forward for reality television, demonstrating "the kind of thing the reality show can really do." Producer Jon Kroll agreed, noting that his show conveyed "a truth to the masses in a format that will be seen."[13] The big question is: What truth? Perhaps as a kind of pop sociology, *Amish in the City* is a step forward, but it is hard to imagine a show called *Muslims in Montana* having the same kind of cachet. Despite the novelty of seeing Amish young people in a reality television show, the main distinction of *Amish in the City* is that, in media aesthetic terms, it is a throwback to the era before shows like *The Osbournes* upped the ante for bad behavior on reality television. That's what critics liked about it—and what they didn't like.

What Truth?

Even though *Amish in the City* is not half as tasteless as it might have been, we still might ask (along with sociologist Donald B. Kraybill and others), "What's the point?" As I argue in chapter 2 of this volume, one measure of the value of a documentary is the extent to which it punctures popular prejudices by providing surprising revelations. So, what revelations does *Amish in the City* hold out to the viewer?

That Amish culture is sexist, for one thing. Randy is so accustomed to being picked up after by women that he leaves empty cereal bowls and dirty laundry lying about the house, which leads to one of the few genuine culture clashes of the series. We learn a few more things about Amish life along the way too, but not much. For example, in episode seven, the city kids ask the Amish, "Why would you ever go back?" Mose explains that his family can never accept him unless he returns to Amish ways. When Ruth adds that leaving the Amish church is seen as breaking a promise to God, the city kids find this surprising. One even calls it "shallow." Mose sums up his dilemma, which essentially parallels the dilemma of many Amish teenagers: "I have to make a choice between my family and the outside world. It's very hard."

Apart from such small insights into Amish culture, what we mainly learn from *Amish in the City* is how shallow, rude, self-indulgent, and even ignorant most of the city kids are. The moral of *Amish in the City* is not, as some critics feared, that Amish kids are backward bumpkins. In fact, the series takes pains to take the cast to a working dairy farm, where the Amish kids are in their element and the city kids seem hopelessly bewildered. Whereas the Amish seem very willing to try new experiences, some of the city kids flatly refuse to do farm chores. The Amish kids are open-minded, resourceful, and adaptable throughout. The city kids are the ones who seem parochial.

The Amish are not depicted as ignorant either. In fact, if anyone in the cast is depicted in this way, it is the vegan, Ariel, who calls eggs "chicken abortions" and implies that Abraham Lincoln died because he ate too many of them. With the exception of the Amish guys' occasional slovenliness, when somebody comes off looking bad in this series, it is always a city kid and then, almost invariably, because he or she is intolerant, inflexible, and judgmental about something. It seems clear that one of the main intended morals of *Amish in the City* is that prejudice is bad. By this measure, the Amish kids come off looking very good. They are not objects of ridicule, as critics of the series initially feared, but role models. Still, even though "prejudice is bad" is a worthy sentiment, it is debatable whether it warrants filming a bunch of Amish, not to mention making Ariel look stupid.

Another of the ostensible themes of *Amish in the City* is the spiritual quest. Mose's dilemma—needing to choose between family and the outside world—is not just a point of information; it is supposed to be the dramatic engine of the series. The central premise of the show is that it is helping its young protagonists make difficult life choices. For the Amish this choice is supposed to be a matter of faith, hence the Baptist church, the visit to a seminary, and so on. But as I mentioned earlier, none of this speaks to Mose's actual dilemma. Mose's parents want him to embrace their lifestyle and rejoin their community, which is what faith means to them, not to find theological clarity by going off to seminary. This, of course, reveals the show's premise for what it is: a pretense. The fact is, the overwhelming majority of this show is nothing like a spiritual quest. It is just a fabulously expensive, highly choreographed vacation—a couple of months away from "real life."

Here, then, we see the real moral of *Amish in the City,* albeit one that is regarded as so self-evident and natural that critics rarely comment on it: the purpose of life is not salvation but consumption. The presumption of the show is that everybody naturally wants to ride in limousines, eat at expensive restaurants, and attend Hollywood premieres, and that their lives would be enormously enriched thereby. *Amish in the City* implies that what Mose and Ruth and Miriam have mostly been denied, growing up among the Amish, is not the opportunity to seriously explore other cultures and religions, but the opportunity to spend serious money. A swimming pool on the roof, an expensive hair stylist—*this* is what the Amish are really missing, the show suggests. And *this,* presumably, is what the typical viewer is also missing.

Granted, conspicuous consumption is the unspoken norm of television. Indeed, it is the be-all and end-all of network television: network television exists for the commercials. And most reality television shows (with a few notable exceptions, like *Survivor*) are, for all intents and purposes, extended commercials for materialistic living. The participants are put up in mansions, wear high couture, have face-lifts, and so on. Is that reality? No, but it's the way things are on television. In this respect, the Amish and Hollywood are at opposite ends of the American cultural landscape. What could be more alien to Hollywood's preoccupation with lavish living, idle entertainment, vanity, self-indulgence, and escapist fantasy than an Amish lifestyle? What could be further from Los Angeles than a culture that extols simple living, humility, family, community, and faithfulness to such an extent that it renounces even cars and television?

In its potential to probe that contrast, the decision to film Amish young people in Los Angeles seems genuinely inspired. However, in *Amish in the City,* Amish life is not represented as a real alternative to a life of consumption; it is a foil—a means and an excuse to play up "the good life." This is a shame, a squandered opportunity. True, some critique of mainstream culture sneaks through, not least in the way we are made to cringe at how spoiled and self-indulgent most of the city kids seem in contrast to the Amish. Is this a sufficient answer to Kraybill's question, "What's the point?" Does it warrant exploiting Amish young people? Maybe.

In any case, What's the point? is not the question Leslie Moonves asks himself when deciding his network's fall lineup. The point for him is obviously profits, and he, like other network executives, is acutely aware that sensationalism sells. Thus, the operative ethical question for television programmers and producers is not What's the point? but What's the harm? If Amish young people freely consent to take part in a reality television show, then why *not* film them?

What Harm?

In any discussion of the ethics of nonfiction filmmaking, it is helpful to keep three maxims in mind:

1. *Nonfiction filmmakers have an obligation to make movies.* This obligation goes beyond an ethical one. It is a matter of their livelihood. It is an obligation to their employers, their families, and themselves. It also entails an obligation to their prospective audiences: if nobody watches their films, they have let everybody down. So in a sense, nonfiction filmmakers have an obligation to entertain, even if they also aim to instruct or edify with their films.

2. *Nonfiction filmmaking is, by nature, exploitative.* The makers of movies, fiction and nonfiction alike, shape stories and advance arguments. But the producers of nonfiction movies shape stories and advance arguments using, as raw material, other people's lives and likenesses. They choose and

frame, edit and organize representations of other people—*real* people. This inevitably has consequences for those people, including some that cannot be predicted and some that may be unpleasant or even harmful.

3. *Nonfiction filmmakers want to be helpful, not harmful.* If you count among nonfiction movies reality television shows like *Survivor* and *Fear Factor,* this may seem incredible, but in my experience, it is true. Although corporate executives like Leslie Moonves may be consumed with the bottom line, the people with cameras (and even the people overseeing the people with cameras) depend on a relationship of trust and goodwill with their subjects. On the rare occasions that they deliberately expose somebody to derision or harm, as when Michael Moore goes after Charlton Heston at the end of *Bowling for Columbine* (2002), it is because they think their targets deserve it—and usually because they genuinely believe they are serving some greater good.[14]

These three maxims lead, inexorably, to a fourth: *nonfiction filmmaking is an ethical tightrope act.* There is no simple way to balance the interests of audiences and the interests of subjects, to sort out the potential for harm from the potential for good. The ethics of nonfiction filmmaking have to be worked out in the trenches. Legitimate criticism of documentary ethics needs to take the filmmakers' predicament into account. Nevertheless, nonfiction filmmakers are not exempt from moral and ethical responsibility for harm they may cause, even unintentionally. It is no different from stepping on somebody's toes in a darkened theater. Even if I do it by accident, I have an obligation to apologize. I may even be liable for damages.

Does *Amish in the City* step on anybody's toes? We may not approve of the way it advertises a consumer lifestyle, but that is the right of a television show—its business, even. We might regret that the program is not more "serious" in tone, but that is not its purpose. These are judgments about the show's morals and aesthetics, not legitimate criticisms of its ethics. Ethics has to do with real harm done to real people. Does *Amish in the City* cause any such harm?

I have already pointed out that, like other reality television shows, *Amish in the City* in effect treats its subjects as television lab rats. This is clearly exploitative, but does it cause them harm? How can we judge? As it happens, there are widely acknowledged guidelines on how to treat humans as experimental subjects. In the United States, these principles are laid out in the Belmont Report, written in 1979 by a federal commission and routinely upheld by review boards at universities, hospitals, and other research institutions.[15] The central guideline, called the Common Rule, is "that people should not (in most cases) be involved in research without their *informed consent,* and that subjects should not incur increased risk of harm from their research involvement, beyond the normal risks inherent in everyday life." Harm is said to include not just physical injury, but embarrassment and discomfort. The Common Rule rests on three underlying principles: *respect for persons* (meaning that subjects are free to choose whether to take part, based on adequate understanding of the likely consequences); *beneficence* (positive outcomes, on balance, for the subject and society); and *justice* (meaning that no group is singled out for unfair benefit or harm). The second principle, beneficence, serves as the overriding principle, since it is supposed to be the raison d'être of research.

The crux of ethical decision making in research, in short, is to balance the potential for harm to *individuals* against the potential for good to the *social collective.* This is precisely the balancing act described by my fourth maxim: weighing the interests of subjects against the interests of audiences. When these two interests are aligned, as is arguably the case when contestants vie for the "privilege" of being humiliated on *American Idol,* there is no real ethical issue. When the two interests are at odds, as when Michael Moore humiliates Charlton Heston in *Bowling for Columbine,* then which of the two interests should take precedence is open to debate.

The producers of *Amish in the City* would no doubt assert that their situation is more like the *American Idol* example: their Amish subjects were eager to take part in the show, plus they got paid handsomely for it. In fact, nobody in the series is filmed without their express permission. When one of the Amish girls drops by her family's farm in the show, members of her family are kept offscreen, even though there is no legal reason not to show them. *Amish in the City* does put Amish young adults in somewhat sensational situations, to be sure, but it goes out of its way to avoid demeaning them. In sum, if the Belmont Report is taken to be the guideline for ethical filmmaking, there is nothing wrong with the treatment of Amish people in *Amish in the City.*

In fact, *Amish in the City* appears to conform more closely to the Belmont Report's guidelines than *Devil's Playground* and *The Amish: A People of Preservation,* two of the more serious documentaries on Amish life. *A People of Preservation,* first filmed in 1976 and revised in 1991, shows pictures of Amish people taken without their consent and even without their knowledge, using a panel truck as a blind. *Devil's Playground* shows Amish youths using illegal drugs, putting them at risk of legal consequences and perhaps subjecting them to lifelong embarrassment. Why then the flap about *Amish in the City?* Why the whiff of sleaziness that attends it in the minds of many viewers and critics?

The answer to these questions is pretty straightforward. Whereas the first purpose of reality television is *business* (profits), the ostensible first purpose of documentaries like *Devil's Playground* is *beneficence* (social commentary and the pursuit of knowledge). If, in the making of *Devil's Playground,* Amish people were embarrassed or put at risk, that was strictly collateral damage—an accident suffered en route to a noble end. That does not necessarily excuse it, but it does entitle the filmmakers to some latitude with respect to their means. Reality television is not entitled to the same latitude because, plainly put, it does nobody any good beyond lining the pockets of its producers and providing idle entertainment for its viewers. People understand this difference intuitively and make ethical judgments accordingly.

The Belmont Report was designed to safeguard the rights of individuals. But what about communities? Are the Amish entitled to special consideration *as a group* because of their cultural differences from the mainstream, including their desire to be left alone and their religious scruples against allowing themselves to be filmed or photographed? The general presumption seems to be that they are. For example, some of the same critics who take offense at the notion of making fun of an Amish person have no qualms poking fun at the girl who is a vegan in *Amish in the City.* What's the difference?

Double Standard or Due Respect?

When the idea for *Amish in the City* was first announced, an Amish leader wrote a letter to CBS's Leslie Moonves calling the show "a serious infringement of our privacy."[16] He may have meant something like this: We do not want you to put Amish young people in your television show. We think it will harm them. Apart from that, it will bring unwanted attention to the rest of us. We prefer to be left alone. Moreover, the very idea of putting Amish people on television for the purpose of entertainment is deeply insulting. Not only does it belittle our faith, it directly opposes values and practices that we hold dear.

This is a reasonable complaint. It involves three additional issues beyond the issue of "harm" addressed by the Belmont Report. First is the issue of *privacy*. What right do people have to shield themselves from unwanted attention? Second is the issue of *cultural and religious freedom*. What right does a community have to preserve practices and beliefs that it values, even if those are out of step with the dominant culture? Third is the issue of *respect*. Are groups of people like the Amish entitled to the same kind of respect that, according to the Belmont Report, is due individuals?

With regard to the privacy issue, a body of case law exists that helps to clarify conventional wisdom, at least in the United States. Since this is neatly summarized elsewhere, I will limit discussion here to one especially illuminating case.[17]

In 1978, an African American businessman, Clarence Arrington, had his picture snapped while walking down the street. *New York Times Magazine* bought the photo and printed it on the cover of an issue to illustrate an article entitled "The Black Middle Class: Making It." Arrington was unaware that his picture had been taken and had not authorized its use; he eventually sued. The New York Court of Appeals ruled that, since the use of the photograph was editorial, since it showed Mr. Arrington in a public place, and since it did not malign him personally, *New York Times Magazine* had not invaded his privacy and was justified in using the photograph. On the other hand, the court ruled that, since the photographer and the photo agency had profited by using his likeness without permission, they were financially liable (a decision that the state legislature later overturned under pressure from media concerns).

This case illustrates two things. First, in U.S. law, a person's likeness is first and foremost property.[18] What that means, as a practical matter, is that if I were to film an Amish funeral from a public street, it is likely that the only grounds on which I might be successfully sued (were Amish inclined to sue) is that I stood to make money thereby. As this example shows, what is legal is not necessarily ethical. But legal precedent helps to make clear what values are commonly held in highest regard. In the United States, what matters most is very often money.

Second, the Arrington case illustrates that, by and large, privacy is held to be something that affects *individuals*. The claim that the privacy of *all* Amish people is compromised when a handful of Amish people are featured in a television show just does not compute in American law, and certainly not in the minds of American television producers. This is an example of the way the values of two communities can collide. For the Amish, privacy and property are both, in some measure, community matters. In mainstream American culture, they are strictly private affairs.

This brings us to the second ethical conundrum: What happens when the values of two communities are out of sync? Does a minority group like the Amish have a right to be left alone? Is it entitled to special consideration? Most of us would say that depends. The Amish as a group are entitled to more consideration than vegans because . . . Why? The truth is that such judgments depend on where one's sympathies lie. That is why, as an ethical issue, the question of community rights is especially vexing.

Consider the following example, which, although it has nothing to do with media portrayals of the Amish, clearly illustrates the problems of "special consideration." In Amish communities, twelve-year-old boys often handle heavy farm equipment such as harrows and balers. Having young children learn to do real work is an important cultural value to the Amish. As a result, serious injuries to children are not uncommon. When these happen, they are regarded as tragedies in the Amish community but also, in a sense, as acts of God. In the wider culture, however—in the eyes of the law, in fact—these events are sometimes regarded as criminal negligence.

Should the Amish be left alone in cases like this to pursue their traditional practices and to suffer the consequences in their own way? Or should the outside community step in to restrict the kind of work that Amish children may do? In American law and custom, the rights of individuals are generally held to outweigh the rights of religious communities. Even the constitutionally granted right to religious freedom is interpreted as the right of individuals to be free of religious persecution, not the right of religious communities to be left alone.

Is any community, any culture, entitled to special consideration? In liberal societies, the simple answer is no.[19] Communities and cultures do not exist in seclusion, even communities and cultures that desire seclusion. If I live next to a privacy-seeking community of bigots, I have no ethical obligation to respect their culture and protect it from public view. Individuals in that community are entitled to the same protections from harm as anybody else, of course, but there is nothing wrong with my exposing or criticizing their way of life. The Amish are in the same boat. To hold Amish culture out to public view, to criticize it, or even to make fun of it is no different, in principle, from treating a community of bigots that way. It just seems different because we typically hold Amish culture in such high regard.

But what if some Amish people find that sort of treatment insulting or offensive? This brings us to the third ethical issue mentioned above, the matter of "respecting" a particular group or culture. In U.S. law, there are two kinds of insult: insult that causes harm (e.g., libel), and insult that is merely immoral or offensive. For better or for worse, the second kind of insult—the "merely" immoral or offensive kind—is not only allowed, but it is protected. As media ethicist Matthew Kieran writes, "The foundation of any liberal conception of law is the presumption that the mere immorality of a particular act, whatever it is, cannot justify any legal proscription against it, for the point and purpose of the liberal state is to maintain the rights and just conditions required for individuals to lead their lives as they freely choose. This includes the right to act immorally as long as such acts do not harm or infringe the rights of others."[20] The bottom line here is protection of the rights of individuals, even at possible expense to the values and standards of communities.

One important implication of this ethical framework is that there is a difference between moral values and ethical responsibilities. That many Amish people find *Amish in the City* to be offensive may make the program seem impolite or even immoral, but it does not make it unethical. The responsibility of the producers to *their* community is to make profitable television shows, not to respect Amish sensibilities.

A second implication is that cultures and communities have no intrinsic rights, including the right to freedom from outside interference. Communities are entitled to their own values and standards, of course, and they are even entitled to encourage others to embrace those values and standards. For instance, the Amish community has the right to exert pressure to keep a program like *Amish in the City* from being produced, but in the end, such "rights" are a matter of political negotiation. Neither cultural norms nor religious principles can be regarded as an ethical trump card. Even the American Anthropology Association takes this view, charging anthropologists with responsibility to the individuals whose lives and cultures they study, but none to those cultures per se.[21]

To be sure, liberal societies do sometimes ban hate speech, for such speech can cause actual harm to individuals. For example, racist language has been used to incite violence. It also breeds prejudices that perpetuate systemic injustices. It is conceivable that a television show might harm Amish people in such ways, but *Amish in the City* tiptoes around this danger by avoiding any hint of criticism of Amish customs and beliefs.

In general, as in the case of *Amish in the City,* it appears that the Amish tend to *benefit* from popular prejudices. The Amish are, as a rule, supposed to be hardworking, peace-loving, honest, deeply religious, and so on. That is probably the reason why critics rushed to the defense of the Amish in *Amish in the City* while hanging the poor vegan Ariel out to dry. We all "know" that vegans are a little "out there" to begin with. What we all "know" about the Amish, in contrast, is that they are "good." Leaving good people alone when they wish to be left alone may seem reasonable to most people, but as an ethical principle for filmmaking, it is fatuous. It is also condescending. The Amish are entitled to the same consideration as everyone else, no more and no less.

The Moral

All movies, fiction and nonfiction, are forms of social discourse. All discourse, even the most apparently benign, involves power relationships. And wherever power is involved, ethical questions follow. Is it right to show a grieving parent crying on the evening news? Is it right to depict women as sex objects? Is it right to spend millions of dollars on a movie (or even $8.50) when children in Africa are starving?

The only logical and fair way to resolve such questions—indeed, the only ethical way—is to ask, Who is likely to be hurt? Is this avoidable? and, if not, Is there some positive outcome that compensates for or justifies the hurt? The only obvious uncompensated hurt caused by *Amish in the City* is that of Amish individuals, such as the one quoted earlier, who regard the show as an invasion of their privacy and an affront to their faith. This is a legitimate grievance, but not actual and substantial harm.

On the other hand, *Amish in the City* could cause actual and substantial harm if it were to draw such flocks of tourists to Amish communities that it impeded the ability of Amish people to make a living and invaded the privacy of Amish individuals. Indeed, something like this happened when the feature film *Witness* was shot in Lancaster County in 1984. Streets were clogged, and some Amish people were filmed without their permission. *Witness* was a major Hollywood production and painted a very alluring picture of Amish life, so it brought a great deal of attention to the Amish community of Lancaster County. Many Amish people were annoyed and inconvenienced by this attention; some even felt stalked and frightened as a result.[22]

Sociologist John A. Hostetler maintained at the time that the movie would have harmful long-term effects on the Amish of Lancaster County. The director, Peter Weir, responded that the movie "will come and go like a summer breeze."[23] With twenty years' hindsight, it is clear that they were both partly right.

Witness turned out to be a huge box office success, reviving and arguably boosting a stagnant tourist industry. From the standpoint of the local Chamber of Commerce, that is an entirely positive outcome. From the perspective of the Amish, it is decidedly mixed. Heavy automobile traffic on Lancaster County's roads has only increased in the past twenty years, as have the number of people lining up to take pictures of the Amish as they work. That said, many Amish have reaped considerable financial rewards from the tourist trade. I have talked to more than a dozen Lancaster County Amish about the impact of tourism on their community. While all of them said they find tourists and tourist traffic annoying at times, most of them also felt that tourism has had, on balance, a positive impact on their community because of the economic benefits it has brought. So even if *Amish in the City* does draw attention to Amish communities in the form of more movies and more tourism, whether that is good or bad for the Amish depends on one's point of view. Even the Amish are ambivalent.

In any case, like tourist traffic in Lancaster County, exploitation television has become a fact of life in America. The reason is that many people enjoy watching it. If others find some of it offensive on aesthetic grounds, they can change the channel; better yet, they can do like the Amish and get rid of their televisions altogether. If they find a program harmful or distressing on moral grounds, they can boycott the companies that advertise on it. They can exercise their power as part of the community of television viewers to influence the practices of the community of television producers and programmers. That has worked in the past to keep reality television shows off the air, including *The Real-Life Beverly Hillbillies*. The proliferation of reality programming in which willing participants eat worms, handle snakes, and fight like cats and dogs suggests that this is increasingly a long shot—a longer shot, even, than the Amish kids in *Amish in the City* returning to their Amish communities. Still, that is the only ethical way to resolve morally complex issues. For better or for worse, it is the way moral issues are resolved in liberal societies.

Notes

1. The story recounted here is gleaned from approximately two dozen reports in *The Hollywood Reporter, Variety, Washington Post, New York Times,* several Associated Press wires, and other newspapers, accessed through the database Lexis-Nexis.

2. Qtd. in Lisa de Moraes, "The TV Column," *Washington Post,* 21 February 2004, C01. Lexis-Nexis.

3. Ann Donahue, "TV Reviews," *Variety,* 2 August 2004, 31.

4. Gloria Goodale, "'Amish in the City': Nobody Drives Buggies in L.A.," *Christian Science Monitor,* 26 July 2004, 12.

5. Dick Benner, "Thank You, Hollywood," *Mennonite Weekly Review,* 9 August 2004, 4.

6. Qtd. in Rich Preheim, "Amish 'Reality' Show Misleads, Experts Say," *Christian Century,* 24 August 2004, 14.

7. Qtd. in Marc Peyser, "Amish Out of Water," *Newsweek,* 2 August 2004, 57.

8. Les Troyer, "'Amish in the City' Is Not Our Reality," *The Budget,* 11 August 2004, 14.

9. Robert Bianco, "'Amish in the City' Wrongs a Rite," *USA Today,* 28 July 2004, D3. Lexis-Nexis.

10. Qtd. in Julie Salamon, "Trading Buggies and Bonnets for Stardom," *New York Times,* 28 July 2004, E1. Lexis-Nexis.

11. Lisa de Moraes, "UPN Gets the Critics 'Amish' Up," *Washington Post,* 21 July 2004, C01. Lexis-Nexis.

12. See Rob Owen, "Amish Give 'Real World'-Style Show a Twist," *Pittsburgh Post-Gazette,* 22 July 2004, C1. Lexis-Nexis.

13. Qtd. in Goodale, "'Amish in the City': Nobody Drives Buggies in L.A.," 12.

14. There are, regrettably, a few striking exceptions to this third maxim, such as paparazzi, who are to the photographic profession what ambulance chasers are to the legal profession. But the common ideal is reflected in the 1999 Code of Ethics of the National Press Photographers Association, which reads, "[I]n every responsibility that comes before us, our chief thought shall be to fulfill that responsibility and discharge that duty so that when each of us is finished we shall have endeavored to lift the level of human ideals and achievement higher than we found it." Even though uplift is hardly the goal of *Fear Factor,* because the show earnestly endeavors both to provide good entertainment and to avoid harming or insulting anyone, its producers can honestly claim to adhere to the same ethical guidelines. The 1999 NPPA Code of Ethics can be found on the Web site of the American Society of Newspaper Editors, www.asne.org/ideas/codes/nppa.htm (accessed February 2004).

15. These principles can be found at http://ohsr.od.nih.gov/guidelines/belmont.html.

16. Qtd. in de Moraes, "The TV Column," C01.

17. Privacy law in general, and this case in particular, is outlined in Larry Gross, John Stuart Katz, and Jay Ruby, "Introduction: A Moral Pause," in their *Image Ethics: The Moral Rights of Subjects in Photographs, Film, and Television* (New York: Oxford University Press, 1988), 1–33.

18. For a deeper discussion of this issue, see John David Viera, "Images as Property," in *Image Ethics,* 135–62.

19. As a matter of practical policy (as opposed to philosophical ethics), certain accommodations to religious groups are sometimes made. The Amish have sometimes benefited from various accommodations over the years.

20. Matthew Kieran, *Media Ethics: A Philosophical Approach* (Westport, CT: Praeger, 1997), 129.

21. For the American Anthropological Association's Code of Ethics, see www.aaanet.org/committees/ethics/ethcode.htm.

22. John A. Hostetler and Donald B. Kraybill, "Hollywood Markets the Amish," in *Image Ethics,* 220–35.

23. Qtd. in "Hollywood Markets the Amish," 227.

Part II

The Old Order Amish as Media Producers and Consumers

In the early 1970s, senior administrators at Herald Press, a Mennonite publishing house in western Pennsylvania, began receiving complaint letters from a handful of Amish writers. The letters targeted two Herald Press novels, the first one already released *(Jonathan)* and a second one on the way *(Amish Soldier)*, each of which featured the antics of wayward Amish teens. One chagrined Amish writer recounted the meeting of an "Amish Concerns Committee" before concluding with the not-so-subtle reminder that Amish customers helped to make Herald Press's "success possible." Initially dismissing the complaints as overly sensitive, Herald Press changed its course when the controversy did not subside. By early 1975, the publishing house had destroyed all of its unsold copies of *Jonathan* and, in advance of the second novel's publication, changed the title from *Amish Soldier* to *Mennonite Soldier.*

The Amish response to Herald Press's novels was more activist than the Old Order Amish tend to be, but it nonetheless illustrates the central theme of this volume's second part: the Amish are not just images to be consumed; they are actors in history. It is true, of course, that compared to most of their North American neighbors, the Old Order Amish tend toward public reticence and political passivity. At the same time, Amish people do talk, write, debate, and act. They are not only represented by the mainstream media, but they produce their own media, consume media of various sorts, and in some cases respond to and shape mainstream media accounts of their lives. Part II explores that reality, limning the ways in which Amish people and their communities engage the media, both the mainstream media and their own.

And engage it they do. Although some outsiders may imagine the Amish sitting at home with only their Bibles to read, studies of Amish literacy reveal that the Amish consume a wide variety of printed materials. For instance, in *Amish Literacy: What and How It Means,* Andrea Fishman lists the books she found on her host family's shelves, which, in addition to containing *Martyrs Mirror,* the church's German-language songbook (the *Ausbund*), and three different versions of the Bible (the King James Version, *The Living Bible,* and a German Bible), also contained reference works (e.g., bird identification books), children's classics (e.g., Anna Sewell's *Black Beauty*), and inspirational nonfiction (e.g., Corrie ten Boom's *In My Father's House*). Just as prominent in the home were subscription periodicals: a general interest daily newspaper *(Lancaster Intelligencer Journal),* an Amish-readership weekly *(Die Botschaft),* two farm-oriented periodicals, and five children's publications. Surprisingly, one of the teenagers in the household had even begun to purchase (with her mother's knowledge) drugstore copies of *True Story,* a magazine telling maudlin tales of romance and unrequited love. In sum, Fishman found that her Amish host family was not isolated from the mainstream print media. At the same time, they were more selective in their consumption of it than were most of their English neighbors, and in many cases they interpreted what they read in ways that were peculiarly Amish. For instance, whereas Amish readers took certain texts at face value (e.g., their church's religious texts and some secular reference books), they displayed considerable skepticism toward texts produced by mainstream journalists.

We will explore some of these issues in the chapters that follow, though it may be good first to ask the question, Why? Why not expand part I of this volume to include even more genres of media in which the Amish appear? We have two answers to this question. First, a book on the Amish and the media that considers only mainstream media portrayals of the Amish runs the risk of further objectifying Amish culture. By underscoring the agency of Amish people and communities in the work of producing and consuming media, we hope to qualify that objectification, bringing Amish actors and their voices closer to the foreground. Second, we believe that a comparative approach, one that sets mainstream media endeavors beside Amish media endeavors, holds promise for probing the relationship of religion and the media. Even as the media are a variegated reality, so too is religion. Part II allows us to see how one particular religious group thinks about and responds to the media, which in turn enables us to make more nuanced claims about the relationship of religion and the media.

We launch this section, then, with a consideration of Amish cultural values. In chapter 7, Donald Kraybill identifies key cultural components of Amish life that set the Amish at odds with most North Americans in general and with mainstream media culture in particular. More than simply making the Amish culturally peculiar, these cultural features make Amish-related news stories a particularly challenging (and therefore rewarding) "get" for the news media. Still, as Kraybill points out, some Amish persons do participate with mainstream journalists in their efforts to write about Amish life—though, at least in some instances, participation with the mainstream media comes at a price to the Amish informants.

Chapters 8 and 9, written by Steven Nolt and Karen Johnson-Weiner, respectively, explore a different form of Amish agency: the production and consumption of their own media. For his part, Nolt focuses on two Amish-affiliated weekly newspapers, *The Budget* and *Die Botschaft,* both of which publish Amish-written columns and letters, and both of which are mainly read by other Amish people. According to Nolt, these two newspapers provide a sense of "imagined community" among geographically disparate, locally organized Amish communities; that is, they help "Amish people recognize one another as Amish and claim a connection across time and space." At the same time, the two newspapers, which diverge from one another in significant ways, create and sustain two "competing correspondence communities" that reflect different conceptions of Amish life.

The same can be said for the two publishing concerns that Johnson-Weiner examines in chapter 9. The Old Order Amish have a number of publishing or printing concerns in North America, the two most prominent being the Gordonville Print Shop in Gordonville, Pennsylvania, and the Pathway Publishing Corporation in Alymer, Ontario. These two publishing houses provide Amish people (and some non-Amish readers) with a variety of reading materials, some devoted to traditional schooling endeavors, others devoted to family life and spiritual edification. But even as both publishers diverge in their missions from mainstream publishers, so too do they diverge from one another, both reflecting and reinforcing the particular Amish communities they serve.

The last chapter in part II might well have been included in part I. In chapter 10, Diane Zimmerman Umble examines the news coverage of the 1998 arrest of two Amish teenagers for distributing crack cocaine to other Amish youth. Even as the feature film *Witness* shaped the contours of mainstream conversation about Amish life in the 1980s, the "Amish drug bust" shaped that conversation at the turn of the twenty-first century. Indeed, subsequent television and film endeavors such as *Devil's Playground* and *Amish in the City* may never have been produced had not the drug bust captured so much attention in the summer of 1998. Still, as Umble points out, the media frenzy that followed the drug bust was more than an occasion for English journalists to produce an interesting story; it was also an occasion for Amish people to exert themselves in response to the mainstream media's efforts. Drawing on interviews with a local journalist, one of the defendants' lawyers, a prominent scholar of Amish life, and various Amish participants, Umble seeks to illumine the representational dilemmas faced by various parties in the aftermath of the drug bust—dilemmas that provide a context for some of our concluding observations.

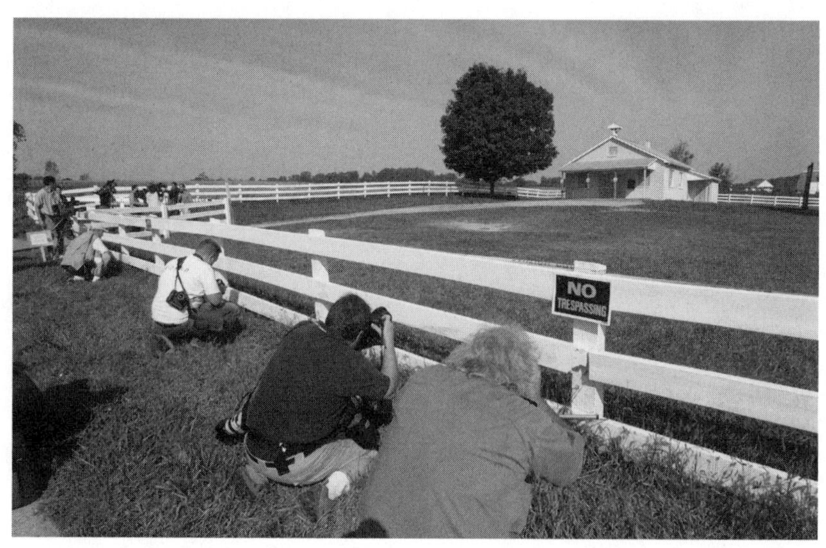

Photographers work to get images of the Amish schoolhouse near Nickel Mines, Pennsylvania, where ten Amish schoolgirls were shot in October 2006.
Photo by Mel Evans; used by permission of AP / Wide World Photos.

Chapter Seven

Amish Informants

Mediating Humility and Publicity

Donald B. Kraybill

We don't want to be placed on a pedestal.
—a Lancaster County Amish bishop

My home phone rang at 7:00 a.m. while I was skimming the local newspaper. "We don't need any more books on the Amish," grumbled an Amish leader with a strained voice. He was responding to a morning newspaper story detailing a lecture I had given the day before on my research for a forthcoming book on the Amish. Unaware that a reporter was in the audience, I had spoken too directly and freely. Now I faced the consequences of my indiscretion on the newsprint in front of me, where I was quoted at length and often out of context. "We don't want our way of life exposed any more [than it already is]. We shun publicity," the Amish caller continued. Moreover, he concluded, "It's not true that the bishops approved cell phones."[1] In my lecture, I had noted that if cell phones continue to slip into use among the Amish, they will gradually be accepted by default. The caller was annoyed about the prospect of more publicity and because he thought that I had given erroneous information about the acceptance of cell phones.

"We shun publicity" were his words, putting the modest Amish on a collision course with the news media, whose mission is to educate and inform the public, to create publicity. This cultural clash goes beyond a mere difference between Amish preferences and the mission of the news media; many people share the Amish proclivity for operating below the radar of public life. The Amish-media tension reflects fundamental differences between two cultural systems. In this essay, I identify some of the points of opposition between the two systems and explore the role of Amish informants who negotiate this delicate cultural terrain by providing the news media with information about Amish life.

Creating and Shunning Publicity

The media market is driven by public curiosity, and the Amish provide attractive images for public consumption for a variety of reasons. As Crystal Downing notes in chapter 1, many images associated with the Amish are pastorals—idealized depictions of rural life. The stark cultural differences of Amish life make the Amish interesting, and their traditional patterns of life invoke idyllic images of the American past. Their stubborn refusal to accept cars, computers, and television as well as their ability to adapt technology for the purposes of their community also stir interest. Moreover, their strong sense of family, rootedness, identity, and community solidarity fascinates those disenchanted with modern life. The pastoral images tantalize media markets and "make Amish stories play well," in the words of an Associated Press reporter.[2]

Sensationalism also sells Amish images. Especially sensational are stories that fracture images of Amish piety, exposing them as fallen saints who sin just like other humans. *Devil's Playground,* a Cinemax documentary featuring rebellious Amish youth, and *Amish in the City,* UPN's reality television series, provide two examples. Stories of sexual abuse, teenage rowdiness, and angry defectors feed the consumptive appetites of the American public, who are sometimes gratified to learn that beneath the apparent self-righteous veil of plain clothing are real bodies that vibrate with sexuality and emotions of anger, spite, and envy.[3] In some ways the Amish reticence for publicity makes them an even more tantalizing target, promising a bigger payoff for enterprising reporters who can puncture the veil of mystery.

Not only do the Amish have little interest in telling their story publicly, but they also have no organized ways of coping with publicity about them. A loosely connected network of some fifteen hundred different congregations and various subgroups in twenty-seven states and the Canadian province of Ontario, they operate without any centralized structure of control. The authority of the church rests in each local congregation and with hundreds of bishops across the country. They have no national publicist, central office, or official head who can speak on their behalf. They do not, for example, produce news releases of any kind, let alone those designed to put a positive spin on Amish-related stories. Amish reticence to produce publicity about themselves is not primarily because they lack the infrastructure; rather, it is rooted in a deep cultural objection to placing their community on a public pedestal. Ironically, their aversion to publicity likely generates more of it than they could ever create for themselves—given all the exposure they receive from tourist establishments and various news media already—even if they desired it.

Some Amish people do occasionally respond to Amish-related stories that they have read in local newspapers and to television coverage that they have seen in an English neighbor's home or have heard about from English friends. If an Amish story appears in a local newspaper, some Amish may discuss it in informal settings, at work, during family reunions, or at community social events. Newspaper coverage about a public protest by animal rights supporters of so-called puppy mills owned by some Amish farmers certainly stirred informal discussion among the Amish, but no letters to the editors.[4] Occasionally a member may send a letter to the editor of a local newspaper, but it more often offers an opinion on a local issue such as zoning than responds directly to an Amish story. Although ordained leaders may discuss a particular story in informal gatherings, they rarely if ever convene special meetings to discuss media issues. The Amish response to a particular news report will vary by the content of the issue as well as the views of local leaders.

A High-Context Society

Social scientists make a distinction between low-context and high-context societies.[5] Modern societies typify low-context settings because highly mobile individuals move across different contexts in a day or lifetime without being anchored in one local setting where all their roles and identities coalesce.

A high-context society like the Amish has dense social networks with many functions—work, family, education, church, neighborhood, and recreation—woven into a single fabric in which everyone knows everything about everyone else. All dimensions of an individual's life are thus ensconced in the community's crisscrossing networks.

The behavior of Amish people is embedded in this thick social fabric—a specific context. "Jake's Anna's Mary" is identified by her extended family's reputation in the community. The details of dress and the color and design of one's carriage only make sense within the context of subgroup affiliation and the local church's *Ordnung,* the unwritten rules that govern behavioral expectations. Behavior is interpreted against the rich social backdrop of family, community, and church; the virtual realities of modern communication simply do not exist among the Amish.

Modern communication typically decontextualizes social life, creating a "pseudo-context," to use the language of Neil Postman.[6] Both telephones and radios transmit voices that are extracted from the symbolic texture of their real-life contexts. Images on television appear in an artificial frame or are seen from a perspective that hides the full context. Internet communication strips context from message and creates a virtual reality that blurs the boundaries of reality itself. Television advertising creates the best example of decontextualized images that are morphed into a kaleidoscope of ever-changing virtual realities.

The technological decontextualization of life was advanced significantly in the nineteenth century by photography. Still photographs extract images from their social contexts and present them from one particular perspective—the photographer's. To the Amish, a photograph is a symbol of pride and vanity, but viewed from a sociological perspective, the Amish taboo on photographs of people arose because an individual cannot be understood alone (as just an individual) but only in the context of a tightly woven cultural fabric that provides full symbolic meaning. Seeking biblical legitimization, the Amish considered photographs of individuals "graven images," a symbolic form of idolatry.[7]

In his classic critique of media culture, Postman argued that electronic communication creates a "peek-a-boo world, where now this event, now that, pops into view for a moment, then vanishes again." With fragments of reality and little coherence, media images and snippets are, in his words, "like a child's game of peek-a-boo, entirely self-contained . . . but also endlessly entertaining."[8] Driven by entertainment, individualism, consumerism, and sensationalism, media values collide with the virtues of Amish life. Not only the values but also the methods and techniques for gathering news often offend Amish sensitivities.[9]

From recorded voices on radio stripped from context to somersaulting images of people on television sets, the technology of modern life severs voices and images from their social moorings. Communalists to the core, the Amish seek to keep voices, people, and images tethered to specific social settings. Given that contemporary media by its very nature decontextualizes life, it threatens the implicit assumptions of the high-context, face-to-face nature of Amish society.

"Keep Your Head under the Covers"

"In Amish life," one elder advised, "it's always best to keep your head under the covers." This metaphor for Amish humility successfully captures the Amish reticence to go public. If the Amish impulse is to pull the covers up, the media impulse is to pull them down to reveal information about the quiet, semi-reclusive Amish. Two fundamental values of Amish life wrap the cultural tarp tightly around their society: *separatism* and *humility*. These Amish principles often oppose and obstruct media interests in gathering and publicizing information about this religious community that prefers to live in the shadows of public life.

Separatism

The Anabaptist movement that gave birth to the Amish church faced severe religious persecution when it formed in sixteenth- and seventeenth-century Europe. The suffering galvanized a sharp separation between the Anabaptists and the larger world that the Amish still embody today. As an ethnic minority on the fringe of contemporary society, the Amish continue to draw boundaries of separation between the church and the larger world.[10] Members are admonished to avoid entanglements in the larger society such as holding public office that will compromise their faith. Worldly values and behaviors are considered a threat that in time will undermine the purity and integrity of the church. Legitimizing their separatist beliefs with scripture, members are taught to "love not the world neither the things that are in the world" (1 John 2:15) and reminded that "that which is highly esteemed among men is an abomination in the sight of God" (Luke 16:15). Another frequently quoted scripture cautions them: "And be not conformed to this world" (Romans 12:2).[11]

The theme of separation from the world runs deep and strong in Amish life. Its practical expressions take many forms—speaking a German or Swiss dialect, wearing distinctive forms of dress, using horse-and-buggy transportation, boycotting public schools, avoiding politics, and insisting on endogamy (marriage within the group). All of these practices underscore the social and cultural boundaries between Amish life and the larger society.

Separation does not necessarily mean isolation or avoidance, however. Amish people, especially those involved in business, interact freely and frequently with the outside world in the realm of commerce. Many Amish enjoy friendly contact with their English neighbors. Separation does mean, though, that news media attempts to report Amish life face hurdles constructed by religious conviction. The Amish prefer to be left alone, out of the public spotlight.

Leaders in the Lancaster Amish community, for example, initiated several meetings with the editors of the Lancaster daily newspapers because they felt that the papers were printing too many Amish-related stories and photographs. Moreover, the leaders objected to identifying people in some of the stories as Amish. For example, a pedestrian hit by a car would have typically been identified as an Amish pedestrian. "They would never say a Jew was hit by a car, but they always say Amish in their stories," said one Amish leader. As a result of the meetings, "the editors," according to one Amish spokesman, "agreed to be more sensitive to Amish feelings and print fewer Amish stories."[12]

Unlike many other religious bodies, the Amish have little interest in public relations, in having their stories told to the larger world. Some leaders express satisfaction in seeing newspaper stories that report on Amish life in a positive way, but Amish people will rarely, if ever, try to place stories in the news media or take the initiative to feed information to reporters for a possible story. "We shun publicity" is the singular message on the "No trespassing" signs posted on the borders of Amish society.

Humility

Although drawing lines of separation is central to Amish identity, it is not the primary cultural distinction. The most fundamental difference between Amish and mainstream American culture lies in their respective views of individualism. Unlike the robust individualism of American culture, which champions personal choice, mobility, fulfillment, freedom, and self-actualization, the Amish argue that personal fulfillment comes through subordination to a redemptive community. The collective welfare takes precedence over individual choice; communal guidance constrains individual behavior.

In lieu of achievement, acclaim, and individualistic pursuits, the Amish are taught the disciplines of self-denial, humility, and obedience. These cultural traits contribute to personal fulfillment under the canopy of community life. Pride is strongly condemned. Considered an offense to God, pride comes in many forms: posing for photos, attaching one's name to a written essay, seeking credit for things, showing off one's knowledge of scripture, dressing in worldly clothing, and—God forbid—appearing on television or in newsprint.

Humility, the highest virtue of Amish life, means not calling attention to oneself or one's people. Such forward, assertive behavior signals a proud and vain heart—an abomination in the eyes of God. The virtue of humility and the vice of pride are underscored by numerous scriptures cited by Amish preachers and leaders.[13] Members who cooperate too freely with the news media may face not only their own guilty consciences and the anger of the church but also the frown of God. Thus, a decision to speak with a reporter carries potential religious consequences for an Amish informant.

Amish people who agree to talk may baffle some journalists because they typically refuse to have their names appear in stories. Pressed by their editors for clear lines of attribution, reporters are often caught between the demands of their editors and the reticence of their Amish sources. I am often asked by exasperated reporters why Amish people refuse to permit their names to appear in print. The answer is that, in the context of a communal society that shuns publicity, an individual who steps forward with his or her name violates several taboos and will likely face the ire of the church and some form of censure.

Going public with one's name reflects a proud heart and violates Amish teaching on humility. It also transgresses the cultural norm of shunning publicity and the symbolic line of separation from the world. Obviously, individuals who knowingly violate these community standards seek to do so anonymously to avoid censure by their community. For reporters operating under the assumptions of an individualistic, publicity-seeking culture, this Amish reticence is hard to grasp.

Unlike many people in the larger world, Amish members live within the cultural constrictions of their ethnic community and are held accountable to them by the elders of the church. Indeed, at baptism adults agree to follow the *Ordnung*, the rules of the church, ranging from dress and use of technology to participation in public life. Although these are not written rules and their interpretation varies among congregations, they are nevertheless clearly understood guidelines for behavior. These oral understandings of the cultural expectations that govern behavior across the spectrum of Amish life include not posing for photographs, appearing on television, or promoting Amish life in public ways. A member who violates these norms will face informal criticism by members or formal reprimand by church officials and, depending on the severity of the offense, may be expected to make a public confession in front of the church.

One Amish man complained, for example, that another member of his extended family "talks to the papers too much and embarrasses us too much."[14] Typical Amish informants are usually sensitive to the cultural constraints of their communities. An Amish man who had spoken with several reporters was reprimanded by his bishop. Later, when he was again asked to grant an interview, he confided, "If I do it, everyone [in my church] will say, 'There's that guy blowing off steam again.' And I don't want to get my bishop upset again. He's already said that I'm doing too much of this stuff."[15]

Recalcitrants who persist in speaking openly with reporters will face some form of censure, possibly even excommunication and shunning until they repent. Nevertheless, many Amish members provide information to reporters without being sanctioned by church officials. They avoid sanctions by remaining anonymous and by withholding comment on controversial topics. However, those who violate the norms of humility and step across the moral boundaries by giving their names or speaking about controversial church issues will hear from church leaders.

Amish Informants

Quiet Voices

Journalists seeking reliable information and working under tight deadlines often do not have the time or the resources to research Amish culture in depth. Thus they struggle with how to gather information quickly in the face of Amish reluctance or even resistance. This is especially challenging because most Amish do not have easy access to phones. As much as the news media may seek to convey news and trustworthy information, media success is also about better ratings, increased readership, and greater advertising sales. The commercial interests of the media as well as the journalistic goals of reporting news fly in the face of Amish pleas to be left alone and undisturbed.

Despite this clash of cultural values—the clash between humility and publicity—the Amish are in the news. Moreover, in some cases it is evident that a given reporter has succeeded in gaining information, insights, or comments directly from an Amish person. How does this happen?

Amish cooperation with journalists takes various forms. Some members are curious and willing to speak, depending on the circumstances. Others will never speak with a reporter. Lay members will typically speak more freely than ordained leaders, who feel a greater obligation both to protect the church and to uphold its norms against publicity. The willingness of *some* informants to speak *sometimes* depends on the identity of a reporter. In general, Amish informants are more likely to speak with a reporter they know and trust than with a complete stranger, but not always.

International journalists are sometimes an exception. Some Amish people seem more willing to speak with international reporters than local ones for several reasons: the Amish are curious about the reporter's country and culture, they feel obligated to help foreign reporters because they traveled such a long distance, and they assume that the information they give will not appear in their local paper. Often local journalists without strong connections to the Amish community face the most difficulty obtaining information because Amish informants worry that the story will appear in the local paper where other Amish will read it and chide them for seeking publicity.

On the other hand, those local reporters who have developed a measure of trust with Amish informants over several years are likely to have easier access to information. Indeed, some reporters based near Amish communities have a network of several Amish lay members whom they consult when working on an Amish-related story. These informants may assist journalists on a regular basis. These are not the one-time informants who happened to be cornered by a journalist on a street or in a public store; these are seasoned, sometimes media-savvy Amish with previous experience dealing with reporters. Although such informants may serve a helpful function in their community by providing accurate information to reporters, their role is not approved by leaders because in almost all cases the leaders would prefer less, not more publicity about Amish life. Why then do these self-appointed spokespersons cooperate with reporters if they know their community frowns on their role?

Motivations for Speaking

Several factors may motivate Amish informants to speak with reporters. Sitting on the cultural fence between Amish and mainstream society, some worldly-wise Amish are familiar with the outside media culture through their work and travel. One member was described by another Amish man as having "one toe inside the Amish community and two feet out." Such Amish people, curious about the outside world, enjoy interacting with reporters; they are stimulated by the questions that are posed, and they also learn about the larger culture through the conversations. Despite Amish prohibitions against pride, these self-appointed informants enjoy being considered expert sources of Amish wisdom.

Often, however, the motivations for speaking are more complex than mere pleasure-seeking. Although most Amish abhor publicity, some will cooperate with journalists reluctantly, believing that if they do not, the headlines and stories will misinterpret their culture—a charge that Amish people frequently levy at tourist books and promotional pieces. In justifying their behavior with concerns for the truth, they may claim that if they do not speak out, the true facts of Amish life will be distorted. And because the story will likely be told in one way or another, they "want to make sure that it's told truthfully."

Complicating this mix of motivations even more is the fact that many Amish informants who collaborate with reporters on a regular basis stand on the margins of their communities. They sometimes tell their stories in ways that do not necessarily reflect the mainstream views of their people. In almost all cases these spokespeople are more progressive in their lifestyles than other members of the community. Their views and commentaries, while representing their personal perspectives, may not reflect the mainstream practice or majority opinion of their community. For example, an Amish man who owns a cell phone, speaking with reporters, said, "So many of our people have cell phones that it will be impossible for church leaders to ever get rid of them." Other members of his community would strongly disagree. Like other communities, the Amish hold a diversity of opinions, but the regular informants who provide commentary for reporters typically represent the more liberal segment of the community.

Marginal Voices

In some cases, the willing informants are ex-members or rebellious youth headed out of the church. This was the case with three of the four lead characters profiled in *Devil's Playground*. One joined the church during the filming and then refused to continue cooperating with the production. Two of the most talkative characters were the wildest of the wild and had turned their backs on the church with no intention of returning. The Amish youth who appeared in UPN's *Amish in the City* were also exiting from their communities. While both of these shows provided true stories of the wild and rebellious, they were not representative of most Amish youth. Nevertheless, these images shaped the perceptions and impressions of millions of viewers.[16]

News stories of illegal Amish activities that may involve distraught members or ex-members often reflect the perspective of the victims, who are eager to tell their stories. Reporters often gain easy access to disgruntled ex-members or victims who want to vent their frustration and anger. Church leaders and perpetrators of crime are of course very reluctant to speak. Thus a public story of Amish blight that appears on television or in print typically tilts in the direction of Amish victims or ex-Amish sources who suffered in the incident. The case of a young Amish woman in Wisconsin who was repeatedly raped by two of her brothers over several years illustrates an extreme case. As a young adult, she left the community and became the prime informant for an ABC *20/20* program on the sad story and subsequent trial of her brothers.[17] Although her mother offered a few cryptic comments to a reporter, the Amish leaders refused to speak and explain how the church had dealt with the abuse before the story hit the press.

Exceptional Circumstances

A sudden major news event can test the rules of Amish-media engagement. The October 2006 shooting of ten Amish girls in a one-room school by a deranged English neighbor brought down an avalanche of publicity on a small Amish community in Pennsylvania. Dozens of media crews swarmed the rural crossroads of Nickel Mines within hours of the shooting. The Amish, stunned by the deaths of five children and serious injuries to five more, were overwhelmed by hundreds of reporters who lingered for five days to cover the shooting and the subsequent funerals. Reporters felt pressure to speak with Amish people as quickly as possible to meet their deadlines. The Amish, overwhelmed with grief, wanted above all to be left alone.

Generally speaking, the basic Amish rules of media engagement remained intact during this exceptional event, though not entirely so. Few if any Amish people directly faced television cameras for interviews, and Amish people did not provide statements or news releases to the media. Several English neighbors spoke on behalf of the Amish, and some Amish people spoke with the media, noting with sympathetic understanding that "reporters have a job to do too."[18] The most obvious departure from standard Amish practice was the fact that many Amish people provided their names to reporters—or at least, in the heat of the spotlight, forgot to request anonymity—which produced numerous quotations attributed to specific Amish persons. Several Amish people wrote and signed letters to the editors of local papers to express their feelings about the shooting. For their part, church leaders seemed quite willing to overlook members' transgressions with the media during this horrific and unprecedented event. Had the story involved the exposure of Amish deviance, such as the drug bust of 1998, church leaders would undoubtedly have been less sympathetic to members who cooperated too freely with the media.

Voices of Remorse

What happens in more normal circumstances when upright members exercise poor judgment in speaking with reporters? If confronted by church elders, their only recourse to avoid excommunication is confession. A Swiss television producer who had lived near an Amish community in Pennsylvania as a high school exchange student returned to the United States to shoot a documentary film on Amish life. An Amish friend who knew him during high school agreed to assist in the production, thinking the film would only be shown in Europe for educational purposes. Surprisingly, the

Amish man even agreed to appear on camera several times—assuming that local church leaders would never learn about his deviance. All went well until PBS purchased the rights to show the video on PBS stations in the United States. To his shock and consternation, English neighbors began calling the Amish man a "Hollywood TV star" when the documentary appeared locally.[19]

Realizing that news of his error would spread rapidly in the Amish community and could bring censure, he quickly begged for forgiveness. "I headed straight to my bishop that same day to explain what happened," he reported. The next Sunday he made a confession at a members' meeting following the church service. A repentant heart and remorseful spirit typically bring forgiveness and full restoration into Amish life. Had this unwitting "Hollywood star" balked and defended his appearance on television, he would have surely faced excommunication and shunning.

Another Amish man did receive a six-week probationary exclusion for his involvement with the media during the so-called Amish drug bust of 1998, an incident that culminated in the arrest of two Amish youths for buying cocaine from members of the Pagans motorcycle gang and selling it to their Amish friends. This sensational story that married the most unlikely of images—barefoot Amish lads and black-jacketed Pagan cyclists—created a feeding frenzy among journalists.[20] Some of them found their way to the home of an Amish man who supplied them with a frank and sometimes humorous spin on the story. Trying to control the swelling influx of reporters, this self-appointed Amish publicist announced that "I have to be very careful who I talk with, and I won't talk with reporters in marked cars or with TV trucks, and [will allow] no recorder and no use of my name."[21] His self-imposed limits were not strong enough, however, to control the damage. He too was soon confessing his errors in front of his local congregation and facing a six-week probationary exclusion from church activities. The temporary censure ended when he confessed his transgressions and promised to use better judgment in the future.

In a third case, an Amish man who used a clandestine computer in his business, a clear violation of Amish taboos on technology, agreed to speak with a reporter doing a story on Amish technology for a major regional newspaper. When the story of his computer, his photograph, and careless comments about his bishop appeared in a front-page story, this wayward Amish man was soon confessing his transgressions to his local congregation. Moreover, in an unprecedented move taken because the issue had become so public, he wrote a letter of apology to the local newspaper for his indiscretion. In his written apology, he said, "I am embarrassed and humiliated. . . . I was misquoted and words were taken out of context. I, however, blame no one but myself. In the future, I will try to be more careful with my words."[22]

These stories illustrate the church's response when Amish members cooperate too freely with the news media and the consequences of excessive cooperation. In some other religious communities, these stories might have offered moments of fame in the media spotlight but probably not censure by church leaders. Amish informants most likely to face scorn are those who permit their names to be used and who make reckless comments about sensitive issues that embarrass the church. Many Amish laypeople provide helpful information to news reporters, but usually under the cloak of anonymity. Both those who cooperate quietly with journalists and those who display some vanity nevertheless are accountable to the authority of the community and are expected to exemplify the virtues of humility that they affirmed at their baptism.

Bridging Humility and Publicity

The role of Amish informants is more than simply providing information. It often involves negotiation with the journalists. An Amish informant may grant an interview with various stipulations. Virtually all Amish spokespeople will insist on anonymity. Some will speak, but not on a recorder. Others may be willing to answer questions but insist on no note-taking. One Amish leader, sought out by an NPR reporter, agreed to speak but insisted, "I don't want my voice recorded," effectively terminating the interview because radio was the medium. Another informant agreed to speak with a national reporter at an undisclosed site away from his home so his family and neighbors would not see the reporter's car. Unless they know and trust the reporter, seasoned Amish informants typically set boundaries for discussions with journalists by clarifying at the beginning of the interview what they will talk about and what limits they will place on the story—always aware that a reckless quotation could stir the ire of the church.

Amish informants may cooperate only with a clear understanding that no photographs are taken and no camera crews accompany the reporter. Many Amish people will permit photos of buildings, animals, and landscapes, but the typical moral boundary on photos forbids pictures of people who appear to have posed—suggesting the subject was cooperating. On some occasions, an Amish person, pushing hard against the cultural fence, will consent to be photographed from the back or the side, as long as his or her face is not photographed from the front. The more gregarious and adventuresome informants sometimes grant a variety of "un-posed" poses.

On the other side of the bargaining table, reporters often need to make concessions as well. A primary one is that they must travel and conduct face-to-face interviews because they typically cannot interview by phone, teleconference, or e-mail. Apart from conducting interviews by phone, they rarely can even make an appointment by phone. Rather, they are forced to travel to the Amish community and spend several days scouting the local area in search of Amish informants. This is especially true for international and national reporters but is usually not the case for local journalists, who have reliable sources inside the Amish community. In any event, journalist-informant interactions are often negotiated in a variety of creative ways.

Amish gatekeepers are an important form of Amish agency; their voices offer insider perspectives to the content of Amish-theme stories. Indeed, Amish informants open the doors that provide access across the cultural chasm that separates public curiosity from Amish realities. News media want accurate information about the Amish in order to inform and educate the public about Amish life, whether in daily news or in feature essays. But the search for inside information always proceeds in the face of cultural reluctance to disclose it.

Amish spokespersons must negotiate the cultural terrain between the norms of their community and sincere requests for information and Amish commentary. Amish informants often find themselves in the awkward and uncomfortable role of mediating requests from the news media and the restraints of humility in their own community. The informants are often caught between their own willingness to be good neighbors by accommodating reporters' requests for assistance and Amish leaders who advocate privacy and seclusion.

Bridging the deep cultural divide that on one side celebrates publicity and transparency and on the other side advocates humility and seclusion, Amish gatekeepers often walk a tight line. They want to be helpful by providing reliable information so that Amish stories will, in their words, "tell the truth," yet they must be ever cautious, ever careful to cooperate in ways that respect the values of their culture and its leaders' aversion to publicity.

Notes

1. Telephone conversation with author, 31 October 2003.

2. Telephone conversation with author, 2 June 2004.

3. For an extended discussion of the construction and consumption of Amish images, see David Weaver-Zercher, *The Amish in the American Imagination* (Baltimore: Johns Hopkins University Press, 2001). For another discussion of Amish representations, see Daniel W. Lehman, "Graven Images and the (Re)presentation of Amish Trauma," *Mennonite Quarterly Review* 72 (1998): 577–87.

4. The three major Lancaster newspapers (*Intelligencer Journal, New Era,* and *Sunday News*) all reported a daylong protest of puppy mills in Lancaster County on September 17, 2005. The protest, which featured national celebrities, specifically targeted Amish puppy growers.

5. Edward T. Hall, *Beyond Culture* (Garden City, NY: Doubleday, 1976), 74–96.

6. Neil Postman, *Amusing Ourselves to Death: Public Discourse in the Age of Show Business* (New York: Elizabeth Sifton Books/Penguin Books, 1985), 76.

7. For a series of objections to photographs, see the minutes of the National Conference of Amish Ministers meeting in 1876, recorded in Paton Yoder and Steven R. Estes, eds., *Proceedings of the Amish Ministers' Meetings, 1862–1878* (Goshen, IN: Mennonite Historical Society, 1999), 218–21.

8. Postman, *Amusing Ourselves,* 77.

9. The production of the feature film *Witness* provides one example of the clash between Amish sensitivities and media interests. Despite Amish objections to shooting this film, director Peter Weir demonstrated remarkable sensitivity to Amish values in his portrayal of their culture as discussed in chapter 1 of this volume. For additional discussion of this story, see Kraybill, *The Riddle of Amish Society,* rev. ed. (Baltimore: Johns Hopkins University Press, 2001), 280–84; and John A. Hostetler and Donald B. Kraybill, "Hollywood Markets the Amish," in *Image Ethics: The Moral Rights of Subjects in Photographs, Film, and Television,* ed. Larry Gross, John Stuart Katz, and Jay Ruby (New York: Oxford University Press, 1988), 220–35.

10. For an overview of Amish origins, persecution, and the emergence of the

theme of separation, see John A. Hostetler, *Amish Society,* 4th ed. (Baltimore: Johns Hopkins University Press, 1993); Steven M. Nolt, *A History of the Amish,* rev. ed. (Intercourse, PA: Good Books, 2003); and John D. Roth, *Letters of the Amish Division: A Sourcebook* (Goshen, IN: Mennonite Historical Society, 1993).

11. All quotations are from the King James Version of the Bible. Other typical biblical passages that are cited by Amish leaders to support the principle of separation from the larger society include John 17:14, 1 Peter 2:9, James 4:4, and John 17:15. For a discussion of these verses, see *1001 Questions and Answers on the Christian Life* (LaGrange, IN: Pathway Publishers, 1992).

12. Interview with author, 3 June 2004. The meetings with the news editors occurred in the spring of 2004.

13. Typical biblical passages that are used by Amish leaders today to support humility include Psalm 51:17, Matthew 18:4, Luke 18:13–14, John 1:27, Philippians 2:5, 8, and 1 Peter 5:5–6. Often-cited scriptures that warn of the dangers of pride include Jeremiah 13:15–16; Proverbs 6:17, 16:5, 21:4; Matthew 11:28–30; and James 4:6.

14. Interview with author, 20 July 2004.

15. Telephone interview with author, 27 February 2003.

16. Although these two examples are outside the realm of news media, they illustrate the way in which Amish people on the margins of their culture can distort public perceptions of mainstream Amish practices.

17. This story aired on ABC's *20/20* on December 10, 2004.

18. Interview with author, 15 November 2006.

19. This fifty-five-minute video, *The Amish Riddle,* was produced by François Jeannet and Vincent Mercier of EKIS, Agence de Reportages, and was shown periodically on many PBS stations in the late 1980s and early 1990s. By special arrangement to protect the Amish accomplice, it was not shown on WITF, the PBS affiliate in Harrisburg, Pennsylvania, whose signal covers the Lancaster Amish settlement.

20. Media that covered the story included ABC World News, Australian Broadcasting, CNN, NPR, BBC, *Time, New York Times, New Yorker Magazine, London Daily Mail,* and various European television networks. When the story broke, I received more than fifty media inquiries in three weeks' time.

21. Telephone conversation with author, 26 June 1998.

22. The story and photograph appeared in the *Philadelphia Inquirer* on July 30, 2000. The confession in the local newspaper was printed as a letter to the editor in the *Lancaster Intelligencer Journal* on August 4, 2000.

NOTICE

REVISION OF GUIDELINES

By the *Die Botschaft* Committee

1. Please avoid unreasonably long letters of news not of interest to majority of the readers, as we wish to keep the cost of *Die Botschaft* down. Not more than one sheet is allowed.
2. Scribes approved by the committee are entitled to free envelopes and subscriptions. Please ask for them in beginning of year.
3. For prompt delivery have 6 or more subscribers to one postal address.
4. For extra slow delivery contact local post office. If you are convinced that it is not the local post office, contact Circulation Department of *Die Botschaft*.
5. Unaffiliated or improper letters, murder or love poems or stories will not be printed in *Die Botschaft*.
6. Letters of religious discussions or criticism or unsigned letters will not be printed in *Die Botschaft*.
7. Questionable advertisements in *Die Botschaft* should have the approval of *Die Botschaft* committee.
8. No money showers will be printed in *Die Botschaft*.
9. No photos of people in ads.
10. Old Order Amish and Old Order Team Mennonite scribes only.
11. No faxed letters accepted.
12. Mysteries, War & Love stories will NOT be accepted. To advertise other books, please send a copy of the book to *Die Botschaft* and it will be reviewed by the Committee for suitability to be advertised in the paper. Books are not returned.

Yours truly,
Die Botschaft Committee
192 Sproul Road
Christiana, PA 17509

Die Botschaft
420 Weaver Road
Millersburg, PA 17061

Editorial guidelines governing what can appear in Die Botschaft *shape the community that the paper engenders.*

Used by permission of *Die Botschaft*.

Chapter Eight

Inscribing Community

The Budget *and* Die Botschaft *in Amish Life*

Steven M. Nolt

No photos of people in ads.
—publishing guideline for *Die Botschaft*

Each week tens of thousands of readers across North America eagerly await the delivery of newspapers devoid of headlines, feature stories, comic pages, and sports sections.[1] Instead, the news that these subscribers anticipate is contained in hundreds of letters that fill the papers' pages. Regular correspondents, known as "scribes," submit weekly or biweekly accounts of events in their neighborhoods to *The Budget* or *Die Botschaft,* two Amish-affiliated correspondence weeklies.[2]

"Our church service at Robert A. Troyer's yesterday was well attended with many visitors," reported one scribe from Baltic, Ohio, in the summer of 2004, before listing a dozen of the visitors. Two columns to the left, another Ohio writer noted that "we were blessed with a beautiful day after the area received 3 or more inches of rain" and that "John and Ruth Raber say 'It's a boy.' They have named him Bruce. He has two sisters and one brother to greet him. Grands are Abe J. C. Rabers and Wayne M. Millers." Other entries on the same page informed readers that "women are busy with sweet corn, apples, peaches, etc." in Holmes County, Ohio, and that "Bishop Ammon J. Miller's came for a Hochstetler reunion." A page earlier, Lavern Stoll of Conneautville, Pennsylvania, "received the shocking news . . . of the passing away of his grandmother, Mrs. Elizabeth Slabaugh."[3]

These entries, taken from *The Budget,* and similar offerings in *Die Botschaft* (which, despite its German title, is also an English-language publication), serve up page after page of community life detail from Amish and Mennonite communities in more than thirty states and Ontario. Published since 1890 in Sugarcreek, Ohio, on the eastern edge of the large Holmes County Amish settlement, *The Budget* has a circulation of about 19,000 and includes some 450 letters in each issue. *Die Botschaft,* launched in 1975 and long published in the sizable Amish community in Lancaster County, Pennsylvania, is issued to just over 10,000 subscribers and prints about 300 letters per week.[4]

Scribes' letters, often running eight to twelve inches of column space, fill the vast majority of both publications. An assortment of paid advertisements, obituaries, and exchange columns comprise the rest of the contents.[5] *The Budget* typically runs forty-two pages, while *Die Botschaft,* with its smaller page dimensions, can have up to sixty pages.

Although non-Amish firms have issued both papers, readers regard them as all but essential Amish reading matter. One eighty-five-year-old Indiana Old Order woman chuckled over a conversation she witnessed in Sarasota, Florida—a winter haven for some older Amish adults—between her husband and an Amish woman from another part of the country. When the woman referred to something in *The Budget* and the man admitted he currently did not read the paper, "the woman gave him the strangest look—as if we didn't have a Bible or something!"[6]

Observers have often remarked on the place of correspondence papers in Amish society. For example, William Schreiber believed *The Budget*'s pages accurately reflected Amish values. Scholar John A. Hostetler called *The Budget* and *Die Botschaft* mechanisms of "adult socialization," while

Donald B. Kraybill has said that writing for and reading these periodicals is a "public form of bonding."[7] Yet these weekly publications do more than mirror Amish society or connect readers to an existing community. The papers are in fact agents in the creation of that community.

Inscribing Community

Popular perception to the contrary, the North American Amish world is remarkably diverse—geographically, ethnically, economically, and in terms of technological and cultural practices.[8] Even the horse-and-buggy-driving Old Order Amish, the largest and most tradition-minded segment of the church, do not always agree on the permissibility of things such as farming with tractors, traveling by airplane, or having telephones in their homes. Such differences abound, and they extend from dress and deportment to the implications of church discipline. Overlaying these issues are other sorts of variety. For example, some Old Orders farm, but more men work in small shops or are employed in industry. In addition, beyond the Old Order pale, there are progressive Amish church affiliations such as the so-called Beachy Amish, who drive cars, might attend high school, and engage in vigorous English-language proselytism.

Given this diversity, the basis and nature of Amish *unity*—the fact that Amish people recognize one another as Amish and claim a connection across time and space—has long puzzled scholars. Formally organized only at the most local, congregational level, Amish society has no national or denominational structures and is remarkably free of the rational bureaucracy that constructs commonality for most moderns.

In this organizational vacuum, *The Budget* and *Die Botschaft,* although not singular sources of Amish solidarity, engender and sustain Amish community in critical ways. On one level, the two correspondence papers serve as mechanisms for shaping and maintaining an "imagined community" among Amish readers. The shared parameters of imagined communities, as theoretician Benedict Anderson has explained, allow people who have never met to feel themselves part of a common way of life.[9] Such sentiments can bind sprawling nation-states or scattered participants in cyberspace chat rooms. In their ongoing cultural conversations, imagined communities also function as "interpretive communities" that construct, share, and validate meaning for their members.[10] If Amish correspondence papers seem strikingly different from the technology that facilitates Webloggers, the imagined interpretive communities that each create and support bear important similarities.[11] As is the case among online interest groups, the subjects about which Amish scribes write—and those that they avoid—combine to create a world of insider knowledge, assumed taboos, and a shared sense of larger society. For example, *Budget* letters casually refer to horse-drawn transportation ("We buggied over to Seth Miller's place"), while advertisements for driving harnesses or hired "taxi" services further normalize the absence of drivers' licenses.

But *The Budget* and *Die Botschaft* are not only vehicles for transporting an interpretive community through the mail. The papers' very format and content produce this community by functioning as collective diaries, spaces in which order is brought to bear on group life, highlighting particular commonality and suppressing certain types of diversity. In this regard, correspondence papers function for the imagined community much like personal diaries do for individuals. The personal diary, literary and communication theorists argue, is a creative historical record.[12] In the leaves of a diary, a writer can retrospectively impose order on the otherwise disorderly mix of events and unpredictable contingencies that comprise human life.[13] The sometimes monotonous nature of diary entries belies a teeming world of activity even as it reveals the sorts of stability writers sought to mark. Assigning order to the unpredictability of weather, health, finances, or the activities of one's neighbors has been a central function of diaries. Reading such patterns suggests approaches to making sense of life's daily diversity.[14]

Although scribes who record news for *Budget* and *Botschaft* readers write personally, their letters are not private. In published form they create a sort of public, collective diary. Like its private counterpart, the public diary abstracts certain themes from life's myriad events and imposes a frame for understanding and bringing order to them. But given their public profile, the scribes' reports also serve to shape other peoples' means of making sense of life. This dialectical process of creating and recreating meaning to be shared among scribes and readers is *mediation,* as Diane Zimmerman Umble and David Weaver-Zercher outline in this volume's introduction.

Even the physical composition of the correspondence papers symbolizes and helps to shape a shared Amish world. Although scribes mail handwritten letters to editorial offices, editors transform submissions into neat type, with identical fonts and spacing, aligned in straight columns. Photographs occasionally accompany advertisements for books, tools, nutritional supplements, and farm supplies, but otherwise no illustrations break up pages of dense text. Behind the papers' orderly layout and somewhat formulaic content is a yeasty mix of Amish diversity, yet each week the printed pages present submissions from settlements of varying and even conflicting conviction side by side as a cohesive whole.

The public diaries printed each week in *The Budget* and *Die Botschaft* come from the pens of hundreds of scribes who agree to submit weekly or biweekly letters in exchange for envelopes and stamps provided by the publishers and a free subscription to the periodical itself. Both papers limit the number of regular scribes geographically to avoid duplication in letter content. Smaller settlements typically have one scribe, while larger communities have several representing different neighborhoods. Both papers receive more offers from potential scribes than they can commission and must therefore turn away most would-be scribes. When a commissioned scribe decides to discontinue writing, she or he usually nominates a replacement to the editor, and since such nominations typically are honored, the scribal system is largely self-perpetuating. Turnover is uneven; some scribes write for only a couple of years, while others continue for decades. One popular *Budget* scribe, Noah Gingerich, of Uniontown, Ohio, has been writing for more than thirty years. Several *Botschaft* scribes have contributed since that paper began in the mid-1970s.[15]

"Budgetland" and "All you *Botschaft* readers"

The correspondence communities created by *Budget* and *Botschaft* letters coalesce around shared values and common interests that displace potentially disparate themes in readers' lives. At a most basic level, the papers are testimony to the universal English literacy among all Amish groups. While the majority of Amish speak a German dialect commonly known as Pennsylvania Dutch as their first language, an important segment of ethnically Swiss Amish speak a very different dialect. Both populations, however, use English for written communication, and Amish schools are conducted almost entirely in English. Although *The Budget* includes a Pennsylvania Dutch column, it is authored by a non-Amish linguist and is not central to the paper's success. To be sure, nonstandard English usage appears in some letters—especially in *Die Botschaft,* which is edited less vigorously than *The Budget.* A phrase such as "A friendly line with love to younce ['you ones,' or you-plural] again," is not uncommon. But in any case, English is the middle ground on which Amish of different ethnic and dialect backgrounds meet.[16]

The lack of polished English not only suggests a practical rather than a literary approach to communication but also demonstrates the writer's humility, presenting a posture of diffidence through the pen that in face-to-face interaction would come through plain clothing and a reserved demeanor. "Excuse mistakes" and "Enjoy the mistakes" are common closing lines. Some writers offer opening disclaimers for their poor writing ability, apologies that mirror the statements by Amish ministers who begin their sermons by stating their unworthiness to preach. Letters are rarely introspective or deeply autobiographical. Although their letters are not anonymous and they typically share events from the scribe's personal and family routine, scribes do not call attention to themselves, but focus on the events of their neighborhood. As Donald Kraybill explains in his essay on Amish informants (chapter 7), communal sensibilities routinely take precedence.

Regular reporting from a dispersed network of neighborhoods creates a shared geography among readers, even though the correspondence community unites people who have never been in the same space.[17] Amish travel typically is limited to excursions by bus, rail, or hired van to other Amish settlements in which the travelers have extended family. Scribal reports, however, offer the possibility of learning about life in a much wider range of places that then become familiar territory. Indeed, the papers' imagined communities evoke spatial metaphors for themselves. "Budgetland" is a common term in that paper: "Greetings to all you in Budgetland" or "Does anyone in Budgetland know where I can purchase ——?" Similarly, *Botschaft* scribes address "all you *Botschaft* readers," as if speaking to a group assembled in a single room.

Nor are inhabitants of the correspondence world passive recipients of scribal news. The community is intensely interactive, with those from all corners participating in "card showers" and "money showers" in which writers ask readers to cheer or assist other readers. "Let's have a thinking of you shower for Enos Yoder. He will be 74 March 15. He cannot do anything and has many long days," begins one typical entry. "Let's have a get well or whatever you wish shower for Mrs. Andy L. Hershberger," urged another. "She had hip replacement surgery. Let's fill her mailbox."[18] Judging by the notes of thanks that such recipients submit to subsequent issues of the papers, these showers stimulate correspondence between people whose only point of contact is the pages of one of the papers.

Nevertheless, the success of the correspondence communities rests not only on the generation of geographic and interpersonal connections. Its durability also lies in the assumptions, content, and omissions of the public diaries that present a consistent collective life. For example, since Old Orders hold church services in private homes instead of church buildings, scribes consistently report which family hosted worship and who the visitors were. In addition to relaying the routines of ritual life, the most common subject taken up by scribes in both papers is the weather and the status of crops—and together they serve as more than formulaic means of introducing letters. Attention to such concerns actually grows in significance as fewer and fewer Amish families make their living from the land. Even in settlements that can claim virtually no full-time farmers, scribes comment on features of life that would be critical to an agrarian existence. Virtually all Amish continue to claim that the farm is the best place to raise a family and the proper setting for living Amish life—nonfarmers often express such sentiments most strongly—and the correspondence papers promote such ideals and keep them at the center of the Amish imagination. Meanwhile, writers rarely discuss the details of workdays in small manufacturing shops, on long-distance carpentry crews, or on factory floors—employment options that occupy an increasing majority of Amish men. The silence surrounding such work and the continued universal discussion of agriculturally related themes creates a community in which farming remains the ideal despite a dearth of farmers.

Discussion of women's household work also appears in many letters. Here the discussion reiterates traditional tasks, and even when such writing is in the first person, it is as much description of gendered roles as personal statement. "I must go. Work is waiting. It's my job to feed cows with Levi gone, plus always sewing to do," closed one *Botschaft* scribe. "I'm alone with 3 little ones today," reported another. "I should go gather the eggs and soon time to get dinner ready for scholars so it's ready when they come."[19]

Such statements are all the more common because women apparently comprise a majority of scribes in both papers. Forty-six percent of *Budget* letters are signed in a woman's name, such as Edith Mullet, Mrs. Levi Stoltzfus, or The Wickey Sisters. Another 35 percent are signed ambiguously under a family name such as The Schmuckers or Ed and Vera Lehman. Only 17 percent of the letters are signed only by men. Letters to *Die Botschaft* display a similar profile. Less than a fifth of letters are submitted by men alone, 31 percent come from women, and 49 percent are signed as household submissions.[20] Moreover, analysis of letters signed by couples or families as well as anecdotal reports suggest that a majority—perhaps a large majority—of such letters are actually written by women, despite patriarchal propriety that dictates a plural signature. In any case, women fashion much, if not most, of the published public diaries.[21] This is not entirely surprising, since the Amish have long considered writing and clerical work to be women's skills. Amish women comprise the vast majority of teachers in Amish schools; their hiring by the male school boards demonstrates the belief not only that women are suited to nurture children but also that they possess academic ability in contrast to men's mechanical acumen.

Whatever its roots or rationale, the gendered nature of scribal activity is one avenue of empowerment for women in a culture in which they otherwise lack formal leadership roles. Not only is their authorship publicly acknowledged in a culture that typically puts an accent on anonymity, but in mediating their communities to others, women scribes provide the stories, themes, and explanations that shape the resulting imagined communities in significant ways.

But power is a curious creature in Amish society. Even as scribing empowers Amish women, it is their lack of formal power positions that is fundamental to the success of the imagined communities they help create. By writing in English about rural life, traditional family tasks, and the hospitality that undergirds patterns of visiting, women's public diaries focus on themes that cut across borders of place, ethnicity, custom, and practice, and can more easily skirt potentially controversial topics. Amish community is most brittle at the boundaries of church *Ordnung*, the unwritten but binding regulations of personal and social life monitored by male church leaders. Perhaps not surprisingly, few ordained men serve as scribes. Conversely, a remarkable number of scribes come from the ranks of those lacking much formal influence in Amish society: women, physically disabled men, and lay members. Since such people have less structural power to enforce social norms, they also bear less responsibility to police those norms or to pass judgment on inter-Amish relationships.[22]

Yet judgment has not been entirely absent from the worlds created by these newspapers. In fact, disagreements over where the correspondence community's boundaries should rest led to the creation of *Die Botschaft* in the mid-1970s as an alternative to *The Budget*. Similar as they are, the two papers have come to foster two different definitions of Amish community and identity.

Competing Correspondence Communities

The Budget only gradually evolved into an Amish correspondence newspaper, and its development shaped the sort of interpretive community—and broadly Amish identity—it has nurtured. Initiated in 1890 as a local publication for the town of Sugarcreek, Ohio, *The Budget* served a religiously mixed clientele. During the early years, former residents of the Sugarcreek area—a few of whom were Old Order Amish—wrote letters to the paper as a means of keeping up contacts with old friends, thus establishing a precedent that would eventually come to dominate the paper. Through the 1920s, though, most subscribers and letter writers were progressive Amish Mennonites (who had split with the Old Orders in the 1860s) from Ohio or related midwestern communities. They filled the paper with feature writing, letters promoting Mennonite mission work, and advertisements for Goshen College, a Mennonite-affiliated college in northern Indiana. None of these things especially appealed to Old Order readers, but they apparently read and occasionally wrote for *The Budget* because they were interested in local civic news and in the smattering of Old Order letters. Then too, the nineteenth-century division between the Old Order and progressive wings of the Amish church was still fairly fresh, and many conservatives had relatives and friends in the progressive camp. Family boundaries remained fluid despite churchly differences, and *The Budget* reflected that social fluidity.[23]

As progressive Amish Mennonites found their way into Mennonite circles and discontinued their *Budget* subscriptions in favor of explicitly Mennonite denominational periodicals, *Budget* circulation dropped, and Old Order readers became a larger slice of the paper's pie. By 1938 more than three-quarters of the letter writers were Old Order Amish. The paper then took on its now characteristic shape as a forum for scribes, and feature articles were phased out.[24] Significantly, however, the paper continued to carry correspondence from non–Old Order scribes such as the more technologically permissive Beachy Amish, and its circulation base remained largely (though never exclusively) Ohioans and their midwestern kin. The paper's father-and-son team of editors after 1920—Samuel A. Smith (1884–1960) and George R. Smith (1906–2000)—were Lutherans who had warm friends among the Old Orders, but they kept the paper open to a range of Amish and Mennonite religious expression.[25]

That range widened and intensified during the 1950s and early 1960s when a vigorous and evangelically inclined "Amish mission movement" emerged within Old Order circles. Arguing both for moral reform within the Old Order church and evangelism and service to the wider society, advocates were keen to interpret the strengths and shortcomings of their people in a way that mixed a brand of evangelical piety with a critique of certain Old Order traditions.[26] Some scribes' letters cast their church life, young people's activities, and interaction with the wider world in terms of the mission movement's repertoire—a repertoire not all readers recognized.

Jacob J. Hershberger (1908–1965), an Old Order–turned–Beachy Amish minister and dairy manager from Lynnhaven, Virginia, was one such scribe. From 1953 to 1965, his weekly entry, titled "Lynnhaven Gleanings," held a prominent place as a boxed entry in the upper corner of the front page (the only scribe ever to receive such status). Many readers, including some Old Orders, looked forward to Hershberger's entries because of his interesting observations on life. But Hershberger also used "Lynnhaven Gleanings" to solicit money for overseas mission work and promote the doctrine of "assurance of salvation," the notion that one could publicly claim one's standing before God.[27] In Old Order circles, such sentiments were frowned upon as arrogant, and so, not surprisingly, some tradition-minded scribes sought to rebut Hershberger and introduced competing efforts to order Amish religious life in the pages of the paper.

By the early 1970s the intense heat from such controversy had subsided, but in place of the most explicit scribal entries, the more evangelically inclined members of *The Budget* community—Beachy Amish, just-emerging New Order Amish, and conservative Mennonites of Amish background—took to running paid advertisements for religious books and musical recordings. Such ads, along with the continued presentation of non–Old Order religious conviction (seen, for example, in letters from Beachy Amish missionaries stationed in other parts of the world) were too much for some conservative readers. Adding to their disenchantment was the growing number of business advertisements that included close-up photographs of people or that otherwise mocked *Ordnung* boundaries.

In October 1974 deacon Ezra Wagler (1916–1983) of Bowling Green, Missouri, and a small group of self-consciously conservative associates suggested establishing an alternative paper. Convinced of the merits of a correspondence weekly but "concerned that the *Budget* is becoming too large and [has] too many news letters written by people that did not have the same opinion in many things, as the Old Order Amish," Wagler floated the idea of a paper for scribes only from horse-and-buggy-driving groups.[28]

Die Botschaft began the next summer, but it got off to a slow start. After all, the correspondence community created around *The Budget* had proven its durability, and its interpretive authority—fraught with some tensions, to be sure—was more real and compelling than an appeal to imagine a new community constructed along exclusively Old Order lines. Interestingly, after a year of having *Die Botschaft* issued by the same firm that printed *The Budget, Botschaft* backers arranged to transfer ownership to the National Amish Steering Committee. Organized in 1966, the Steering Committee was an ad hoc Old Order liaison to government and had no experience in publishing. Yet it too was a novel attempt to speak on behalf of horse-and-buggy Amish.[29] Not surprisingly, the appeal of *Die Botschaft* was strongest in Pennsylvania and in midwestern communities with more tenuous ties to eastern Ohio—in short, places where Old Order sensibilities could trump historic migration or genealogical ties to the region around Sugarcreek, Ohio.[30] By 1980 the new paper was printing 150 letters per issue, and since then it has continued to expand.

A five-member board of deacons monitors *Die Botschaft*'s content and advertising, overseeing "what is acceptable to be printed and who is acceptable as writers."[31] A set of explicit guidelines, which are periodically printed in the paper, list prohibitions on "murder or love poems or stories" and "letters of religious discussion or criticism." Significant too are the restrictions on advertisements: "No photos of people in ads," "No books on positive thinking or how to get smart," "No books as living or revised Bibles," and no "wild west," romance, or mystery novels. Indeed, all books advertised in *Die Botschaft* must first be vetted by the paper's deacon board.[32]

Over time, the guidelines have evolved in ways that reinforce traditional Old Order expectations. During the mid-1990s, for example, the deacons declared that letters could not be faxed to the editorial office; only surface mail would be accepted. Adding the fax prohibition to the printed guidelines highlighted for subscribers the expectations of the conservative community.[33] Likewise, when the paper's non-Amish editor allowed an advertisement for cell phones in late 2003, the deacons intervened to discontinue it. Although some Old Orders in the editor's Lancaster, Pennsylvania, area had cell phones—and the advertiser was a Lancaster firm with Amish accounts—the wider *Botschaft* readership was not ready to accept such innovation in the *Ordnung*. Cell phones were a divisive matter and had to be excluded from the medium that held the imagined community together if that community were to remain intact.[34]

Similarly, *Die Botschaft* prohibits discussion of explicitly theological matters—such as the nature of salvation or the implications of church discipline—on which Old Orders themselves might disagree. "*Die Botschaft* is considered a newspaper. . . . Religious matters are not to be discussed in the news letters or in ads," reports a notice the committee frequently inserts in the paper. "*Die Botschaft* is not a gospel paper!"[35] Paradoxically, a deeply religious people must shun explicit religious discussion to avoid troubling community waters and keep the focus on shared Old Order ideals and practices.

Reading Amish Identity through *The Budget* and *Die Botschaft*

Like diarists who abstract order from a whirl of weekly activity, scribes write about their communities in particular ways, highlighting certain ideals and activities and ignoring or reordering others. In that sense, the repeated rehearsal of particular details is not the propagation of marginal "gossip" as mainstream journalists and critics have contended.[36] Nor is it, on the other hand, an exact record of the things that matter most to the scribes themselves.[37] Rather, the selection, exclusion, and repetition of material serve to shape local Amish experience so as to incorporate it into broader interpretive communities of discourse about what it means to be Amish.[38]

Although some scribes write for both papers—submitting identical letters, in fact—the collective result of each publication is subtly but significantly different. The Amish world created by *Budget* correspondence is one whose coherence comes especially through generations of shared history that somehow tie to eastern Ohio. Letters from ultra-conservative Swartzentruber Amish, now living in upstate New York but stemming from Wayne County, Ohio, appear next to communications from Beachy Amish missionaries from Minerva, Ohio, who now live in Ireland or Kenya. Mainline Old Orders, New Order church members, and conservative Mennonites of Amish background share space on *Budget* pages in a way that suggests a sort of Amish ecumenism rooted in history and governed by a general orientation to "plain" living.

To be sure, Old Order scribes report distinctive religious rituals, such as biweekly worship in private homes or semiannual all-day communion services. But in *The Budget* the exposition of that faith occurs in the company of a sizable percentage of non–Old Orders (perhaps as many as one-third of letter writers) whose religious values and evangelical fervor are distinctly different. Although no scribes mention watching television, some write about airplane travel, verbal proselytism, or their children's high school studies.[39] Advertisers assume that readers not only are interested in buying and selling farms but also might listen to *a capella* hymn recordings or read Christian romance novels.[40] The Amish community that comes through the pages of *The Budget* is one in which Old Orders are but one segment—a legitimate and numerically dominant segment, to be sure, but hardly the exclusive definition of being Amish. This sort of imagined community has fostered the more irenic Amish identity characteristic of many midwestern settlements.

In contrast, the Amish community that emerges from the pages of *Die Botschaft* is more limited and explicitly Old Order. A proclivity for plainness may provide a backdrop to the ties that bind *Botschaft* subscribers, but contemporary commitments trump genealogical or historical links to those outside the Old Order orbit. Advertisements are tightly proscribed, and letters discussing technological or theological innovation cannot order the public diary of the community's collective life. Yet if limiting its scribes and advertisers to Old Orders narrows *Die Botschaft*'s constituency, the paper also expanded its correspondence community by making direct appeals to Old Order Mennonites—who had never really participated in *The Budget*—to write for *Die Botschaft*. Today almost one-fifth of the paper's regular scribes are horse-and-buggy-driving *Mennonites*.[41] By restricting discussion of religious subjects that might divide tradition-minded Mennonites and Amish while also printing life experiences arranged in Old Order terms, the paper has replaced some historic Amish connections and contexts with new Mennonite ones, rewriting community along Old Order lines that transcend denominational traditions and form another viable version of Amish identity.

Two overlapping but distinct Amish communities emerge from the pages of *The Budget* and *Die Botschaft,* ordered and repeated by hundreds of scribes each week. Since none of the actual local neighborhoods represented by individual scribes exactly matches either of the two papers' imagined communities, scribes must mediate their home communities carefully, perhaps overlooking expressive evangelical piety in one paper, or hiding fax or cell phone use in the other, as they write themselves into one of the ideal worlds. Along the way, references to visitors to and from certain places, attention to agrarian life and traditional gender roles, and the absence of allusions to popular culture create and normalize additional community boundaries, constructing and reconstructing Amish commonality amid persistent diversity.

Notes

1. The combined circulation of *The Budget* (*TB*) and *Die Botschaft* (*DB*) is about 30,000, but given the large size of households and the fact that some households share a single subscription, the number of readers is probably 100,000.

2. *DB* was biweekly, 1979–82.

3. Quotations taken from *TB*, 25 August 2004, 1–2. Observations in this chapter are based on the author's familiarity with *TB* and *DB*, systematic reading of the years 2003 and 2004, heavy reading of the years 1999 through 2002, and skimming of earlier issues.

4. Jim Weaver, editor of *DB* from 1976 to 2005, telephone interviews with author, 17 December 2004 and 2 February 2007; and Fannie Erb-Miller, editor of *TB* (National Edition) since 2000, telephone interview with author, 20 December 2004. *DB* was published in Lancaster from 1976 to 2005; since then editorial offices have been in Dauphin County, Pennsylvania, an Amish settlement closely tied and geographically adjacent to its Lancaster "parent" settlement.

5. Exchange columns in *TB* are Classified Ads, Death Notices, Information Please, Cookin' with Maudie, Showers, Cards of Thanks, and Es Pennsilfaanisch Deitsch Eck. In *DB*, these are Classified Ads, Births, In Memoriam, Exchange Column, and Ivverich und Ender [odds and ends]—Here's a column for the Hausfrau.

6. F.S.H., interview with author, 9 March 2000. Non-Amish publishers issued *DB* until July 2005, when ownership and editorial control transferred to an Amish group.

7. William I. Schreiber, *Our Amish Neighbors* (Chicago: University of Chicago Press, 1962), 145–46; John A. Hostetler, *Amish Society*, 4th ed. (Baltimore: Johns Hopkins University Press, 1993), 377; Donald B. Kraybill, *The Riddle of Amish Culture*, rev. ed. (Baltimore: Johns Hopkins University Press, 2001), 154.

8. Steven M. Nolt and Thomas J. Meyers, *Plain Diversity: Amish Cultures and Identities* (Baltimore: Johns Hopkins University Press, 2007).

9. Benedict Anderson, *Imagined Communities: Reflections on the Origin and Spread of Nationalism* (London: Verso, 1991).

10. Stanley Fish, *Is There a Text in This Class? The Authority of Interpretive Communities* (Cambridge: Harvard University Press, 1980). Thomas R. Lindlof, "Media

Audiences as Interpretive Communities," *Communication Yearbook* 11 (1988): 81–107, and Barbie Zelizer, "Journalists as Interpretive Communities," *Critical Studies in Mass Communication* 10 (1993): 219–37, explore the theory with two specific social groups.

11. Ravi Kumar et al., "Structure and Evolution of Blogspace," *Communications of the ACM* 47 (2004): 35–39, and K. Ann Renninger and Wesley Shumar, eds., *Building Virtual Communities* (New York: Cambridge University Press, 2002) offer examples of communities created through Internet technology, and particularly those fostered by educational institutions.

12. Robert Fothergill, "One Day at a Time: The Diary as Lifewriting," *A/B: Auto/Biography Studies* 10 (1995): 81–91.

13. Walter Ong notes that writing permits a certain type of control over one's world and even over time: "Time is seemingly tamed if we treat it spatially, . . . mak[ing] it appear as divided into separate units next to each other." This is even more so with diaries in which retrospection allows one to impose order. See Walter Ong, *Orality and Literacy: The Technologizing of the Word* (New York: Methuen, 1982), 42, 81, 104.

14. "To know what they chose to record is also to know something of their culture, that is, the symbols and systems of meaning constructed by ordinary people in their everyday lives to make sense of life" (Royden Loewen, "Introduction," in *From the Inside Out: The Rural Worlds of Mennonite Diarists, 1863 to 1929*, ed. Royden Loewen [Winnipeg: University of Manitoba Press, 1999], 20).

15. Author interviews with Weaver and Erb-Miller; *TB*, 17 November 2004, 25.

16. *DB*, 26 November 2003, 4. German usage in both papers is extremely uncommon; on German in *TB*, see David Luthy, "A History of *The Budget*," *Family Life*, June 1978, 21–22.

17. Some *Budget* scribes do meet one another at one of two "scribe reunions" that are by-products of the paper's cultivated community. *TB* itself hosts a gathering every five years in Ohio. Each winter scribe Noah Gingerich organizes an unofficial gathering of older scribes who are spending time in Florida.

18. *TB*, 3 March 2004, 19.

19. *DB*, 3 March 2004, 55, 51. "Scholars" is a common Amish term for school-age children.

20. Based on a count of all 1,833 letters in *TB* and all 1,146 letters in *DB*, included in their respective 3 March, 2 June, 1 September, and 1 December 2004 issues. Two percent of *TB* letters were signed with initials and could not be categorized.

21. In an unusual case, writing for *TB* served as a springboard to national syndication for one woman. Elizabeth Graber Coblentz (1936–2002) of Geneva, Indiana, who had begun as a scribe when she was a teenager, began authoring "The Amish Cook" in 1991 as a weekly syndicated feature in mainstream newspapers across the country. Coblentz served up recipes and observations on everyday life.

22. For several months after an Amish group assumed responsibility for publishing *DB*, an Amish minister served as its editor.

23. Harvey Yoder, "*The Budget* of Sugarcreek, Ohio, 1890–1920," *Mennonite*

Quarterly Review 40 (1966): 27–47; David Luthy, "History of *The Budget*," *Family Life*, June 1978, 19–22 and July 1978, 15–18.

24. Since 1946, Sugarcreek Publishers has issued two very different weekly papers under the name *TB*. The "Local Edition" of *TB* is not a correspondence paper, but a standard weekly newspaper of the sort published in many small towns in middle America; its circulation is all but exclusively in the greater Sugarcreek area. The "National Edition" of *TB* is the correspondence paper described in this essay and sent to some 19,000 addresses across North America.

25. S. A. Smith was editor until 1936; George R. served as editor of the National Edition from 1936 to 2000. See David Luthy, "History of *The Budget*," *Family Life*, July 1978, 17; and *TB*, 25 October 2000, 1.

26. Steve Nolt, "The Amish 'Mission Movement' and the Reformulation of Amish Identity in the Twentieth Century," *Mennonite Quarterly Review* 75 (2001): 7–36.

27. See, e.g., "Assurance," *TB*, 7 July 1955, 1. On Hershberger, see William R. McGrath, ed., *Lynnhaven Gleanings from the Life and Writings of Jacob J. Hershberger (1908–1965)* (Minerva, OH: Christian Printing Mission, 1991). See also [Jacob J. Hershberger], comp., *Our Youths: A Collection of Letters Pertaining to the Conditions Among Our Youths, the Amish Mennonites* (Lynnhaven, VA: Amish Mennonite Church, [1955]), which included forty-seven letters in response to a polemical Hershberger *Budget* column.

28. Andrew S. Kinsinger, *A Little History of Our Parochial Schools and Steering Committee from 1956–1994* (Gordonville, PA: Gordonville Print Shop, 1997), 232; "Founder of *Die Botschaft* Dies," *DB*, 28 December 1983, 7.

29. Marc A. Olshan, "The National Amish Steering Committee," in *The Amish and the State*, 2nd ed., ed. Donald B. Kraybill (Baltimore: Johns Hopkins University Press, 2003), 67–85. In early 1976, when *DB* subscriptions had been slow to materialize during the paper's first year, the Sugarcreek Budget, Inc., suggested discontinuing the paper and converting all outstanding subscriptions into subscriptions to *TB*—a proposal to which *DB* supporters vigorously objected and which led them to transfer ownership to the Steering Committee. Thereafter *DB* was a joint enterprise of the Steering Committee and Brookshire Printing of Lancaster until 2005, when the Steering Committee purchased Brookshire's interest in an "amiable transfer" and arranged for an Amish group to begin editing and publishing the paper. Author interviews with Weaver.

30. A full third (114 of 351) of the towns frequently represented in *DB* letters are in Pennsylvania, and only 10 percent are from Ohio. The plurality of letters in *TB* are from Ohio, and Pennsylvania addresses comprise a relatively small segment.

31. Kinsinger, *Little History*, 232. The deacon board is self-perpetuating and is made up of men from around the country, although the secretary must be from the Lancaster settlement to facilitate communication with the publisher and printer located nearby. In contrast to the practice at *TB*, where scribes are approved by the non-Amish editor, the board must approve every scribe for *DB*. Author interviews with Weaver and Erb-Miller.

32. "Notice of Revision of Guide Lines, effective July 1990 and thereafter," reproduced in Kinsinger, *Little History*, 233. Author interview with Weaver.

33. Author interviews with Weaver and Erb-Miller. *TB* prints faxed letters with some frequency, and occasionally one sees the editorial note "Incomplete Fax" at the end of a letter cut off mid-sentence.

34. Author interview with Weaver. The offending ad from a Lancaster County (New Holland) Radio Shack appeared in *DB*, 3 December 2003, 37; 10 December 2003, 52; 17 December 2003, 46; 31 December 2003, 55; and 7 January 2004, 58.

35. Frequently included under the heading "Attention Scribes," e.g., *DB*, 6 January 1999, 1; and 1 October 2003, 2. A curious exception to the general prohibition of controversial content was the fall 2004 inclusion of partisan political material by one scribe. The large majority of Amish do not vote, and those who do are asked to do so quietly and not "electioneer." Nevertheless, polemical paragraphs supplied by a Republican Party operative and ex-Amish relative of one Lancaster scribe were inserted into some letters (e.g., *DB*, 1 September 2004, 68).

36. Luthy, "History of *The Budget*," 17, gives examples of Associated Press feature stories on *TB* that cast it as a forum for "gossip." Even the highly appreciative Elmer S. Yoder, *I Saw it in the Budget* (Hartville, OH: Diakonia Ministries, 1990), 5–10, assumes *TB* must be defended against charges of gossip-mongering.

37. However, some Amish treat *TB* as a faithful archival record, compiling and reprinting in chronological order letters from particular communities to create a sort of narrative history. See, for example, John J. Byler, comp., *Amish Directory and History of the Atlantic Settlement in Crawford County, Pennsylvania, 1924–1997* (Hartstown, PA: J. J. Byler, 1998), 76–125, which reproduces *Budget* letters for the years 1924–1951.

38. A small number of Old Order Amish churches do not read either paper. These church districts, part of a loose network of highly self-conscious ultra-conservatives, do not write for or subscribe to the correspondence papers, arguing that if one has free time for such reading, it would be better spent reading the Bible. Not reading *TB* or *DB* isolates these Old Orders socially from other Amish, but their highly sectarian stance resists such interaction in any case. N.G., interview with author, 27 October 1999, and David Luthy, letter to author, 9 December 2004.

39. For a horse-and-buggy-driving Amish person traveling by plane, see *TB*, 25 August 2004, 1.

40. See a range of ads in *TB*, 3 March 2004, 16 (Bible studies); 2 June 2004, 27 (Christian romance novel); and 1 December 2004, 28 (music recordings).

41. A count of all 1,146 letters in the 3 March, 2 June, 1 September, and 1 December 2004 issues of *DB* revealed that 198 (17%) were from Old Order Mennonites. In 1977, when *DB* ownership migrated to the National Amish Steering Committee, *DB* supporters solicited Old Order Mennonite financial support and treated them as partners in the enterprise. See Kinsinger, *Little History*, 234, and Luthy letter to author.

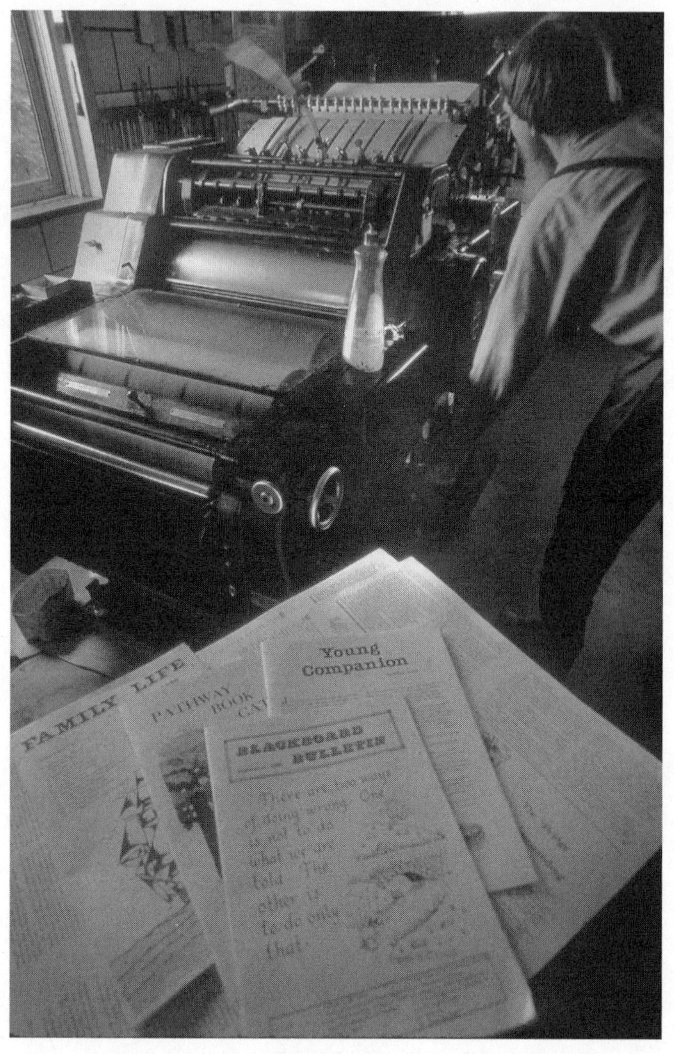

A Heidelberg printing press is used to produce Pathway publications for Old Order readers.

Photo by Blair Seitz; used by permission.

CHAPTER NINE

Publish or Perish
Amish Publishing and Old Order Identity

Karen Johnson-Weiner

How to Ruin a Child #6: Let him read any printed matter he gets his hands on. Be careful that the silverware and drinking glasses are sterilized, but let his mind feast on garbage.
—Amish editor Joseph Stoll, writing in the *Blackboard Bulletin*

Amish entry into publishing was motivated by the development of Old Order private schools. In the mid-twentieth century, in response to changes in the public school system—the consolidation of rural one-room schools, an increase in the length of the school year, an increase in the number of years of mandatory schooling, and the addition of new subjects to the curriculum—many Old Order Amish began to withdraw their children from public schools.[1] Insisting that eight years of formal education were sufficient and that schools remain under the watchful eyes of parents and church leaders, they began to establish one- and two-room schools that would keep children close to home and apart from non–Old Order peers. These schools needed suitable texts, and Old Order entrepreneurs began to provide them.

Nevertheless, what constituted appropriate texts for an Old Order Amish school soon became a matter of debate as church-communities struggled to determine what kind of education the new private schools should provide. Established in one-room school buildings bought from public school districts and employing retired public school teachers, the first Old Order schools used the same schoolbooks as their public counterparts. Initially, many Old Order parents saw private schools as a means of providing their children the same education that Old Order youngsters had always received in public one-room schoolhouses. Others, however, soon began to see in Old Order schools the opportunity to educate their children in Christian values.

Private schools not only allowed but encouraged Old Order church-communities to shape pedagogy and curriculum, and their decisions about how they would educate Old Order children began to reflect different orientations toward each other and the dominant society. For example, by limiting the curriculum to reading, spelling, arithmetic, and German and by making no place in the school day for devotions or the Lord's Prayer, the ultra-conservative Swartzentruber Amish have structured formal education to provide the minimal book learning that children need to earn a living in a church-community that limits contact with the dominant society.[2] In contrast, schools in more progressive Old Order communities help to prepare Amish children to compete economically with their non–Old Order counterparts on a playing field that may be only marginally in the Old Order world. Schools in these church-communities often begin with morning devotions, emphasize Bible verse memorization, and offer an expanded curriculum that includes geography and art. As Old Order education has evolved to reveal diverse notions of what it means to be Old Order, Old Order printers and publishers and the materials they produce have come to reflect and shape this diversity.

This essay explores two major Old Order Amish producers of school texts: the Gordonville Print Shop in Lancaster County, Pennsylvania, and the Pathway Publishing Corporation, in Aylmer, Ontario, and LaGrange,

Indiana. Both publishers provide "appropriate reading materials." Yet in doing so, they reflect different community-based notions of what it means to be Old Order, how the Old Orders must interact with the dominant society, and, most importantly, what values are to be reinforced through the schools.

The Gordonville Print Shop

The first notable Old Order printing and publishing venture, the Gordonville Print Shop in Lancaster County, Pennsylvania, was founded by Andrew S. Kinsinger in 1956. Kinsinger had become familiar with printing while working in the shop of a local non-Amish man, J. G. Fisher, and he acquired the printing equipment after Fisher's death, "thinking that maybe someday it would be a good retirement."[3] The business began modestly, printing "broadside objects [such] as bills, business cards and feed tags. His first sign read: 'Printing Plain and Fancy.' His first business card said, 'I would be pleased to do any or all of your printing. Anything.' "[4]

As the name makes clear, the Gordonville Print Shop[5] is not a publishing house. From the beginning, Gordonville has printed items as requested by its predominately Old Order clientele, producing a wide range of materials, including family histories, songbooks, cookbooks, coloring books, forms, and small pamphlets. Often filling the need now served by photocopiers, it has allowed print runs of as few as a dozen copies of pamphlets, letters, diaries, family histories, and pages of advice.

Gordonville's entry into schoolbook printing came in response to demands for texts from the growing number of Old Order private schools that were finding it increasingly difficult to rely on cast-off books from the public schools. As the number of private schools multiplied, the supply of texts became sparse. Moreover, as secular publishers continued to revise and update texts for the public schools, many Old Order communities were finding the cast-off texts less desirable. As John Martin, a retired Old Order Mennonite schoolteacher, noted, the result was that "we [Old Order church-communities] weren't so satisfied, and we thought we should have our own."[6]

Formed in an attempt to "keep unity" among the different Old Order schools, the Old Order Book Society of Pennsylvania first met in May 1957 to discuss the standardization of books and curriculum.[7] Kinsinger was elected Book Society chair in 1958, and in the same year he acquired the rights to reprint a number of editions no longer in use by the public schools and began to supply Old Order private schools with books.[8]

Kinsinger chaired the Old Order Book Society from 1958 to the late 1970s. While the Old Order Book Society recommended texts for private school use, the Gordonville Print Shop helped to make those texts available, encouraging an Old Order school curriculum that changed little from what it had been in the old one-room public schools. For example, all of the books listed in the 1967 *Book List: School Books Most Generally Used in Our Amish Parochial Schools in Pa.,—Ohio—Ind.* (prepared by the Old Order Book Society and printed by Gordonville Print Shop) were texts that had served the public schools in previous years. Teachers could order books from Old Order dealers in either Ohio or Indiana, or they could order them directly from the Old Order Book Society in Gordonville, Pennsylvania.

Andrew Kinsinger's daughter Susan has noted that while "custom printing is worked in day by day . . . , school material printing is the overall large job at this print shop."[9] Today the Gordonville Print Shop continues to produce report cards and other forms used in Amish private schools and to supply schools in the most conservative Old Order communities with texts that were standard in public schools in years past, including the 1919 *Essentials of English Spelling* and the 1934 Strayer-Upton Practical Arithmetic Series, which the Old Order Book Society had approved for the parochial schools in 1959. When, under Kinsinger's guidance, the Print Shop did develop and make available a new work, it was generally one derived from available texts such as the *Teachers' Manual to Book Three* of the Strayer-Upton Practical Arithmetic Series or *Plain and Fitting English,* a collection of English exercises Kinsinger compiled from a variety of published sources.[10] "We knew these were good texts because school boards had approved them, so why change?" argues Andrew Kinsinger's son-in-law, who continues to operate the Gordonville Print Shop. "We print what the schools ask for."[11]

Archaic Texts and Reinforcing Values

In several important ways the Gordonville texts strengthen the roles of church, home, and family in Old Order communities. In supplying Old Order schools with reprints of archaic texts, Gordonville and similar Old Order print shops reinforce Old Order traditions by maintaining the status quo. For the most conservative Old Order Amish, commitment to the *Alte Ordnung,* the Old Order of their ancestors, is revealed in a lifestyle that signals devotion to God's unchanging truth by maintaining patterns of behavior linked to previous generations. Old public school texts from Gordonville allow children to follow the same lessons in the same books their parents and grandparents used, reinforcing a sense of continuity with the past and reaffirming the values of the church-community. Thus, Gordonville textbooks, like other symbols of Old Order life, unite community members across generations.[12]

Equally important, according to one Old Order teacher, reprinting the old books is "a conscious attempt to keep separate." The lessons in these archaic texts help Old Order children learn to speak, read, and write English and do arithmetic, necessary skills for an Old Order life; but the archaic examples and illustrations in the text teach children little about the world outside their church-community. For example, the eighth-grade word list from the 1919 *Essentials of English Spelling, Part Two* offers "household" terms such as *emetic, gimp, chiffonier,* and *poultice,* and "rural" words, including *Bordeaux, sulky,* and *whiffle tree.* In an essay on the stock market in the third book of the Strayer-Upton Practical Arithmetic Series, which is used for seventh and eighth grades, a picture of a biplane portrays airmail service.[13] Illustrations in the McGuffey's Eclectic Readers show little girls in petticoats and ruffled bonnets, their brothers in knee-length trousers, and their mothers in floor-length skirts. Using these turn-of-the-century texts, children in the most conservative Old Order schools do story problems in which prices bear no resemblance to those in modern-day markets, and they memorize vocabulary words and sentence structures no longer used by their non-Amish neighbors.

Moreover, divorced from both the local non–Old Order world that children see and the Old Order world in which they live, Gordonville texts support a pedagogy that encourages rote learning of basic information and downplays critical thinking.[14] The more conservative Old Order communities that use these texts tend to draw a sharp distinction between "schooling" (or "book learning"), in which one acquires basic skills or information, and "education," in which one learns to live according to the values of the church-community. These conservative communities believe schools should offer the less-valued book learning. Children are expected to learn to read, write, and do arithmetic, because if they do not, they will be unable to earn a living and participate fully in the church-community. But they will become truly "educated" only as they learn to farm, run a business, keep house, and raise a family through sharing labor and enjoying fellowship at home and at church.[15]

Finally, although some of these archaic texts, such as the McGuffey's Readers, are "oppressively didactic," depicting "an idealized version of mainstream, white, middle-class Protestant American culture,"[16] they are not overtly linked to any particular denomination. Most are religiously neutral, emphasizing the view held by many in more conservative Amish communities that "religion is nothing to play with" and should be the responsibility of parents and church leaders, not a young (female) teacher in the schools.[17]

Rethinking Old Order Education: The Pathway Publishing Corporation

By the late 1950s, while the Gordonville Print Shop and the Old Order Book Society remained committed to the unchanging practices of their church-communities and wondered "how to keep the same texts . . . [when] . . . publishers kept putting out new texts and new editions,"[18] others had begun to redefine Old Order education as education in a *Christian* context. In Old Order schools, one Amish man wrote, "we have the privilege of teaching the regular branches, and at the same time we can interweave the doctrine of God, Christ, and the Church in all our studies, even in arithmetic."[19] Questioning the suitability for Old Order schools of *any* texts written for a secular, non–Old Order world, the founders and editors of the Pathway

Publishing Corporation began to prepare texts designed specifically for Old Order students and representing Old Order values and religious ideals.

The Pathway Publishing Corporation traces its origins to a "circle letter" started in the early 1950s by a group of Old Order Amish teachers in Ontario, Ohio, and Indiana. A circle letter is actually a packet of letters, the contents of which are always being updated. Upon receiving the circle letter, each participant takes out the page he or she had written for the previous circle, writes something new, adds it to the letters from the other participants, and sends the whole packet on to the next person on the list; if there are ten participants, there will be ten letters circulating. The teachers' circle letter offered all participants the opportunity to seek help, share tips, and keep in touch with the others. Nevertheless, the circle letter format limited the number of those who could be involved. Mrs. Mose S. Byler of New Wilmington, Pennsylvania, suggested that the letter should become a periodical like *The Budget,* which, as Steven Nolt describes in chapter 8, has helped to create a sense of community among diverse Amish groups. The idea for an "Amish schools paper," which would feature letters from parents and teachers, was discussed for some time before final arrangements to publish it were made at the 1957 Teachers' Meeting held near Selinsgrove, Pennsylvania. Circle letter founder Joseph Stoll became the first editor of the *Blackboard Bulletin.*[20]

The staff of the new paper was not large. In addition to Stoll, Lydia F. Beiler, a teacher from Ronks, Pennsylvania, served as secretary-treasurer, and Crist M. Hershberger of Burton, Ohio, was the printer. The first volume, written for the 1957–58 school year, had six issues, all printed by spirit duplicator. From the beginning, the *Blackboard Bulletin* relied on readers for letters, articles, poems, and stories. A teacher in Ephrata, Pennsylvania, for example, wrote a question-and-answer article on "tattling," while others sent in articles on discipline, school history, public relations, and teaching methods. Although Stoll argued later that the private school movement was already starting to spread and that rather than creating it, the *Blackboard Bulletin* "just got in on the beginning and it mushroomed,"[21] the *Blackboard Bulletin* helped to redefine education for a number of Old Order church-communities, encouraging a different, more interactive pedagogy that saw teaching as preparing future church members. As one of the first issues proclaimed, the goal was "to teach children to live that they may have life!"[22]

A few years later Stoll and some Amish colleagues expanded their publishing work by founding Pathway Publishers. Working with David Wagler, who had recently started the Pathway Bookstore to supply the Aylmer, Ontario, Amish community with suitable reading material, and Jacob Eicher, a local Amish minister, Stoll incorporated Pathway Publishers as a nonprofit organization. The three men had different hopes for the new publishing corporation. Stoll remembers that, while he was looking forward to sharing with others some of the responsibility for publishing the *Blackboard Bulletin,* "Wagler's primary interest was in reprinting old books no longer in print, plus also publish[ing] new titles (he had a bookstore and had become aware of the demand for certain books)."[23] Before long, Pathway found a U.S. distributor for its products when Levi J. Lambright, who lived in LaGrange, Indiana, but had cousins in the Aylmer settlement, agreed to take on the job. Lambright had published pamphlets on his own, and as current Pathway editor David Luthy remembers it, he "had an interest in improving the moral life of young folk."[24]

Today Pathway Publishing is chartered in Ontario as a nonprofit organization and in the United States as a public charity. The staff employees at Pathway are paid for their work, but the directors, who are not considered employees, are not.[25] It is not a large company. The *2000 Aylmer Amish Directory* notes that Pathway Publishing employs ten workers, but most are employed part-time. Teenage girls from the community help to assemble and address the magazines, and the editors do most of their work at home.[26] Nevertheless, with this small staff Pathway Publishing continues to produce the *Blackboard Bulletin* as well as two other magazines, *Young Companion* and *Family Life*. It also publishes two texts for teachers (*Tips for Teachers* and Uria R. Byler's *School Bells Ringing*) as well as a series of school readers and accompanying workbooks and a variety of other works, including storybooks for children and books on Anabaptist history.

Challenging Long-standing Assumptions

Unlike Gordonville and other print shops, the Pathway Publishing Corporation fosters the production of new texts and, through the creation of a distinctively and consciously Old Order literature, actively examines Old Order beliefs. As the editors put it, "We at Aylmer feel very strongly that our church is not becoming a 'dead' culture; therefore, we try to instruct our young people in the whys and wherefores of all practices."[27] For instance, the first Pathway periodical, *Blackboard Bulletin,* with a current circulation of approximately twenty-four thousand, continues to publish articles on education, reports and letters from teachers, original poems and stories, and editorials on matters of concern to Old Order educators and parents. As it did in the beginning, the journal gives all in the church-community a stake in the education of children as future church members.[28]

Other Pathway periodicals continue to help define what it means to be Old Order and to reinforce the ties binding the individual to the larger group. In 1966 Pathway began production of the *Ambassador of Peace,* a journal directed at "youths in the USA serving their 1-W terms of alternative service." Like the *Blackboard Bulletin,* the *Ambassador of Peace* was a response to a perceived need—in this case, the need to reach out to Old Order men with 1-W selective service classifications, meaning those who, as conscientious objectors to military service, were working away from their home church-communities in civilian jobs that contributed to national health or safety. Although Pathway editors were concerned that publishing the journal would be taken by some as support for the 1-W system, one editor wrote, "If it would be possible to encourage the boys to be steadfast in the faith, and to be a witness to the world, without exactly endorsing the 1-W program, I think it could be done."[29]

In 1971 the *Ambassador of Peace* became the *Young Companion,* reflecting how, in the five years since the magazine's first issue, it had become a more general magazine for young people. It continues to be published monthly and has an average circulation of twenty-seven thousand. Many of the articles focus on issues of importance to young folk who are no longer in school but have not yet married and settled down. Often the stories are reminiscences from older readers told to guide the decision making of younger ones. For example, in "The Girl I Asked," the anonymous author tells how he dealt with a young girl's rejection by learning to depend daily on God's help. The author ends by noting, "I learned that it can be comforting to just 'wait on the Lord' and trust that He will lead us and show us what is best for us."[30] Other stories, editorials, and question-and-answer columns focus on issues of concern to Old Order young people, including the temptation of non–Old Order activities and "impure thoughts."

Pathway's third magazine, *Family Life,* first appeared in 1968, and, as its name suggests, it was designed to be "a paper of general interest for the whole family." As the editors asserted in a notice announcing the new periodical, the magazine sought to have "lots of articles from all our different communities, which will be of interest to our plain people." The notice also promised content that would make clear "that the Bible is at the heart of our everyday living."[31] In an editorial twenty-six years after the founding of the magazine, editor Joseph Stoll observed that the magazine has always focused on "what its name suggests—family life. This would include scriptural child training, love, and unity within the family."[32]

All of these Pathway periodicals offer Old Order readers across North America original stories, histories, games, poetry, news, and reprints of articles the editors judge to be interesting and informative. Although most of the selections are written by Pathway editors, many come from the readership, and each journal offers interactive question-and-answer columns that help to draw readers together. The "Problem Corner" in *Family Life,* for example, offers readers the opportunity to seek advice from others in the *Family Life* audience.

Marketed together in the "three-for-one" plan, these periodicals—*Blackboard Bulletin, Young Companion,* and *Family Life*—seek to present to Old Order readers a picture of what an Old Order life informed by Christian values ought to be. This active engagement with Old Order culture is also evident in Pathway's book publishing. In 1964 the company published its first hardcover book, *Worth Dying For,* a story of the persecution of the Waldensians in Italy before the Reformation. An early big-seller was David Wagler's *A Mighty Whirlwind,* about the 1965 Palm Sunday tornadoes in Indiana. Among Pathway's other book titles are *On Fire for Christ,* a collection of stories retold from *Martyrs Mirror; How the Dordrecht Confession Came Down to Us,* a booklet by Joseph Stoll presenting the history of the Dordrecht Confession; Uria Byler's *School Bells Ringing: A Manual for Amish Teachers and Parents;* the Benjie and Becky Books, stories of five-year-old Benjie and nine-year-old Becky that teach children important lessons and values; and David Luthy's *Amish in America: Settlements that Failed 1840–1960.*

The Pathway Readers: Made for Amish Schools

Pathway became involved in textbook publishing as well and, only four years after the company was founded, began to publish the Pathway Readers, a series designed specifically for use in Old Order schools. In the initial stages of preparing the Pathway Readers, the editors attempted, like the Gordonville printers, to select appropriate editions of out-of-date public school texts that could be reprinted. As Stoll wrote in 1966, "What we have in mind is to prepare a set of Christian readers, at least for the upper elementary grades, for our parochial schools. We would choose selections from these old readers and from other sources; in other words pick off the cream."[33] Although the older texts first seemed acceptable to Pathway (because many of the selections were "moralistic"), some editors found that "the kind of stories, fairy tales etc. which they contain . . . has no place in a Christian School."[34] As Stoll lamented, "even with these old books we find a good many war stories and political speeches, and articles with an objectionable slant on patriotism."[35]

In the end, the Pathway editors decided to follow the example set by Uria R. Byler, one of the original circle letter participants, who in 1963 had written an eighth-grade history text, *Our Better Country,* specifically for Old Order schools. As a writer to the Amish newspaper, *The Budget,* noted at the time, "*Our Better Country* is the first book ever written by an Amishman as a textbook for Amish children. As you would expect of an Amish text on history, there is more of peace than war, more of love than hate, more of God in man than of the devil in him."[36]

"I am convinced," Stoll asserted, "we are missing a golden opportunity if we don't . . . get up our own set of readers. We could add a touch of Anabaptist history, with selections from the *Martyr's Mirror,* etc. The possibilities are endless."[37] The first of the Pathway Readers, a series designed specifically for Old Order schools, appeared in 1968, and there are now thirteen textbooks and sixteen workbooks. As editor David Luthy notes, "The workbooks were totally compiled by Amish people, most of whom are [Pathway] staff members."[38]

Like the Gordonville texts, the Pathway Readers separate Old Order life from the dominant society, but they do so with pictures and stories of Amish farms and Anabaptist history, not with archaic language and pictures of a world that no longer exists. For example, *Our Heritage,* the eighth-grade reader, includes a reading on sixteenth-century Anabaptist martyr Dirk Willems; selections from *Martyrs Mirror,* a record of Anabaptist martyrdom first published in 1660; and "One Dark Night," a retelling of the "Hochstetler massacre," a defining event for the Old Order Amish in which an eighteenth-century Amish farmer, Jacob Hochstetler, forbids his sons to take up arms in self-defense against attacking Indians. The seventh-grade reader, *Seeking True Values,* offers a section on Anabaptist history featuring a piece by Nicholas Stoltzfus on the Waldensians ("Trek Across the Mountains"); several selections from *Martyrs Mirror;* a story about the Amish in Waldeck, Germany, in 1759; and a story about the Ephrata Cloister's printing of *Martyrs Mirror.* The first-grade primer, *Days Go By,* introduces children to storybook Amish children, their pets, and the farm. Although illustrated, the Pathway Readers contain no images of people; drawings portray the farms and other unchanging elements of Old Order life.

The goal of the readers, noted a series editor, was to produce books "that teach lessons without being preachy and which deal with human values and virtues found among all Christians. . . . [O]ur stories do not promote our religion but are religious in the virtues they teach."[39] Moreover, as a letter to Old Order congregations advertising the series pointed out, the readers contained "the atmosphere of farm life and the country one room schoolhouse. These stories will come alive to your children and the lessons will be meaningful, for Amish children will feel right at home with these stories. . . . And why not? They are for our schools!" Insisting that "every day of the year the world stares your children in the face in the stories they have in their readers," the editors argued further that parents concerned enough to withdraw their children from the world's schools should "go all the way" and remove the world from school.[40]

"In church schools," asserted a 1962 editorial in the *Blackboard Bulletin,* "we control the environment, and should be able thereby to make a lasting contribution to each child's spiritual development."[41] With readers that offer stories about Old Order life and history, many set in Old Order communities with Old Order characters, Pathway editors work actively with parents, teachers, and ministers to prepare Old Order children to withstand the temptations of the world. In doing so, however, Pathway blurs the distinction between schooling and education that is so carefully reinforced in schools in less-progressive church-communities.

"Anti-Pathway Bias": Different Ways of Being Old Order

The Pathway Readers and other Pathway texts have acquired a following outside the Old Order community. In 1994, for example, Pathway Publishers was awarded first place in the Readers Category by the *Practical Homeschooling* 1994 Reader Survey. The summer 1994 issue of *Practical Homeschooling* announced that the Pathway Readers "outdistanced the competition so thoroughly that there is no Honorable Mention in this category."[42] Learning Things, an online store for parents who homeschool their children, suggests that "parents appreciate the Pathway Readers Phonics Curriculum for its wholesome moral principles and traditional Christian values."[43] Similarly, the Timberdoodle Company, which caters to homeschoolers, suggests that parents, "weary of the brashness that is evident in readers with contemporary story lines," will find the Pathway Readers "solidly wholesome, with none of the fantasy that is commonplace in both Christian and secular readers."[44] Commenting on the popularity of Pathway, a longtime Pathway employee noted that she "never expected to see a non-Amish audience when we made them."[45]

Yet while Pathway books are popular outside the Old Order world, Pathway founder Joseph Stoll acknowledges what he has called "an anti-Pathway bias in more traditional [Old Order] communities."[46] As Stoll points out, for example, Lancaster Amish schools and others served by the Old Order Book Society have been slow to adopt the new Pathway Readers. Some Amish have observed that Andrew Kinsinger, as chair of the Old Order Book Society, influenced many of the Old Order Amish church-communities against the Pathway texts. Given that Kinsinger's own textbook business stood to lose with competition from another Amish publisher, some have even suggested that there was a financial conflict of interest on Kinsinger's part.

Far more likely, however, is that Pathway's challenge to entrenched beliefs and active exploration of Old Order assumptions—evident in editorials, the stories in its periodicals, and the types of books it was publishing—alienated members of more conservative church-communities, who felt that doing things in the way previous generations had done them showed commitment to Old Order values. One Lancaster Old Order Amish man notes, for example, that Pathway attempted in the beginning to have representation on its editorial board from a variety of Old Order communities and that, when he was asked to serve, he happily agreed. However, he found it impossible to continue his association with the Pathway board in the face of Pathway's stand against tobacco farming, a longtime practice in the Lancaster Amish community.[47] Similarly, Mennonite historian Amos Hoover notes, "The Pathway people wanted stricter dating rules and an end to tobacco farming, two things the Lancaster people objected to."[48]

Asked why conservative communities often limit the use of Pathway Readers (particularly in the younger grades) and more conservative teachers seldom read the *Blackboard Bulletin,* Pathway editor Joseph Stoll answers, "Too much religion. They might be afraid of Pathway influence. There's the threat of more progressive influence."[49] Although the Pathway texts do not overtly teach religion, it is pervasive in the Pathway texts in their discussion of Old Order values, history, and lifestyle, and this may have made it difficult for even some of the more progressive groups to adopt Pathway publications. Despite Levi Hershberger's assertion in a 1963 *Blackboard Bulletin* editorial that "our parochial schools would hardly be worth the extra expense and effort spent, were it not for the important teaching of God's Word somewhere in the program,"[50] many Amish leaders have been inclined to agree with Andrew Kinsinger that "the word of God should not be used to play with or as school text matter, as it can become so familiar . . . that it no longer makes a special impression when used."[51]

From the first, Pathway has served a different kind of Old Order community, one whose commitment to the *Alte Ordnung* is realized both in a more overt emphasis on spirituality and in a greater openness to lifestyle change, even as it reinforces the boundary between church-community and dominant society.[52] As sociologist John A. Hostetler has noted, many of the Pathway texts articulated in print for the first time basic Old Order Amish beliefs and assumptions, sensitizing readers to "customs they never before considered 'bad.'"[53] Members of more conservative church-communities, who identify the maintenance of the status quo with strict obedience to the church and who restrict discussions of matters of faith to ministers, objected to "having too much of their way of life in print."[54]

In contrast, those in the more progressive church-communities that are the audience for the Pathway products are more tolerant of technological innovation and more open to individual spiritual exploration within church guidelines. Pathway editors and writers have challenged those who read their publications to evaluate their lives and actions in light of biblical teachings and Christian values, and in doing so, they have created what Hostetler has called "a new self-consciousness."[55] Commenting on the Pathway influence, one observer noted "a genuine spiritual life among the Old Order brethren" and expressed his belief that "this will continue to transform what is merely traditional."[56]

Conclusion

Gordonville and Pathway both serve the needs of communities that consciously and deliberately separate themselves from the dominant society. Whether the approach to publishing is to reprint old texts (because what is good does not change) or to develop new texts (in order to bring the church-community's own unchanging beliefs overtly into the schoolhouse), these publishers reflect and reinforce the assumptions, values, and beliefs of the communities whose schools they serve. Furthermore, by creating bodies of Old Order literature that highlight certain cultural practices and downplay others, these publishers actively foster very different Old Order identities.

Although the conservative Gordonville Print Shop and the more progressive Pathway Publishing Corporation helped to define Old Order publishing in the twentieth century, they are only the beginning of the story. As the number of church-communities multiplies and Old Order young people face demands different from those that shaped their parents' world, new Old Order publishing enterprises, such as StudyTime in Indiana, are responding to changing notions of "Old Order." Old Order publishing will likely further evolve to reflect and reinforce the diverse assumptions, values, and beliefs of the communities they serve.

Notes

Epigraph: "How to Ruin a Child," in Joseph Stoll, ed., *The Challenge of the Child: Selections from "The Blackboard Bulletin," 1957–1966* (Aylmer, ON: Pathway Publishing Corp., 1967), 42–43.

1. Old Order education varies from one church-community to another. In some Old Order church-communities, Amish children continue to attend public schools. This article focuses on those communities that have invested in their own private schools. For a more in-depth study of the diversity of Old Order schools, see Karen Johnson-Weiner, *Train Up a Child: Old Order Amish and Mennonite Schools* (Baltimore: Johns Hopkins University Press, 2007).

2. Unlike members of other Old Order groups, members of Swartzentruber church-communities will not work "in town," a stand that keeps them from setting up stalls at village farmers' markets, nor will they work for hourly wages in non-Amish-owned factories, restaurants, and retail businesses. Refusing to hire drivers and vans for long-distance travel, a common practice in most Old Order communities, Swartzentruber Amish rely on public transportation to travel distances too far for horses and buggies. Unlike many groups, the Swartzentruber Amish have kept telephones off their farms, choosing to rely on pay phones or non-Amish neighbors' phones in emergencies.

3. See Andrew S. Kinsinger, *A Little History of Our Parochial Schools and Steering Committee from 1956–1994,* comp. Susan A. Kinsinger (Gordonville, PA: Gordonville Print Shop, 1997), 244.

4. Amos B. Hoover, *Inventory of the A. S. Kinsinger Gordonville, PA, Print Shop Collection. Held at Muddy Creek Farm Library. A Collection which Captures the Heartbeat of the Old Order People.* Unpublished manuscript, 1999.

5. In his 1999 *Inventory,* Amos Hoover notes that the Gordonville Print Shop carried a variety of imprint logos, including "Gordonville, Pa, Print Shop," "Gordonville, Penna. Print Shop 17529," and "School Room Book Supply."

6. John B. Martin, interview with author, 20 June 2001.

7. Among the texts deemed acceptable were the Strayer-Upton Practical Arithmetic Series, the Ginn Series of *Learning to Spell,* the Scott-Foresman Basic Readers, the Silver-Burdette Geography Series, and the Laidlow Brothers History Series. All were public school texts, and by 1967 all were available directly from the Old Order Book Society, whose three-man board was chaired by Kinsinger. See Kinsinger, *Little History.*

8. William Hershberger, interview with author, 18 June 2001.

9. Kinsinger, *Little History,* 245. On the title page to this work, Susan A. Kinsinger indicates that she compiled the book and refers to herself as "a link from the Gordonville Print Shop." As Hoover notes in his *Inventory,* Susan long worked for her father in the shop and helped her sister, Priscilla, and her sister's husband, William Hershberger, after they became sole owners. Susan now has her own printing business.

10. Although Andrew Kinsinger was a good businessman, he was not a teacher and had little personal experience of classroom teaching. When he attempted to create his own textbooks, it appears that he was less than successful. Commenting on *Plain and Fitting English,* for example, one Old Order Mennonite teacher noted that Kinsinger "took some lessons from one [textbook] and some from another. Even if there were good points, they didn't go together" (John Martin, interview with author, 20 June 2001). Another noted that the series was "neither plain nor fitting" because the exercises were too complex. That teachers had difficulty using some of the Gordonville texts was motivation for Joseph Stoll, himself a classroom teacher, to help found Pathway Publishing.

11. William Hershberger, interview with author, 18 June 2001.

12. See Karen M. Johnson-Weiner, "Reinforcing a Separate Amish Identity: English Instruction and the Preservation of Culture in Old Order Amish Schools," in *Languages and Lives: Essays in Honor of Werner Enninger,* ed. J. R. Dow and M. Wolff (New York: Peter Lang, 1997), 67–78.

13. Strayer-Upton Practical Arithmetic Series, *Book 3,* 392.

14. See Albert N. Keim, *Compulsory Education and the Amish: The Right Not to Be Modern* (Boston: Beacon Press, 1975).

15. See Gertrude E. Huntington, "Persistence and Change in Amish Education," in *The Amish Struggle with Modernity,* ed. Donald B. Kraybill and Marc A. Olshan (Hanover, NH: University Press of New England, 1994), 77–96. See also Karen M. Johnson-Weiner, "Community Identity and Language Change in North American Anabaptist Communities," *Journal of Sociolinguistics* 2/3 (1998): 375–94.

16. Elliot J. Gorn, "Introduction: Educating America," in *The McGuffey Readers: Selections from the 1879 Edition,* ed. Elliot J. Gorn (Boston: Bedford/St. Martin's), 1–2.

17. Kinsinger, *Little History,* 246.

18. William Hershberger, interview with author, 18 June 2001.

19. John H. Kauffman, "Why We Have Our Own Private Schools," in *Challenge of the Child,* 69.

20. Joseph Stoll, "Preface," in *Challenge of the Child,* 11.

21. Joseph Stoll, interview with author, 26 January 2002.

22. Epigram in *Blackboard Bulletin,* January 1958, 1.

23. Joseph Stoll, interview with author, 26 January 2002.

24. David Luthy, interview with author, 25 January 2002.

25. David Luthy, letter to D. W. Bowling, 25 November 1995. Letter in Heritage Historical Library, Aylmer, Ontario (hereafter, HHL).

26. *Aylmer Amish Directory, 2000* (Aylmer, ON: Pathway Publishing Corporation, 2000), 40.

27. Qtd. in John A. Hostetler, *Amish Society,* 4th ed. (Baltimore: Johns Hopkins University Press, 1993), 381.

28. See Nathalie Delval, "The Amish Educational System Seen Through the *Blackboard Bulletin:* Maintenance of a Minority Identity," unpublished manuscript, 1986.

29. Author unknown, letter to Sarah M. Weaver, 15 September 1965 (HHL).

30. "The Girl I Asked," *Young Companion,* January 2002, 7.

31. "Announcing—Pathway's Newest Paper: *Family Life,*" *Blackboard Bulletin,* November 1967, 102.

32. "Staff Notes," *Family Life,* May 1994, 5.

33. Joseph Stoll, letter to Ivan Leid, 16 May 1966 (HHL).

34. David B. Peachey, letter to Joseph Stoll, 31 January 1968 (HHL).

35. Joseph Stoll, letter to Mr. and Mrs. John Borntrager, 16 May 1966 (HHL).

36. *The Budget,* 30 May 1963. This was a reprint of an article from the *Cleveland Plain Dealer.* Excerpted from Elmer S. Yoder, comp., *I Saw It in the Budget* (Hartville, OH: Diakonia Press, 1990), 145.

37. Joseph Stoll, letter to Mr. and Mrs. John Borntrager, 16 May 1966 (HHL).

38. David Luthy, letter to D. W. Bowling, 25 November 1995 (HHL).

39. Ibid.

40. David Luthy, letter to Old Order schoolteachers in LaGrange County, Indiana, 3 July 1966 (HHL).

41. "The School Environment," in *Challenge of the Child,* 71.

42. *Practical Homeschooling,* Summer 1994, 63.

43. www.homeschooldiscount.com/hsp/pathway.htm (accessed 11 July 2004).

44. www.timberdoodle.com/index.asp?PageAction=COMPANY (accessed 11 July 2004).

45. Elizabeth Wengerd, interview with author, 30 July 2003.

46. Joseph Stoll, interview with author, 26 January 2002.

47. Ben S. Blank, interview with author, 15 April 2005. Pathway's stand on tobacco, for example, is evident in a 1969 *Family Life* article entitled "Tobacco: A Burning Issue," in which Joseph Stoll condemned tobacco farming, noting that tobacco was a wasteful and expensive habit. Subsequent letters to *Family Life* also called the practice evil. For many Amish in Lancaster County, however, tobacco farming had been a profitable way of life for generations and was particularly favored because it engaged the entire family.

48. Amos Hoover, interview with author, 15 April 2005.

49. Joseph Stoll, interview with author, 26 January 2002.

50. Levi L. Hershberger, "Devotions, An Important Part of Our Program," in *Challenge of the Child,* 166–67.

51. Kinsinger, *Little History,* 246.

52. See Steve Nolt, "The Amish 'Mission Movement' and the Reformulation of

Amish Identity in the Twentieth Century," *Mennonite Quarterly Review* 75 (2001): 7–36.

53. Hostetler, *Amish Society*, 381.

54. Ibid.

55. Ibid., 380.

56. Orland Gingerich, *The Amish of Canada* (Waterloo, ON: Pandora Press, 1972), 166–67.

A couple attempts to shield themselves from newspaper photographers outside the federal courthouse in Philadelphia on October 6, 1998.
Photo by Andrea Mihalik; reprinted by permission of photographer / *Philadelphia Daily News.*

Chapter Ten

"Wicked Truth"

The Amish, the Media, and Telling the Truth

Diane Zimmerman Umble

We forgive those of the world who transgress against us.
In that spirit, we ask to be forgiven.
—Amish man, writing in the *Philadelphia Inquirer*

One headline in large bold letters read: "WICKED TRUTH: The Amish Get a Wake-up Call about Drugs." Another claimed: "Amish Drug Arrests Reveal Secret of Closed Society."[1] The arrests in June 1998 of two Amish-raised young men for buying cocaine from members of the Pagans motorcycle gang and selling it to their peers created a media sensation not only in their home community in Lancaster County, Pennsylvania, but also around the world. Peter Durantine's Associated Press story was carried in newspapers large and small across North America.[2] News organizations from around the world assigned reporters to cover the story, including CNN, BBC, *60 Minutes, London Daily Mail, New York Times, Philadelphia Inquirer,*

Baltimore Sun, Los Angeles Times, Washington Post, New Yorker Magazine, USA Today, Time magazine, CBS Radio in Boston, CKNW Radio in Vancouver, Australian Broadcasting, and a Japanese news agency in Washington, D.C.[3] Out-of-town reporters pestered local journalists for access to sources, rousted Amish scholar Donald Kraybill from his vacation for interpretive comments, and scoured the county with cameras and microphones, looking for members of the community, both Amish and English, who were willing to comment.

The intense interest in the arrests and subsequent legal proceedings produced a plethora of stories that reveals as much about the public fascination with the Amish as it does about Amish society itself. Much could be said about the limitations of the coverage and what it shows about the ideological function of the Amish as a site for the making of meaning in mainstream American culture. One analyst has argued that the focus of North American press coverage on the archaic and quaint aspects of Amish practice distracted attention from their belief system and deflected critical attention to a potential crisis in the community by promulgating the conventional perspective of the Amish as a national treasure.[4] Other essays in this book reflect on the various functions the Amish provide that serve in the making of personal and social meaning.

For the purposes of this essay, I will focus my inquiry closer to the ground by describing how local journalists, scholars, attorneys, and members of the Amish community talked about their roles in the news-making process in this case and by analyzing what their accounts reveal about the conflicting frameworks for truth telling they invoke. I begin by exploring how key players in the drug case describe and perform their roles in relationships with the media. These descriptions are gathered from a variety of settings, including public forums, print sources, and personal interviews. In the process, I will highlight the competing notions of truth at work in their various perspectives and conclude with a reflection on my own search for truth in the process.

I am building on Clifford Christians's notion of truth as a creational concept arising out of authenticity and disclosure. A media ethicist, Christians seeks to offer an alternative to the disputed objectivist model of journalism by describing truth as a rhetorical construction that is produced through authentic interaction between journalists and their sources. Arguing from a communitarian perspective, Christians offers an approach to media ethics that he hopes can help journalists move from Eurocentric models of the press toward alternatives that meet the demands of an increasingly global society based on widely differing and competing national, racial, ethnic, and religious identities. He calls for a cross-cultural ethic that gets "to the heart of the matter" by grounding our theory and practice "in the language, definitions and attitudes of those who are studied."[5] In the spirit of Christians's challenge, I will examine the discourse about truth in this particular case by first focusing on the Amish drug bust story from the perspective of a Lancaster journalist.

"Let Them Set the Terms"

Ernie Schreiber, former reporter and now editor of the *Lancaster New Era,* was among the first of the local journalists to cover the story of the drug bust.[6] His approach to this story was informed by a series of ground rules that he and his newspaper had developed over time in association with members of the Amish community. One rule was that photographers would avoid close-up, frontal photography of Amish people out of respect for Amish prohibitions against photography. The Amish take seriously the biblical commandment against the production of "graven images" and feel that photography undermines their practice of humility. The second editorial practice applied to routine reporting: the newspaper identified religious affiliation only when it was essential to the story. Third, in consideration of ongoing relationships with members of the Amish community, journalists attempted to negotiate clear understandings about the identification of sources. The Amish are reticent to be quoted by name in mainstream media because church leaders consider public pronouncements to be self-aggrandizing—another behavior in conflict with the humility expected of church members. As a result, reporters often rely on outsiders to comment on the Amish: scholars, professionals in the community, or non-Amish persons in the local community. Schreiber's personal preference, however, was to go directly to Amish people themselves rather than to rely on intermediaries.

When Schreiber heard about the drug indictments, he consulted a local Amish directory to determine which church districts the two young men were from and set off to talk to their bishops.[7] Schreiber dressed in black. He parked his car by the road at the end of the lane to an Amish home and walked down the lane "to show respect and give them time to prepare." In his conversations with Amish bishops, he "let them set the terms" and gained off-the-record access to information about the young men and their families. Only then did he approach the families of the two young men.

Schreiber says that journalists have an obligation to make sure the Amish understand journalistic shorthand: "Journalists tend to forget that not everyone understands what they mean by 'background' or 'no attribution.'" Schreiber tried to be clear that he was writing a story that would appear in the newspaper. He made sure that there was an understanding between him and the sources about how they would be identified, often by occupation and general geographic location rather than by name. He tried to make sure that they were comfortable with the identification and to assure them that they could say yes or no to an interview. Schreiber says that the Amish are "eager to please." They are careful to be respectful of those on the other side of an issue, so it is often difficult to discern what they truly feel.

As a result of his visits, Schreiber discovered that the Amish were "concerned and alarmed" by the drug problem. But the fact of drug use did not come as a surprise, nor was it something that was hidden, as headlines suggested. The previous October, a letter written by concerned parents had been circulated to bishops and church districts across the settlement, warning of the dangers of drugs and calling attention to the use of drugs and alcohol at youth social gatherings. Schreiber felt that some in the Amish community were in denial about the presence of drugs among their young people, while others thought their youth groups were "tame" and that drugs were not a problem in their district.

Church leaders told Schreiber that they wanted the wider community to "know of their embarrassment and shame, that the Amish weren't better than others." Leaders reiterated that if someone breaks the law, that person should be punished. One bishop lamented, when asked about one of the young defendants, "His Amish roots weren't showing."

"Letter to Amish Families"

Dear Friends,

This is written with love and great concern for our Amish youth. It is not meant to offend anyone. May the Lord help us and grant us wisdom, strength and grace to work on this problem we have with some of our young people using drugs. Some of you may wonder why any young person would use drugs. It is like some of our other evils that slip in caused by peer pressure. Parents, beware of evil changes which your children could or might be going through. The young folks of today are our future generation. There are drugs out there easily available to our young people in the form of marijuana, heroin, cocaine and other types, that can be smoked, sniffed, or injected into the veins . . . Remember drugs can be life-threatening! They can also damage one's brain cells for the rest of their life.

If we could see all the saddened faces at our local mental hospitals and jails, we would want to say no to drugs. Many of the people are there because of drug use and addiction. We parents have also failed many times in our lives and we are thankful for our precious parents, grandparents, brothers and sisters and ministers, who taught and led us by example to a better Christian life. If we have said too much, please forgive us, as tears roll on from our heavy burdened hearts for our youth of this generation and the generations to come. Let us continue in prayer for each other and for our young people and for our church so that we can be a help to each other and not a hindrance.

Praise God for all His goodness and mercy and praise Him also that there are still young folks who say no to drugs and want to do what is right in the sight of the Lord and the well-beings of their bodies. For our bodies are a temple for the soul to live in. And for those who are caught in the use of drugs, there is still time to change and the time is now! May God bless you all, He loves you!

Closing with heavy hearts,

Concerned Parents of Our Youth Today

In October 1997, concerned Amish parents distributed a letter to Amish congregations, part of which was published in the Philadelphia Inquirer *on June 25, 1998.*

Schreiber's newspaper gained a measure of respect from some members of the Amish community because it was one of the few media outlets to make clear in its coverage that the two young men were "Amish-raised" but were not actually members of the Amish church.[8] Because they were not baptized church members, the two young men were not accountable to Amish discipline to the same extent as church members. They were, however, expected to respect their parents and elders, and their behavior was considered shameful within the community. Though family members of those who were charged had been instructed by legal counsel to avoid discussing the case, Schreiber was one of the few journalists to interview one of the young defendants just before his arraignment.

Meanwhile, the story had captured national attention. Schreiber's newspaper was besieged by calls from out-of-town reporters with requests for access to sources, directions, and especially leads for photo opportunities. Out-of-town television crews were often frustrated by the unwillingness of locals to be interviewed on camera. The British press was particularly "aggressive and scurrilous," according to Schreiber. Local journalists had little respect for "hit-and-run journalism" and for the most part were unwilling to jeopardize their own relationships with locals for the benefit of out-of-town reporters.

Reflecting on the coverage, Schreiber says that it is important to "take time to ferret out the religious underpinnings of what they [the Amish] are saying . . . [and] get to the roots of why they believe what they believe. Surface coverage does not do that. We need to understand their notions of community and their notions of separation from the world. Then we can get behind what seems like inconsistency to explore the underlying basis of rules." From his perspective, lack of such understanding characterized much of the national press coverage of this story.

Schreiber's standard of good reporting required going directly to the Amish themselves in a respectful manner and seeking to reveal the roots of their religious motivations. He measured the quality of reporting by the degree to which the religious basis of Amish culture was revealed and respected.

"Not Guilty"

While many in the Amish community wanted it understood that the two young men were not actually church members, defense attorney John Pyfer had a competing interest in maintaining the "Amish boy" images promulgated by the press. Pyfer felt that maintaining their connections with the community would be instrumental in obtaining a fair sentence.[9] While the press was scrambling to find people to talk, Pyfer was making every effort to control press access to the two young men and their families by encouraging them not to talk to reporters. Pyfer himself fielded questions as much as possible because he feared that in Amish attempts to be accommodating, they might say too much and inadvertently turn public opinion against the defendants.

From his perspective, Pyfer felt the defendants and members of their home community were "naive" about drugs, about the law, about the media, and about how dangerous their Pagan suppliers could be. For five years the FBI and local law enforcement had been building a case against the Pagan drug dealers. The case had all the elements of television drama, with bugged telephones (including the phone shanty of one of the Amish families), surveillance, and undercover agents posing as members of the Pagans. When one of the defendants agreed to wear a wire to collect evidence, Pyfer was convinced that the young man had "no conception of the danger." Pyfer recounts that he did not sleep the night he knew that one of the defendants was helping the FBI to collect evidence by wearing a microphone in his hat. The evidence helped to break the case, and his cooperation became the basis for a subsequent plea bargain.

In preparation for their first court appearance to hear the charges brought against the defendants, the defense teams had a difficult task convincing both young men and their families of the need to enter pleas of "not guilty." Without such a plea, both cases would proceed immediately to mandatory sentencing under strict federal guidelines without the benefits of a plea bargain in negotiation. All the parties involved knew the charges to be true, and neither of the young men was willing to claim otherwise. As a result, on the day of the preliminary hearing, the attorneys entered the "not guilty" pleas on behalf of their clients. Few reporters noticed, but many in the Amish community were upset, feeling that the "not guilty" plea was dishonest. Later, when the case came to trial, the pleas were changed to "guilty."

In intervening months, the attorneys, the two Amish-raised defendants and their families, the local state police, the FBI, and the U.S. attorney embarked on an extraordinary series of drug education meetings in barns, fire halls, and warehouses across Lancaster County, eventually reaching several thousand Old Order Amish and Old Order Mennonite young people and their families. Members of law enforcement explained the addictive properties of drugs, what happens to people in prison, and the mandatory sentencing guidelines for drug possession and dealing, and then each defendant told his story. News of the meetings was passed by word of mouth within the plain community, but no one from the media knew the meetings were happening until they were revealed at the pre-sentencing hearing long after the fact. Journalists were surprised to learn that thousands of plain people had attended meetings across the county. These community service efforts by the two defendants contributed to evidence of their changed behavior presented at the hearing.

While the drug education meetings were held in private, "media circus" aptly describes the scene at the courthouse in Philadelphia during each of the court appearances. Representative of their unusual cooperation in the case, both the prosecution and the defense teams, along with the FBI, collaborated to shield the defendants and their Amish supporters from the cameras with limited success. They planned access routes to the courthouse that minimized the distance the Amish would have to walk in the glare of the press and arranged exits from the courthouse through the basement. Nevertheless, the cameras lay in wait.

Pyfer was motivated by his professional obligation to mount the best possible defense for his client. He sought to control, as much as possible, media perspectives on and access to his client. He attempted to field the media inquiries on behalf of his client by granting numerous telephone interviews and addressing the media before and after the court appearances. "I wanted contacts with the media to be scripted," he said. Pyfer admits he was really upset when one of the young men granted Schreiber an interview published the day before the arraignment. The young man could not understand why. "I was only telling the truth," he told Pyfer. And that was exactly what Pyfer feared.

Pyfer's goal was impression management. He was motivated by his ethical obligation to mount an effective defense. He wanted to be sure the press appreciated how being raised Amish made these young men vulnerable to outside influences, and his goal was to shape and limit the sentences they received. Ultimately, the two Amish-raised men served one year in a detention center in a work-release program and continue to be supervised by a parole officer.

"Time Out"

For his part, sociologist and professor Donald B. Kraybill was also trying to tame an unruly press. Widely considered to be an authority on Amish society, Kraybill was on vacation when his phone started ringing. The juxtaposition of images of Pagan motorcycle gangs and barefoot Amish boys as partners in cocaine trafficking set off what Kraybill called a "media feeding frenzy" that ranged from the serious to the absurd. Television crews were desperately seeking images, despite explanations for why the Amish refused to pose for photographs. One crew wanted to film Kraybill in a buggy, asking, "Would you wear one of those Amish uniforms?" He declined.[10]

Kraybill faced multiple challenges. The sheer volume of requests for information was daunting. He was cognizant of how easy it would be to perpetuate stereotypes. He struggled with how to simplify what was complicated, knowing that there was no one "Amish position." He wanted to correct inaccuracies, particularly regarding the status of the two young men as members of the community but not members of the church. He felt protective of members of the Amish community who might be exploited and was guarded in sharing contact information with the out-of-town press. And he wondered about his own complicity in potential exploitation of the Amish.

Kraybill's public statements sought to counter the myths of Amish isolation and control. His newspaper interviews described occupational shifts in the Lancaster settlement that accounted for greater interaction with outsiders. He tried to counter media images of the two men as "typical Amish boys" by explaining the Amish practice of adult baptism and describing *Rumspringa,* the liminal phase in Amish young people's lives when they sometimes explore aspects of mainstream society. Literally translated as "running around," *Rumspringa* is a time when young people socialize in the context of youth groups, typically engaging in singing, playing games, and eating. Although alcohol and drugs are present in some groups, drug use is by no means universal.

Kraybill was repeatedly pressed for details about Amish youth groups. In one interview he commented: "I think they [the press] see the Amish as a very tightly controlled culture. I found a lot of curiosity that there is some space for people to be in a literal position betwixt and between. The assumption was the youngsters are tightly controlled and indoctrinated by the church."[11]

The media seized on *Rumspringa,* and the notion took on a life of its own. Repeatedly, reporters used the label "time out" to describe this phase of an Amish adolescent's life. "I'd never heard the phrase 'time out' before," says Kraybill. "But I think it was created in this event. Media organizations kept asking me about this time-out period. I found myself using the phrase, then saying, What does time out mean? Time out from what? This is not how the Amish describe it. To them, it was always *Rumspringa,* or 'running around.' To me it's interesting how media coverage actually fabricated a label for this."[12]

Kraybill sought to shed the light of scholarship to corral rampant stereotyping in the mainstream press. His efforts at interpretation met with some success as he was widely quoted on the changing occupational structure of the Amish community. His accessibility most likely deflected some intrusions into the Amish community itself. But in his efforts to explain Amish coming of age practices, a new stereotype was created. The "time out" phrase was repeated and amplified across television and print media.

"They Just Don't Get It Right"

A panel of representatives from plain groups (Old Order Amish, Old Order Mennonites, Hutterites, and Old Order River Brethren) registered several complaints about media coverage of plain communities.[13] "They just don't get it right!" said one panelist. Reporters routinely confused the various plain groups, often mislabeling other plain groups as Amish. Although several groups use horse-and-buggy transportation and practice plain dress, they are nevertheless distinguishable by differences in the shapes and colors of their buggies and variations in clothing styles, to name a few signals. Other groups maintain plain dress while permitting the use of automobiles and electricity, practices rejected by the Old Order Amish.

Panelists also complained about the presumption of uniformity across plain communities. "There is no 'Amish' position," said one panelist. "The media will take the word of a choice few—most of our people really resent that—[they] don't speak for me." There is diversity of opinion and practice among the Amish and among other plain groups. One plain person is not representative of all. One group is not the same as another; two young men are not representative of all Amish young people.

Panelists suggested several guidelines for the press: Do not stereotype, do not put plain people on a pedestal, and do your homework. They suggested that if prohibitions about photography are violated, it is confirmation, from their point of view, that the journalists lack integrity.

The chief complaint about coverage of the drug story was that the media did not recognize that the two young men charged were not members of the Amish church. On the other hand, many Amish persons I have talked to felt that the local coverage was generally fair. One middle-aged Amish woman put it this way: "Most genuine, real Amish felt the way we did. You can't shelter them [the young men]. They committed a crime. We don't want outsiders to get resentful if we get preferential treatment. They suffered because of the shame they brought. They felt bad that they involved our people in this. . . . We believe the verse in Romans, that all things work together for good." She said, "If we get negative coverage, if it's accurate and true, it's good for us. When they [the media] make us look perfect, that's not good. . . . Positive feedback from the world is not good for us—[we] become proud. We may all fail. We have to live with that fear."[14]

The Amish expect the media to operate with integrity. "We are no different than anybody else," said an Amish woman. "I resent it when they purposely misquote us for their own purposes. . . . The bishop says they [the media] say what suits their own agenda. The Amish don't trust the media, TV cameras especially."[15]

One Amish man agreed to talk to the press when the drug story broke. "Ed Klimuska [a reporter for the *Lancaster New Era*] came in all a-flying. . . . He asked me if I heard what was going on. He said two Amish boys were arrested for selling drugs. He wanted to know where they lived." The reporter warned that "a lot of reporters would be coming around." That day, the Amish man remembers, "I didn't get anything done. One man came in the morning and one after lunch. . . . The next day, the *London Mail* came. I told them I was kind of tied up. . . . They came back around 8:30, near sundown."[16]

"I always told them not to use my name, and I think most of them didn't," he says. He refused to have his picture taken and did not permit the use of voice recorders or video cameras. One camera crew set up at the end of his driveway, hoping to sneak some footage, but his neighbor sent them away.

Over the course of the next two days, reporters from Washington, Baltimore, New York, London, and Paris showed up at his door. He says that the media were "mostly respectful." He knew it was a big story, and he feared that if no one from the Amish community talked, "it would make it worse. . . . They would write what they thought." That's what motivated Sam to sit down and write a letter to the editor of the *Lancaster New Era*. "People were gonna think kids are all that way and parents are just sitting back and watching. That's not true." In the letter, he tried to capture how the Amish felt about the news. He recounted the changes the Amish community had experienced in population growth, occupational shifts, and tourist attention. And he asked for prayer and forgiveness:

> We love our children. They are the only things on this earth we hope to take along to heaven; through them, the church will grow. Their spirit and muscle can do a lot of work. But children will also be children; even if they don't obey, parents still need them. So some of the un-Amish behavior, while unwanted and even forbidden, is tolerated—much like the problems in our Washington, which no American likes but everyone tolerates.

Isn't that the way teenage life is in most of outside America? Some kids are more restricted. Their parents care more, pray more. And some kids have more liberties. Faster cars. They can stay out late. So it is among us Amish: We're just human. Our church is not perfect.

Vas kenna ma do? (What can we do?) Pray and pray and pray some more. Live a good example. Pray for us, all you God-fearing folks. Pray for us that we can maintain our way of life.

We forgive those of the world who transgress against us. In that spirit, we ask to be forgiven.

His letter was published in the *New Era* and picked up by the *Philadelphia Inquirer.*[17]

While it is hard to gauge the impact of his cooperation on mainstream media content, the reaction from within the Amish community was clear. "I was accused of not helping the situation," he said. "I got nice letters and some nasty ones too." In his own defense, he believes that journalists "need honest answers," but he acknowledges that some in the community were offended. One elderly family member of a defendant said, "He was disciplined in the church for articles in the paper. The family didn't appreciate it a bit. He wrote an article that took half a page. He could have written one column. It had some silly things."[18] Another person close to the case said that the Amish informant was in trouble "because he talks too much." Another Amish man said, "He doesn't speak for the community; he's not an official spokesman." No one I spoke to within the community volunteered information about how he was disciplined by his congregation.

When I spoke to family members of one of the defendants, they felt local print reporters were "reasonable." But they were deeply offended by the behavior of the photographers and television cameras gathered outside the courthouse in Philadelphia. "The media in Philadelphia didn't treat us right," said one Amish woman. One of the defendants described how intimidating the wall of cameras was and commented: "I thought, if I was somebody else, this wouldn't be happening—if I weren't Amish. I'm just a person." Another family member recalled the first court appearance in Philadelphia:

> The first time was so bad. Pyfer slipped us in through the basement. The media did not see us. A couple cameramen were waiting right at the door. On our way home, we had just got out of the parking lot. Abner was in the front seat. He had the window down. We stopped at a [traffic] light. They [the media] ran right out in front of the car. They all came running. One was laying on the hood with a movie camera. We were surrounded . . . all around the car. We felt cheap. It was disgusting. I just couldn't believe it. They ran across the street in front of cars. I thought they were rude.

At sentencing, she recalled: "There was a whole big flock of us. They [the media] were standing there waiting, mostly trying to photograph. They were thick outside the courtroom. We were surrounded." Yet she acknowledges that the media were "doing their job. We can't tell them how to treat us. When we get in trouble, what can we expect? We're no better than anybody else. They're gonna do what they do."[19]

"It was stressful," one of the defendants recalled. "They [the media] made it a lot worse. Everybody was stressed out—my parents, my aunts and uncles—it didn't help."[20]

Family members I spoke with came through the experience with great respect for law enforcement and limited respect for the visual media. As we looked through the newspapers covering the event, one Amish man described the photos as "painful." An Amish family member cried as she pointed out mistakes in identification in the photo captions. One of the defendants recalled: "The papers had stuff that wasn't true, that didn't happen. You wonder where they got information if it's not even true."[21]

News of the drug arrests traveled quickly through the community. The following Sunday morning "every minister brought it up. . . . We were ashamed. The ministers told us to obey God more," said an Amish woman. "We aren't perfect," an eighty-year-old Amish bishop told me. But he wished the media would "stay with the truth." I asked him if reporters stick to the truth. "I don't think so, not 100 percent," he replied. Another Amish man said, "The media want to sensationalize. . . . You give an inch and they take a yard." Nevertheless, one Amish woman concluded that the media were "more fair than we deserved, sparing us more than we deserved. . . . A lot of people said we deserve this."

Amish people who were involved as press sources or family members shared several perspectives on the media. They expected reporters to be truthful about their intentions and accurate in their accounts and were often disappointed when accounts were not factual or were over-generalized. They were deeply offended by the disrespect and rudeness of photojournalists. Although disappointed by the behavior of some members of the press, they acknowledged that members of the press were "just doing their job." And they saw the events as a lesson for the community.

Getting It Right

Clifford Christians has proposed a definition of truth as created in disclosure and authenticity. To achieve truth in this sense, Christians challenges reporters to practice "interpretive sufficiency" that goes beyond a factual recounting. He calls for accounts that have sufficient depth, detail, and nuance to permit readers to form a critical consciousness of their own.[22]

Participants in these accounts about the Amish drug case present an array of approaches to creating the truth. As a seasoned journalist, Ernie Schreiber knew he could only get authentic Amish perspectives on the events by going to church leaders, family members, and the defendants themselves. To do so, he had to meet them on their terms, especially with respect to Amish sensitivities about photography and source identification. Schreiber worried that the Amish inclination to please would prevent some Amish persons from saying no to press inquiries. Less culturally sensitive reporters interpreted Amish reticence for attribution and photos as stonewalling based on an Amish desire to suppress the truth about drugs in their community. Indeed, many of the headlines conveyed this impression: "Amish Drug Arrests Reveal Secret of Closed Society" or "Cocaine Corrupts the Amish Dream: Elders Break Silence over Cult Members Accused of Dealing."[23]

But Schreiber knew better. He understood that the Amish see themselves as called to be separate from the world and that their mentality is to place the community before the individual. He took time to listen, even as he aggressively pursued the story. For Schreiber, communicating the facts without contextualizing them in the religious practice of the Amish community was insufficient. Appreciating the context not only shaped what he wrote but also how he went about covering the story. The *New Era*'s decision to refer to the defendants as "Amish-raised" was not just a nod to accuracy. It was also a sign of cultural knowledge. Disclosure was informed by cultural sensitivity.

As a defense attorney, John Pyfer was much less concerned about whether the defendants were actually members of the Amish church. He wanted to make sure their Amish roots were clearly communicated. He recognized the utility of stereotypical press images of "Amish boys" for mounting an effective defense. His obligation to manage the facts collided head-on with Amish moral obligations to tell the truth. The struggle over how to deliver the "not guilty" plea represents more than Amish naiveté about the judicial process. It also provides a concrete illustration of Amish religious values in action.

The private drug education meetings orchestrated by Pyfer and others suggest another facet of disclosure. Members of law enforcement saw an acute need for education about the dangers and consequences of drug use for young people in the plain communities. They understood that these meetings had to be held without media attention if plain youths and their families were to attend and feel free to ask questions. Pyfer saw these meetings not only as an educational service but also as an opportunity to improve the options for his client. The fact that the meetings occurred was only revealed in court as evidence of the reformed behavior of the defendants and their investments in community service. Disclosure, for the defense attorney, was shaped by legal strategy.

As a scholar, Donald Kraybill wanted to enlighten and inform. Mindful of the stereotypical images of the Amish in mainstream media, Kraybill sought to explain and interpret Amish faith and practice in the context of this event. Though he could offer expertise, he could not set the agenda or control the spin. As the creation and propagation of "time out" illustrates, a new cultural category that inadequately captures Amish practice and experience was created in the midst of the coverage by sheer repetition. Kraybill's efforts to achieve authentic coverage were undermined in the process, and a new stereotype was born. From this perspective, disclosure sought authenticity, and authenticity was undermined in the process.

For the Amish, the picture is more complicated. Telling the truth is an important cultural value; they expect members of the community to be truthful, and they expect outsiders to be truthful as well. Furthermore, as a people who look to the Bible for guidance, they have faith in the printed word. But they have learned from experience that outsiders do not always understand or appreciate the way the Amish look at the world. Amish history and theology teaches them to expect ridicule and even suffering. Nevertheless, they are disappointed and sometimes indignant when they are treated disrespectfully, misquoted, or misled, or when their faith is overlooked or misrepresented. Many simply do not expect the media to get it right. "We would love to be left to ourselves," is a common refrain.

Because they do not expect the press to understand, Amish who agree to be sources run the dual risk of being misunderstood by the world and criticized by the community. I interpret the Amish criticism of one who cooperated with the media not as an attempt to silence him but as a way of tempering his enthusiasm for speaking his mind—a sign of insufficient humility from an Amish perspective.

Even as he was disciplined, the community was disciplined as well. The case served as a "teachable moment," confirming the fears of some parents and demonstrating a need for Amish families to take the problem of drugs seriously. The events prompted changes in the organization and supervision of Amish youth groups in the Lancaster settlement. The coverage presented stories about the Amish that served as lessons about their vulnerability and shaped Amish perceptions of themselves. Despite what is presented in the media, the Amish do not condone drug use, and they make no excuses for illegal behavior. The judge who sentenced the two young men said letters from the Amish community asked for two things: justice and mercy. For the Amish community, disclosure was instructive and corrective.

"Leave Us Alone"

Christians's emphasis on disclosure challenges me to reflect on my own recounting of these events. I set out to talk with key participants in the creation of accounts of these events with particular focus on their interactions with members of the Amish community and the press as the events unfolded. In the process, I explained my purpose as an effort to foster more culturally sensitive reporting. While I was received openly by participants outside the Amish community, some inside the Amish community were decidedly unwilling to engage in discussion about these events, regardless of my purpose. When I approached one Amish leader, he responded, "In my opinion, there are too many books being written about the Amish." He expressed despair about relationships with the media. He wanted it to be understood that no one person speaks for the entire Amish community. He expressed the Amish dilemma: he does not want to talk to the press, but he does not want to be uncooperative. If he refuses, then no Amish voices will temper the many misconceptions that are perpetuated about the Amish. When he agrees to talk, he wants his identity protected. But experience has taught him that his ground rules are not always respected. What is important to him is often unimportant to the reporter. Ultimately, he feels that the press cannot be trusted and that the media are businesses that "use the Amish for commercial purposes."[24]

Another Amish person close to the case was alarmed and angry that I was trying to return to the past when the young men had served their time, paid their debts, and gone on to rebuild their lives. Members of the community pleaded for the privacy of one of the young men who had joined the Amish church, married, and was living a changed life. They asked that outsiders do what they have done: "It's in the past. We want to go on." "How would you feel if this was one of your children?" an Amish man challenged me.[25]

Amish persons offered several explanations for their reticence to discuss the case. Some fear retribution. There remains for some Amish persons a fear that members of the Pagans motorcycle gang will harm the young men who participated in the arrests and convictions of their Pagan comrades. For others the memories of press behavior, particularly in Philadelphia, were deeply hurtful. One woman reflected, "If someone else behaved this way, they would have been arrested. He [the photographer] pushed me. I couldn't even walk. . . . They were rude." Coupled with the prohibitions against being photographed, the behavior of photojournalists continues to be deeply offensive to those close to the events. The shame of the drug abuse, arrests, and convictions experienced by the community was amplified by the behavior of those covering the story.

The young men, their families, and the Amish community were ashamed. They acknowledged wrongdoing, accepted the consequences, and paid their debts. Their families had forgiven them. Now they just want to be left alone to pursue their lives.

Wicked Truth

The accounts of those who were involved in telling the stories about the cocaine bust in an Amish community illustrate various dimensions of truth as disclosure and demonstrate Christians's notion of truth as creational and rooted in social processes. For a local reporter, disclosure needed to be informed by cross-cultural knowledge and sensitivity—the facts contextualized in culture. For the defense attorney, disclosure was strategic. For the scholar, disclosure was an imperfect means of advocacy for authenticity. For the Amish, disclosure was instructive and corrective, and they were humbled in the process.

"Embarrassment" and "shame" are two words that are often used by the Amish to describe their feelings about the drug arrests in 1998. Although they are often disappointed by the conduct of members of the media, many Amish say that the coverage, while not always accurate, was usually fair. And they believed the outcome was just. Together, the journalists, scholars, attorneys, and members of the Amish community wove the story of two Amish-raised boys who got into trouble, paid the price, and now live with the consequences: the disclosure of a wicked truth.

This case study illustrates the ongoing struggle over meaning-making and the construction of religious identity. The stories told are the product of a series of negotiations shaped by the various and competing motivations of the parties involved and the organizations and communities of which they are a part. The experiences of these two Amish-raised young men have spawned a new genre of stories about the Amish, stories that focus on the coming-of-age experiences of Amish youth. The popularization of "time out" has generated both popular and scholarly discourse about *Rumspringa* and prompted yet another round of documentaries, television programs, and books about the Amish, ranging from a gritty documentary, *Devil's Playground,* to an episode on *ER* and the reality television show *Amish in the City.*[26]

Programs like *Devil's Playground* and *Amish in the City,* and more recent news coverage of sexual abuse in plain communities, child endangerment, and animal cruelty prompt some in the Amish community to feel besieged and betrayed by media seemingly intent on disclosing every possible blemish. They are increasingly wary of talking to outsiders, whether they be scholars or reporters, because the Amish are so often disappointed in the results. While the Amish do not claim to be perfect, they nevertheless often feel singled out. If we were not Amish, they ask, would it even be a story?

Notes

Epigraph: Sam S. Stoltzfus, letter to the editor, "For the Old Order, a New Menace," *Philadelphia Inquirer,* 8 July 1998, A21.

1. These headlines are from the *Altoona (PA) Mirror* and the *Chambersburg (PA) Public Opinion,* respectively, from June 27, 1998.

2. I found 195 clippings of Durantine's AP story in newspapers across the country from June 24–28, 1998, provided by Burrelle's clipping service in the library of the Young Center for Anabaptist and Pietist Studies, Elizabethtown College, Elizabethtown, Pennsylvania. The *New York Times, Philadelphia Inquirer, Los Angeles Times,* and Gannett News also distributed reports across their wires.

3. The "feeding frenzy" was the subject of Ed Klimuska, "Worldwide Media Gripped by 'Feeding Frenzy,'" *Lancaster New Era,* 13 July 1998, A1.

4. See Martin H. Folly, "'The News that Stunned the Most Jaded Americans': The North American Press and the Arrest of Two Amish Drug Dealers in 1998," *eJournal EnterText* 1, no. 1 (Dec. 2000), 212–28, www.burnel.ac.uk/faculty/arts/EnterText/. See also David Weaver-Zercher, *The Amish in the American Imagination* (Baltimore: Johns Hopkins University Press, 2001).

5. See Clifford Christians, "Cross-Cultural Ethics and Truth," in *Mediating Religion: Conversations in Media, Religion and Culture,* ed. Jolyon Mitchell and Sophia Marriage (New York: T & T Clark, 2003), 293–303.

6. Schreiber's observations were gleaned from "Lessons Learned: The Lancaster County Amish Cocaine Bust," a panel presentation at "The Amish, the Old Orders, and the Media," a conference at the Young Center for Anabaptist and Pietist Studies, Elizabethtown College, Elizabethtown, Pennsylvania, June 15, 2001; and interview with author, 9 July 2004.

7. Each Amish settlement is divided into geographical districts or congregations. A district consists of twenty-five to forty families that live in proximity to each other and worship together. Amish worship takes place in the home, and services

are hosted on alternating Sundays by families in the district. There are 278 districts in the entire state of Pennsylvania. See Donald B. Kraybill and Carl Desportes Bowman, *On the Backroad to Heaven: Old Order Hutterites, Mennonites, Amish, and Brethren* (Baltimore: Johns Hopkins University Press, 2001), 105, 110–11.

8. Amish young people typically do not join the church (and thereby embrace its rules and obligations) until their late teens or early twenties. Typically, young women join at an earlier age than young men. See Donald B. Kraybill, *The Riddle of Amish Culture,* rev. ed. (Baltimore: Johns Hopkins University Press, 2001), 117.

9. Pyfer's observations were gleaned from the "Lessons Learned: The Lancaster County Amish Cocaine Bust" panel (cited above, n. 6).

10. Kraybill's observations are taken from "Culture Clashes: Conflicting Values, Interests, and Images," plenary address at the conference on "The Amish, the Old Orders, and the Media," June 14, 2001, and also from the "Lessons Learned" panel.

11. Qtd. in Klimuska, "Worldwide Media," A1.

12. Ibid.

13. Many of the following observations are from "How the Media Affects Plain Groups," a panel presentation at the conference on "The Amish, the Old Orders, and the Media," June 16, 2001. Other quotations are based on personal interviews with Old Order Amish persons and others connected with the cocaine story. Except in the cases where names have already been published, I have agreed to use generic identification at the request on the individuals involved. Most of the interviews were conducted during the summers of 2004 and 2005.

14. Interview with author, 9 July 2004.

15. Ibid.

16. Interview with author, 3 July 2002.

17. Excerpt from Sam S. Stoltzfus, letter to the editor, "For the Old Order, a New Menace," *Philadelphia Inquirer,* 8 July 1998, A21.

18. Interview with author, 14 July 2004.

19. Interview with author, 14 July 2004.

20. Interview with author, 25 August 2004.

21. Interview with author, 14 July 2004.

22. Christians, "Cross-Cultural Ethics and Truth," 299–301.

23. The first headline, with minor variations, appeared frequently with the AP story written by Peter Durantine. The second is from the *London Daily Telegraph,* 25 June 1998.

24. Interview with author, 2 August 2004.

25. Telephone interview with author, 6 September 2005.

26. One example is a book based on research done for *Devil's Playground:* Tom Shachtman, *Rumspringa: To Be or Not to Be Amish* (New York: North Point Press, 2006).

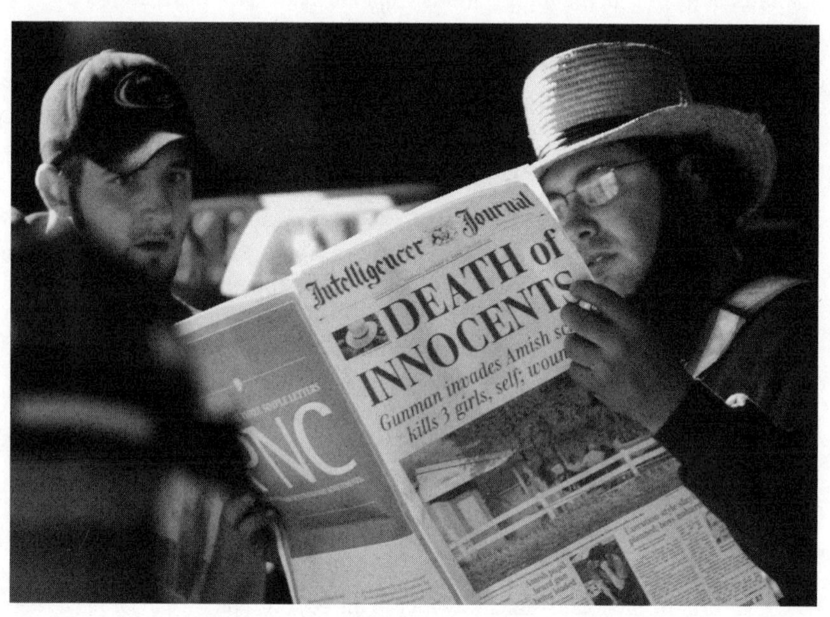

Two men read a newspaper at the roadblock near the scene of the Amish school shootings.

Photo by Mark Wilson; used by permission of Getty Images.

Conclusion

The Amish, the Media, and the Nickel Mines School Shooting

Diane Zimmerman Umble and David L. Weaver-Zercher

Are we worthy of the high esteem the media is piling on us?
—letter in *Die Botschaft* after the Nickel Mines shooting

Although many of the media's portrayals of the Old Order Amish are not rooted in specific events, some of them are. In 1989, for instance, the national news media turned out in force when the first President Bush traveled to Lancaster County to meet with Old Order Amish leaders in the midst of his "war on drugs."[1] The "Amish drug bust," addressed in chapter 10 of this volume, created a similar though more enduring spike in media interest. In terms of its scope, however, nothing compares to the October 2006 shooting at the West Nickel Mines Amish school near Georgetown, Pennsylvania. Ironically—and it is almost impossible to imagine a more heartrending irony—even as we were putting the finishing touches on this book, the biggest Amish-related media event unfolded before our eyes.

The media coverage of the Nickel Mines school shooting, like the event itself, was in many respects unique. At the same time, however, many of the tensions, challenges, and rewards that characterize media portrayals of Amish life in more serene circumstances characterized this most extraordinary incident. In that regard, the coverage of the Nickel Mines school shooting serves as a useful frame by which to underscore themes that appear in earlier parts of this volume. Perhaps most fundamentally, the media coverage of the Nickel Mines shooting reminds us that the words and deeds of real-life actors can make a real—and surprising—difference in the contours of the media's reportage. Conversely, the shooting and its aftermath underscore the fact that, quite apart from the actors and their actions, the media possess enormous power to shape a story and its reception. Moreover, Nickel Mines presents in sharp relief the way the media's work can itself become the raw material by which the media manufactures more news. Finally, the coverage that emerged from the Nickel Mines massacre reveals the close religion-media nexus wherein media accounts become sites for people to make sense of the world, including their own lives and commitments.

Reporting the Story

Despite being more common than we would wish, school shootings in the United States are always "news." Perhaps that is true of all types of lethal violence on the American landscape, though domestic and neighborhood killings rarely get more than a few columns or comments in the local press. But when that lethal violence takes place in a school building with schoolchildren present, the violence quickly becomes fodder for nationwide coverage.

In the case of Nickel Mines, the national coverage quickly assumed epic proportions. Some of that magnitude can be traced to the extent of the violence, which was nothing less than horrifying: ten schoolgirls tied up, threatened with sexual assault, and then systematically shot, five of them fatally. But more significant than the scope of the violence were its context and its victims: a one-room country school filled with Amish schoolchildren. Even persons who know hardly anything about the Amish know that they live relatively rural and secluded lives, and the juxtaposition of the day's violence with this pastoral vision of Amish life made the story particularly poignant. It seemed as if the nation had suddenly encountered the reality of Nicolas Poussin's painting about death in Arcadia: "Et in Arcadia Ego" (Even in Arcadia, there am I).[2]

The news media picked up on this juxtaposition and played it for all it was worth. For instance, an AP wire story for the following day devoted only one sentence to the facts of the shooting before launching into a description of "Lancaster County's bucolic Amish country": a "picturesque landscape of horse-drawn buggies, green pastures and neat-as-a-pin farms, where violent crime is virtually nonexistent."[3] It was not just the national media that emphasized this theme of death having entered Arcadia. "Paradise Lost," trumpeted a large-font headline in the *Centre Daily Times,* a newspaper based near a large Amish settlement in Mifflin County, Pennsylvania.[4] Even the Lancaster newspapers worked hard to accentuate the mythic quality of Amish life in the context of this heinous crime. Most clever in this regard was the *Lancaster Intelligencer Journal,* which used the double entendre "Death of Innocents" to conjure thoughts of pastoral purity (innocence) by using an Amish term for children who are considered innocent before God (innocents).[5] To be sure, the news media devoted attention to many other aspects of the story, in particular the calculated actions and curious motives of the killer, Charles Carl Roberts IV. Still, the story ultimately drew its power from the fact that Roberts enacted his violence on Amish schoolgirls in rural Lancaster County.[6]

It is hardly surprising, then, that the most common question posed to scholars of Amish life in the immediate aftermath of the shooting was "How is this event going to change Amish life?"[7] At least in some cases, the subtext for that question was something like this: The Amish have long lived peaceful, secluded lives. They have been blissfully ignorant that this sort of violence might be perpetrated on them. Now that they have witnessed this intrusion of the larger world on their isolated subculture, they will need to rethink the way they live in the world. What will they do now?

Two observations about this question are in order. First, the content of this question reveals that many of the news journalists covering this breaking story were relatively uninformed about the nature of Lancaster County Amish life—which does not change quickly (especially in response to anomalous events) and which, contrary to popular perception, is not that isolated from the larger world. Then again, why *should* these journalists be well informed about Amish life? There are many good books about Amish life and culture, but most of the journalists who needed to produce a report for their evening broadcasts or morning newspapers did not spend the preceding week reading up on Amish life. Local reporters demonstrated more knowledge of Amish life—understandably so, since Amish-related stories are part and parcel of their work. Their questions about how the shooting might change Amish life therefore focused on small, practical solutions to the problem of schoolhouse security: Will they lock their schoolhouse doors? Will they place cell phones in teachers' desks? Again, national journalists, thrust into the situation with no advance knowledge and precious little preparation, tended to ask open-ended and somewhat grandiose questions about the long-term effects of the shooting.

A second observation regarding journalists' questions about long-term effects is that they were often addressed to non-Amish scholars/students of Amish life, including some who contributed chapters to this volume. As Donald B. Kraybill observes in chapter 7, most Amish persons are reticent to speak to the news media, and some refuse to do so altogether, which means that journalists frequently resort to English sources to gather information for their Amish-theme news stories. This is a sensible and responsible tactic for journalists, particularly in light of pressing deadlines that make it impractical to read a book on the subject at hand. At the same time, some scholars of religion, sound-bited or quoted out of context once too often, refuse to talk to the media about their area of expertise.[8] Like the Amish (though certainly not in every way), these scholars have decided that having attributed quotations in mainstream newspapers may sully their reputations and, worse yet, fail to advance the truth.

Still, many of us who contributed to this volume *did* speak to the press in the aftermath of the Nickel Mines shooting. Some of us even published op-ed pieces that reflected on the tragedy.[9] Which leads us to an important observation that has been mostly implicit in this volume: *scholars are mediators too.* Much like the media enterprises that come under scrutiny in this volume, scholars—particularly those in the social sciences and the humanities—are in the business of discovering, developing, and disseminating information about other people and cultures. For many of us who contributed chapters to this volume, the Others we have studied and written about have been Amish people. So, as much as some of us resist the tag, we too are "the media." We may feel less pressure to tell compelling stories on a daily or weekly basis than do the national news media, and we rarely concern ourselves with advertising revenues or the size of our reading or viewing audiences. Still, like the other media personnel considered in this volume, we need to make decisions about how to gather information and what to do with the information we have. We need to decide which stories to tell and how to tell them. In most cases we have a great deal of time to work through those decisions, and we then tell our stories through small-circulation journals or university press books. In the case of Nickel Mines, however, we provided relatively unpolished information to reporters via phone, radio, and television interviews, which the news media then "re-mediated" to the larger world.

In the course of that process, a new story line came to the fore: the story of Amish forgiveness. This story was not "planted" or generated by English mediators of Amish life—even though, as we noted in this volume's introduction, most people who know something about Amish life know that the Amish are inclined to forgive those who have wronged them. Rather, this story was catalyzed by small, humble acts that the actual Amish actors considered quite ordinary: the extension of the word *forgive* to the family of the killer, the presence of Amish people at the killer's funeral, the decision by members of the Amish community to contribute to a fund for the killer's family, and so on. By virtue of these small acts, the Nickel Mines Amish made news—or, to be more precise, they provided the materials and the opportunity for the media conglomerates who *really* "make the news" to reorient the horrific story from one of utter senselessness to one of spiritual significance, even moral challenge. The story was not possible without the Amish, nor was it "news" without the media. Together, the Amish and the media outlets they largely ignore produced a story with great power—all to the surprise of the Amish actors, who simply did what they thought all Christian people should do.

Indeed, part of our interest in this forgiveness story is the utter lack of calculation on the part of the Amish. In an era when many people crave their fifteen minutes of fame and calculate multiple ways to get it, the Nickel Mines Amish simply lived their lives. But because they lived their lives in such a countercultural way, they caught the attention of English people with the power to make "news." Of course, one could argue that this is really nothing new: for the past one hundred years, the Old Order Amish have generated a great deal of media interest by simply living their lives. What *is* unique in this case is that the specific actions of a few Amish people in a particular context generated conversations about a theological topic—forgiveness—that reoriented standard Amish-theme conversations about the virtues of simple, agrarian living. In other words, unlike *Witness* and so many other media portrayals of the Amish, the currency that emerged from Nickel Mines cannot be reduced to the pastoral. The Amish, with a big boost from the news media, changed the nature of that conversation.

The News Media as Media Critics

There is a second sense in which the media became newsmakers in the aftermath of Nickel Mines. Conscious that the Amish community was wary of, and even disturbed by, the media's presence in Nickel Mines, some media outlets took the opportunity to turn their lenses on themselves. Thus, by late in the week—after Monday's shooting and after the subsequent expression of Amish forgiveness—a wave of news stories began to explore, and sometimes criticize, the work of the media in and around Nickel Mines.

Not coincidentally, these stories began to appear around the time of the schoolgirls' funerals, which took place on Thursday and Friday after the Monday shooting. Even in less notorious circumstances, Amish funerals generate outsiders' interest. In fact, some Lancaster County tour guides have been known to watch Amish cemeteries for open gravesites in order to treat their customers to the solemn ritual of an Amish burial (something many Amish people find particularly offensive). It is therefore not surprising that the media determined to offer up these experiences as well, via words and photographs. Despite some strictly enforced limits on what the media could do in this regard (e.g., the Pennsylvania State Police established a no-fly zone around the homes where the girls' funerals were held), numerous images helped media consumers visualize different aspects of

Amish funeral rites. Most common were pictures of horse-drawn buggies, dozens of them, wending along country roads to Amish cemeteries. Some photographers, however, took a more forward approach, snapping long-range shots of cemeteries filled with black-clad Amish mourners.

The most striking of these cemetery photos was taken from a helicopter by *Washington Post* photographer Linda Davidson. The image, which shows four Amish men carrying a small coffin across a cemetery toward an open grave, caught the eye of the *Post*'s executive editor, Len Downie, who selected it for publication. The photograph effectively captured the emotion of the moment—which is exactly why some of the newspaper's readers objected to it, so much so that the *Post*'s ombudsman, Deborah Howell, felt constrained to respond. In her op-ed piece, "Photographing the Grief of the Amish," Howell quoted some of the complaints the *Post* received, complaints that typically noted the subjects' grief as well as the general Amish reticence toward publicity and photographic imagery. Howell replied that the *Post*'s photos were generally taken "from public spaces," often through telephoto lenses and always with "respect and dignity." Responding more specifically to complaints about the cemetery photograph, she explained that the helicopter was a "half-mile to a mile away," that it "did not fly directly over the cemetery and did not hover."[10]

One might conclude from the foregoing statements that the *Post* was simply trying to get off the hook, but other aspects of the article demand a more sympathetic reading. For instance, Howell opened her piece by noting the ongoing dilemma of covering tragedy: the tension between "the journalistic value of bringing the news to readers" and "the human value of wanting privacy in grief." Later in the article she quoted the photographer, Davidson, who acknowledged that it "bothered" her to photograph the Amish, a discomfort that "has stuck with me all week." Still, Davidson continued, the magnitude of the story warranted "tasteful and sensitive coverage and photo documentation." Moreover, through the story's coverage, "the world has learned so much from the Amish . . . about faith, humility, and immediate forgiveness, all done by example." The implication here, of course, is that the acts performed by the Amish were worth knowing about and that without media broadcasts of these acts practically no one would have learned about them. According to Howell, the cemetery picture, "despite the intrusion," placed an appropriate exclamation point on the week's events, offering a "eulogy to the dignity, the stoic faith and acceptance of the Amish."[11]

Of course, we might still ask whether the *Post*'s eulogy could have been offered in a less intrusive way. Those judgments, which Dirk Eitzen, in chapter 2 of this volume, calls "the cost-benefit analysis" of media endeavors, are notoriously difficult to make and, as we might expect, most media outlets found their own work (if not the work of their competitors) quite satisfactory in that regard. "We must always balance public interest against the need to be compassionate and to avoid any unjustified infringement on privacy," wrote Andrew Steele, the BBC's bureau chief in Washington. "I'm satisfied that this time, despite the difficulties, we achieved the right balance."[12] But what did the Amish think?

The Amish as Media Consumers, Observers, and Critics

Amish persons had a complex and variegated relationship with the mainstream news media in the aftermath of the Nickel Mines shooting. Not only were Amish schoolchildren the primary subjects of the media's story, but Amish people became key sources of information about Amish reactions to the incident as well as about Amish life more generally. Within hours of the shooting, the small, out-of-the-way intersection known as Nickel Mines swarmed with journalists, photographers, television trucks, and countless other vehicles. One spokesperson for the Amish community, himself a non-Amish man, referred to the intense media presence as "the invasion of Nickel Mines."[13] "We were scared," recalled one Amish woman a few months later, because we were "not used to talking to so many people."[14]

Still, the Amish reaction to the mainstream media's coverage of the school shooting cannot be reduced to comments about being invaded or feeling threatened. On the one hand, Amish persons, both those who lived in Lancaster County and those who lived elsewhere, wanted information about the shooting, which they often received through mainstream media sources, particularly newspapers. "We were anxious for the news," said one Amish woman. "We wanted to know what was happening."[15] In addition to wanting details about the shooting itself, they also wanted to see accurate descriptions of Amish life and practice. In more ordinary circumstances, this commonsense desire for accuracy provides sufficient motivation for some Amish persons to become media informants; if anything, the extraordinary nature of the Nickel Mines shooting, which resulted in an unprecedented level of news coverage, increased the willingness of some Amish persons to speak to the media.

Amish persons had mixed views about what was necessary and appropriate in this regard. "Our people need to be willing to say 'no comment,'" said one person who, for various reasons, felt that some Amish community members had been too willing to talk with the mainstream media. Still, this person lamented that the media sometimes failed to verify the information they printed, and it "hurt to see wrong information printed in the paper."[16] This tension—wanting the media to get their facts right, but not wanting to give the media too much help—underscores the difficulty the mainstream media faced in reporting this particular story, and it was never far from the surface in the Amish commentaries that emerged in the tragedy's aftermath. "We thank people from the news media who sensitively reported our tragedy to the world," wrote the Nickel Mines Accountability Committee, a small group of Amish and non-Amish persons assembled to oversee donations that flowed into the community. More than that, the committee thanked media personnel for the various "acts of kindness" they extended to Amish people in the midst of their reporting work.[17] Nonetheless, the spokesperson for the Accountability Committee later complained that the news coverage was excessive, "a disturbing display of crass capitalism" that too often failed to respect the grieving families.[18] An Amish woman concurred, noting that the victims' families had become extremely "wary of the media. . . . They want to get through this grief. They don't want anyone knocking on their doors."[19]

Despite this mounting media fatigue, however, some Amish individuals continued to find meaning—and some degree of satisfaction—in the media's dissemination of news about forgiveness. This perspective came through in the Accountability Committee's statement (the media "helped the world grapple with values that are dear to us," the statement said), and it also appeared in letters to Amish-readership newspapers, *The Budget* and *Die Botschaft*.[20] For instance, one *Botschaft* correspondent from nearby

Georgetown, Pennsylvania, reported that "a non-Amishman said that since this happened, the name of Jesus is being spread all over the world. . . . Is this [God's] way of spreading the WORD?"[21] This correspondent, without dismissing the shooting's horror, suggested that God's work was being accomplished via this strange partnership between the Amish actors, who forgave Charles Roberts, and the mainstream media, who broadcast that expression of forgiveness far and wide. Another correspondent recounted a conversation he had with "a man of the world" who suggested that God "had allowed [the shooting] to happen, so that the whole world and all religions would hear about true Christian forgiveness."[22] More generally, the Amish found comfort in the expressions of support they received as the news of the shooting spread around the world. The whole event "has shown that there are still a lot of caring and helpful people around all over the world," proffered one *Botschaft* letter.[23]

In addition to encouraging Amish people in various ways, the media's coverage of Nickel Mines challenged them to reflect on their own spiritual lives. "Much is being made about the forgiveness of our people," wrote one Amish couple, who then queried their fellow *Botschaft* readers, "Are we worthy of the high esteem the media is piling on us? Are we truly forgiving to each other in the smaller things of life?"[24] Another *Botschaft* writer echoed this viewpoint, first with an expression of humility ("I hope we can be half as good as the world thinks right now"), then with a mini-sermon: "We need to let our light shine as much as possible [since] this is our opportunity to let the world know about God's love."[25] These reflections were not uncommon in the weeks following the school shooting, and many Amish churches in the region devoted their Sunday services to this theme. "Heard on Sunday, Let's be the light the world thinks we are," reported one correspondent. "Gave me something to think about."[26] In this way and others, mainstream media reports about Amish forgiveness, shaped by the actions of Amish people, also shaped the spiritual lives of Amish people.

Navigating Difference, Debating Forgiveness

In his book *The Dignity of Difference: How to Avoid the Clash of Civilizations*, Jewish rabbi Jonathan Sacks makes a plea for "tolerance in an age of extremism."[27] Sacks is not referring, of course, to the "extreme" practices of the Old Order Amish—like rejecting television, dressing plain, and granting forgiveness to the killer of one's children. Rather, he is referring to the need for people from different religious perspectives to find common ground across religious divides. Sacks begins his book by noting the relatively new reality of living in a globalized world: whereas people from past generations lived surrounded by people with whom they shared the deepest assumptions, many now live "in the conscious presence of difference." This, he says, is terribly disconcerting, for whereas former generations inhabited cultural milieus that allowed them to believe that their truth was "the only truth," contemporary world citizens constantly encounter cultures whose ideas are different, a situation that is often experienced "as a profound threat to identity." This is why religion has emerged as such a force in the world, for religion is "one of the great answers to identity."[28] That, in and of itself, is not a problem. It *is* a problem, however, when religious identity becomes calcified into Us-Them dichotomies that reinforce fear and hatred. "Nothing has proven harder in the history of civilization," Sacks writes, "than to see God, or good, or human dignity in those whose . . . faith is not my faith and whose truth is not my truth."[29]

Sacks's book is a profound treatment of this problem, at once sobering and optimistic: sobering because the problem of difference is so deeply entrenched, optimistic because Sacks believes in the possibility of navigating difference in a way that dignifies the Other. He is not simplistic in that regard, though he does see the solution as a relatively straightforward one: "The greatest single antidote to violence is *conversation,* speaking our fears, listening to the fears of others, and in that sharing of vulnerabilities discovering a genesis of hope."[30]

How might Sacks's analysis pertain to the media's treatment of Nickel Mines and, more generally, to its coverage of Amish life and culture? *At their best* the media provide both the context and content for this kind of conversation. As much truth as there is in Sacks's assertions that we live "in the conscious presence of difference," it is nonetheless the case that many Americans do not have much personal contact, let alone sustained personal contact, with people who are different from them. Especially for white Americans, whose families, friendship networks, and religious communities tend to be made up of people who are similar to them, the encounter with the Other often happens at a remove. This is the work of the media. *At their best* the media provide consumers with access to the Other in ways that deepen understanding and thereby enable the discovery of shared hopes and the acknowledgement of mutual fears.

The success of the media in this regard is mixed. We need to look no further than the way Islam has been portrayed by the mainstream American media to discover both the problems and the possibilities of mediated contact with the Other. For instance, whereas many Hollywood films have served to augment American fears of a homogenous "Islamic threat," the proportion of Americans with favorable views of U.S. Muslims actually *increased* after the September 11 attacks, an upswing that is attributable, at least in part, to press coverage of Islam in the attacks' aftermath.[31] Of course, our judgment of whether the media has done its work well cannot be reduced to whether media consumers feel more favorable toward the subject of the media's work. Advancing the truth must also be part of the equation and will sometimes lead to *less favorable* impressions of the media's subject—whether that subject be Islamic militants, U.S. presidents, or the Old Order Amish.

The Amish, despite their relative disinterest in worldly matters, are not ignorant of the media's power to shape outsiders' perceptions of Amish life. Moreover, they realize that the mainstream media shapes *their own* perceptions of themselves. "Are we really as forgiving as the world says we are?" they asked. "Can we—should we—forgive one another as readily as we forgave Charles Roberts?" In light of such questions, Amish publishing enterprises offer crucial resources for the construction and maintenance of Amish identity. Just as portrayals of the Amish in the public media serve as scales for the English to ponder the possibilities of granting forgiveness, Amish publishing efforts function as a means for articulating a discourse about what it means to be Amish and, in the case of the Nickel Mines shooting, what it means to forgive.

We have already noted ways the Amish nurtured that conversation in the weeks following the school shooting. In the English world, this conversation often revolved around this question: What would the larger world be like if non-Amish people forgave as the Amish did? Numerous mainstream commentators linked that question to the U.S. response to the September 11 attacks, a response which, in their eyes, assumed that forgiveness in horrific circumstances was not possible. Other commentaries pointed to the Palestinian-Israeli impasse or to other social issues, such as the retributive nature of the American penal system. In most of these cases, the commentators argued there was something to learn from the Amish response to the school shooting and further argued that persons who weren't Amish themselves could apply some of these lessons in their own situations.

Others, however, begged to differ. In fact, some commentators found the Amish response not only inapplicable to the larger world but inappropriate in all cases. "I wish [the Amish] well," wrote a columnist for the *Boston Globe,* "but I would not want to be like them, reacting to terrible crimes with dispassion and absolution."[32] Not surprisingly, the columnist who wrote these words less than a week after the Nickel Mines shooting generated a strong and negative response. "This is not some softheaded mumbo jumbo," replied one reader. "It's a cultural strategy for self-preservation and mental health."[33] There are, of course, no easy answers to complex questions of forgiveness, anger, and justice. The point we wish to make here is that, in the aftermath of Nickel Mines, the mainstream media provided a context for these questions to be raised, examined, and debated.

Did they do that job well? Just as there are no easy answers to the complicated question of forgiveness, there are no pat formulas for doing mediating work correctly. Still, we are once again helped by Jonathan Sacks, who urges his readers to attend to "the dignity of difference." A common temptation in a world unsettled by difference, Sacks writes, is to look too quickly for commonalities and shared universals. That search is not necessarily wrongheaded, though it must always be done carefully lest we assume our particulars to be everyone's universals. A better starting point for navigating the world's diversity, he writes, is to dignify difference—to allow "our world to be enlarged by the presence of others who think, act, and interpret reality in ways radically different from our own."[34]

The Old Order Amish provide their American neighbors with the proximate presence of Otherness. Scorning the conveniences of numerous technologies, rejecting common wisdom about the importance of higher education, renouncing the assumed rightness of the individual's right to choose, clinging fast to pacifist principles—in these and many other ways, the Amish participate in a radically different reality from most of their American neighbors. On the one hand, this Otherness is not difficult to see, and as many contributors to this volume have attested, these conspicuous traits constitute the grounds for widespread fascination, even valorization, of Amish life. At the same time, countless mediations of the Amish have domesticated this Otherness, shortchanging the radical difference of Amish life. Tourist entrepreneurs, to cite just one example, frequently serve up visions of the Amish that, according to Susan Biesecker (chapter 5), provide middle-American tourists "a coherent and beautiful way to think about where they came from and, thus, who they are." In other words, the Amish, as mediated by certain tourist enterprises, are not so much religious radicals as they are primitive forms of "us" who simply confirm our imagined virtuous past.

There are many explanations, both economic and ideological, for domesticated versions of Amish life. Still, what they fail to do is dignify difference. The Amish have chosen a way of life that at its root is a radical rejection of widely shared American assumptions. In that sense, they do not represent the heritage of mainstream Americans. It is one thing to live in nineteenth-century America without cars and televisions; it is completely another to live in twenty-first-century America without those things, particularly if one has the financial resources to buy them immediately. Similarly, it is one thing to "take one's faith seriously"; it is quite another to demonstrate loyalty to Jesus Christ in such as way that his words about forgiving one's enemies are considered absolute. The Amish are not just peace-loving Americans. As followers of the Prince of Peace, they are willing to let their families suffer harm if war should come their way. They may grieve their children's deaths, but they will consider those losses to be a mysterious outworking of God's plan. They will "forgive their debtors," knowing that their own forgiveness is bound up in their willingness to forgive other people. In all these ways, the Amish are truly Other.

The challenge for mainstream mediators of Amish life is to dignify that Otherness, to recognize it without reviling it. The best mediators of Amish life will do that and more, for they will also help their non-Amish consumers think of *themselves* as Other in the eyes of the Amish.[35] Few

Americans—white Americans, in particular—have devoted much time and energy to thinking of themselves as Other, luxuriating instead in the assumption that their way of life is normal and therefore best. In our estimation, countering that facile assumption provides sufficient grounds for books, films, and other media products that portray Amish life, even when the Amish do not agree (and many times they will not). Helping mainstream Americans enter the world of the Amish, and thereby helping them think of their own social practices as strange, must be the goal of those who wish to mediate Amish life to the English world. The risk, of course, is that these media endeavors will obscure as much as they illumine. Still, in a world where difference is too often quickly and dismissively reviled, it is a risk worth taking.

Notes

Epigraph: Letter from "New Holland, PA; Groffdale," *Die Botschaft*, 23 October 2006, 36.

1. For some attention to this visit, see David Weaver-Zercher, *The Amish in the American Imagination* (Baltimore: Johns Hopkins University Press, 2001), 181–84.

2. For a description and consideration of this 1645 painting, see chapter 1 of this volume.

3. See Mark Scolforo's AP press release, available at www.mclean.harvard.edu/pdf/news/mitn/ap061003.pdf.

4. This headline appeared on the front page of the *Centre Daily Times*, 3 October 2006.

5. This headline appeared on the front page of the *Lancaster Intelligencer Journal*, 3 October 2006.

6. A few hours after the shooting, one television reporter admitted that the news story would have been bigger had the gunman himself been Amish. Phone conversation with David Weaver-Zercher, 2 October 2006.

7. This observation is based on our experience as well as on conversations with other scholars who were contacted by the media after the shooting.

8. This is the stance taken by Robert A. Orsi, the 2003 president of the American Academy of Religion. See Orsi, "On Not Talking to the Press," *Religious Studies News* 19, no. 3 (2004): 15.

9. See, for instance, Donald B. Kraybill, "Forgiveness Is Integral in Amish Faith," *Harrisburg Patriot-News*, 8 October 2006, F1; and David Weaver-Zercher, "In God They Trust," *Pittsburgh Post-Gazette*, 8 October 2006, H1.

10. All quotations in this paragraph are from Deborah Howell, "Photographing the Grief of the Amish," *Washington Post*, 8 October 2006, B6. Howell attributes the words "respect and dignity" to Joe Elbert, the *Post*'s assistant managing editor of

photography; the details she cites about the helicopter flight were provided by pilot Steve Bussmann.

11. Ibid.

12. See Andrew Steele, "Photographing the Amish," 4 October 2006, BBC Newsblog, available at www.bbc.co.uk/blogs/theeditors/2006/10/.

13. Herman Bontrager, videotaped interview with Linda Espenshade; shown at "Trauma: Covering and Recovering," a conference held in Lancaster, Pennsylvania, December 9, 2006.

14. Amish woman sharing at the "Trauma: Covering and Recovering" conference.

15. Ibid.

16. Ibid.

17. Statement from Nickel Mines Accountability Committee, in "Humbled by Outpouring of Love," *Lancaster Intelligencer Journal*, 11 October 2006, A11.

18. Herman Bontrager, videotaped interview shown at the "Trauma: Covering and Recovering" conference.

19. Amish woman sharing at the "Trauma: Covering and Recovering" conference.

20. For information on *The Budget* and *Die Botschaft*, see chapter 8 of this volume.

21. Letter from "Georgetown, PA," *Die Botschaft*, 23 October 2006, 22.

22. Letter from "Kincardine, ON," *Die Botschaft*, 23 October 2006, 16.

23. Letter from "Narvon, PA," *Die Botschaft*, 23 October 2006, 23.

24. Letter from, "New Holland, PA; Groffdale," *Die Botschaft*, 23 October 2006, 36.

25. Letter from "New Holland, PA; Welsh Mt.," *Die Botschaft*, 23 October 2006, 41.

26. Letter from "Stevens, PA," *Die Botschaft*, 23 October 2006, 71.

27. Jonathan Sacks, *The Dignity of Difference: How to Avoid the Clash of Civilizations* (London and New York: Continuum, 2002), vii.

28. Ibid., 10.

29. Ibid., 65.

30. Ibid., 2.

31. See Rubina Ramji, "Representations of Islam in American News and Film: Becoming the 'Other,'" and Mark Silk, "Islam and the American News Media post September 11," in *Mediating Religion: Conversations in Media, Religion and Culture*, ed. Jolyon Mitchell and Sophia Marriage (London and New York: T & T Clark, 2003), 65–72, 73–79.

32. Jeff Jacoby, "Undeserved Forgiveness," *Boston Globe*, 8 October 2006, E9.

33. Mark Davis, letter to the editor, *Boston Globe*, 15 October 2005, E10.

34. All quotations in this paragraph are from Sacks, *Dignity of Difference*, 23.

35. This paragraph is indebted to Crystal Downing, "Tongue in Check: Paralleling the Taliban with the Amish," *CrossCurrents* 53 (2003): 200–208.

Acknowledgments

The impetus for this volume was the 2001 conference, "The Amish, Old Orders, and the Media," sponsored by the Young Center for Anabaptist and Pietist Studies at Elizabethtown College in Elizabethtown, Pennsylvania. The conversations it generated convinced us that a book like this would be a valuable addition to the scholarship on Amish life. Early on we benefited from the encouragement of David Eller, then the director of the Young Center, and we have enjoyed the support of Donald B. Kraybill, series editor of Young Center Books in Anabaptist and Pietist Studies. Of course, our greatest debt is to the contributors, many of whom were working on other projects when we solicited their essays. We hope that our work on this volume has done their contributions justice.

Both of our institutions, Messiah College and Millersville University, provided support for this project, including sabbaticals and publication grants that paid permission fees. We share a great appreciation for the librarians at our respective institutions, consummate professionals who responded to our queries about books, articles, and citations with grace and skill. Similarly, the librarians at the Lancaster Mennonite Historical Society devoted energy and expertise to assist us in our work.

We gratefully acknowledge the following copyright holders who granted permission to reprint poems, all of which appear in chapter 3: University of Pittsburgh Press ("Why We Fear the Amish," by Robin Becker, from *The Horse Fair: Poems*); Cleveland State University Poetry Center ("Uneven

Light," by Roger Mitchell, from *A Clear Space on a Cold Day*); Denise Duhamel ("June," by Denise Duhamel, from the poetry journal *Third Coast*); Texas Tech University Press at www.ttup.ttu.edu ("Ocean City," by Deborah Burnham, from *Anna and the Steel Mill*); and Knopf Publishing ("Amish Phone Booth" and "Shunning," by Mary Swander, from *Heaven-and-Earth House*).

Both of us are blessed with gracious spouses who appreciate the rigors of academic life and support us in our work. We are also blessed with children who challenge, inspire, and love us in more ways than we can count. If this project sometimes preoccupied our minds when we should have been focused on our families, then that is all the more reason to celebrate its completion. We happily dedicate this book to them.

Contributors

Susan Biesecker (Ph.D., University of Pittsburgh) teaches in the English Department at the University of Dayton. In addition to coediting *Anabaptists and Postmodernity,* Susan has published numerous journal articles and book chapters on topics including classical rhetoric, feminist rhetoric, and radical religious rhetoric. She is currently completing a book-length manuscript on the visual rhetoric of tourism in Amish Country in which she explores how the Amish are figured by tourism for tourists' pleasure as well as how Amish resist such figuration, thereby offering a critique of consumer culture.

Crystal Downing (Ph.D., University of California, Santa Barbara) has won both national and international awards for her essays on film. When she moved to Pennsylvania in 1994, she started writing about the Amish, publishing her work in *Christian Living, Conrad Grebel Review,* and *CrossCurrents.* Currently professor of English and film studies at Messiah College in Grantham, Pennsylvania, Downing focuses most of her scholarship on the relationship between postmodernism and faith, an issue that informs her books, *Writing Performances: The Stages of Dorothy L. Sayers* (Palgrave Macmillan, 2004) and *How Postmodernism Serves (My) Faith: Questioning Truth in Language, Philosophy and Art* (InterVarsity, 2006).

Dirk Eitzen (Ph.D., University of Iowa) is head of the Film and Media Studies program in the Theatre, Dance and Film Department at Franklin & Marshall College in Lancaster, Pennsylvania. He is the producer and director of *The Amish & Us* and many other documentaries, some of which have aired across the country on public television and garnered major awards. Eitzen's film-theoretical publications include contributions to *The Emotional Basis of Film Comedy* (Johns Hopkins University Press, 1998) and many film journals, including *Cinema Journal, Post Script,* and *Film History.* He is currently working on a documentary about community trauma healing in the wake of the 2004 tsunami and a book examining the distinctive emotional appeals of nonfiction.

Karen Johnson-Weiner (Ph.D., McGill University) is associate professor of anthropology and chair of the Department of Anthropology at SUNY-Potsdam. She has published articles and book chapters on Old Order women's roles and Old Order parochial schools in *Mennonite Quarterly Review, Journal of Sociolinguistics,* and the *Yearbook of German-American Studies.* She is the author of *Train Up a Child: Old Order Amish and Mennonite Schools,* published by the Johns Hopkins University Press.

Julia Spicher Kasdorf (Ph.D., New York University) is associate professor of English and Women's Studies at Pennsylvania State University, where she teaches poetry and directs the M.F.A. program in creative writing. Kasdorf has published poems, book chapters, essays, articles, and books, including *Fixing Tradition* (Pandora Press U.S., 2002) and *The Body and the Book* (Johns Hopkins University Press, 2001). With Michael Tyrell, she has edited *Broken Land: Poems of Brooklyn* (New York University Press, 2007).

Donald B. Kraybill (Ph.D., Temple University) is distinguished professor and senior fellow at the Young Center for Anabaptist and Pietist Studies at Elizabethtown College in Elizabethtown, Pennsylvania. Nationally recognized for his scholarship on Anabaptist groups, he is the author, coauthor, or editor of many books and dozens of professional articles. His books on Anabaptist communities include *The Riddle of Amish Culture* (rev. ed., 2001) and *On the Backroad to Heaven: Old Order Hutterites, Mennonites, Amish, and Brethren* (2001), both published by the Johns Hopkins University Press.

Steven M. Nolt (Ph.D., University of Notre Dame) is professor of history at Goshen College in Goshen, Indiana. He has authored a number of books, chapters, and journal articles, including *Plain Diversity: Amish Cultures and Identities* (Johns Hopkins University Press, 2007) and *An Amish Patchwork: Indiana's Old Orders in the Modern World* (Indiana University Press, 2005). In addition, Nolt is the book review editor for *Mennonite Quarterly Review* and the editor of the monograph series, Studies in Anabaptist and Mennonite History.

Diane Zimmerman Umble (Ph.D., University of Pennsylvania) is professor of communication and acting director of the Center for Academic Excellence at Millersville University. Her published work includes *Holding the Line: The Telephone in Old Order Mennonite and Amish Life* (Johns Hopkins University Press, 1996), a coedited collection, *Strangers at Home: Amish and Mennonite Women in History* (Johns Hopkins University Press, 2002), and articles and chapters on telephone history and media criticism.

David L. Weaver-Zercher (Ph.D., University of North Carolina at Chapel Hill) is associate professor of American religious history and chair of the Department of Biblical and Religious Studies at Messiah College in Grantham, Pennsylvania. He has published articles in *Church History* and *Mennonite Quarterly Review* and is the author or editor of five books, including *The Amish in the American Imagination* (Johns Hopkins University Press, 2001) and *Writing the Amish: The Worlds of John A. Hostetler* (Pennsylvania State University Press, 2005). With Donald B. Kraybill and Steven M. Nolt, he has written *Amish Grace: How Forgiveness Transcended Tragedy* (Jossey-Bass, 2007).

Index

Young Center Books in Anabaptist & Pietist Studies

Karen M. Johnson-Weiner,
Train Up a Child: Old Order Amish and Mennonite Schools

James O. Lehman and Steven M. Nolt,
Mennonites, Amish, and the American Civil War

Steven M. Nolt and Thomas J. Meyers,
Plain Diversity: Amish Cultures and Identities

Richard A. Stevick, *Growing Up Amish: The Teenage Years*

Diane Zimmerman Umble and David L. Weaver-Zercher, eds.,
The Amish and the Media

Center Books in Anabaptist Studies

Carl F. Bowman,
Brethren Society: The Cultural Transformation of a "Peculiar People"

Perry Bush,
Two Kingdoms, Two Loyalties: Mennonite Pacifism in Modern America

John A. Hostetler, ed., *Amish Roots: A Treasury of History, Wisdom, and Lore*

Julia Kasdorf, *The Body and the Book: Writing from a Mennonite Life*

Donald B. Kraybill, *The Riddle of Amish Culture,* revised edition

Donald B. Kraybill, ed., *The Amish and the State,* 2nd edition

Donald B. Kraybill and Carl Desportes Bowman, *On the Backroad to Heaven: Old Order Hutterites, Mennonites, Amish, and Brethren*

Donald B. Kraybill and Steven M. Nolt,
Amish Enterprise: From Plows to Profits, 2nd edition

Werner O. Packull,
Hutterite Beginnings: Communitarian Experiments during the Reformation

Benjamin W. Redekop and Calvin W. Redekop, eds.,
Power, Authority, and the Anabaptist Tradition

Calvin Redekop, ed., *Creation and the Environment: An Anabaptist Perspective on a Sustainable World*

Calvin Redekop, Stephen C. Ainlay, and Robert Siemens,
Mennonite Entrepreneurs

Steven D. Reschly, *The Amish on the Iowa Prairie, 1840 to 1910*

Kimberly D. Schmidt, Diane Zimmerman Umble, and Steven D. Reschly, eds., *Strangers at Home: Amish and Mennonite Women in History*

Diane Zimmerman Umble, *Holding the Line: The Telephone in Old Order Mennonite and Amish Life*

David Weaver-Zercher, *The Amish in the American Imagination*